Toward Combined Arms Warfare:

A Survey of 20th-Century Tactics, Doctrine, and Organization

by

Captain Jonathan M. House, U.S. Army
August 1984

University Press of the Pacific
Honolulu, Hawaii

Toward Combined Arms Warfare:
A Survey of 20th-Century Tactics, Doctrine,
and Organization

by
Jonathan M. House

ISBN: 1-4102-0159-7

Reprinted from the 1984 edition

University Press of the Pacific
Honolulu, Hawaii
http://www.universitypressofthepacific.com

CONTENTS

FIGURES

MAPS

v

FOREWORD

The history of ground combat in the twentieth century is to a large extent the history of the evolution of combined arms warfare. The impact of technology, the expansion of armed forces, the advent of complex controlling, planning, and organizational structures, and the attendant growth of functional specialization, are all developments which have rendered the conduct of modern war a complex and multifaceted undertaking. Nowhere has change been more evident than on the battlefield itself, where the challenges of combat have simultaneously (and almost paradoxically) mandated greater differentiation and increased integration among the various arms and services.

This study focuses on a key aspect of change, the development of combined arms doctrine, tactics, and organization at the division level and below. Captain Jonathan House begins his treatment with the pre-1914 period, when the various combat arms retained separate functions and required only rudimentary coordination. Through two world wars and numerous lesser conflicts he traces the gradual integration of the different arms and services into a mechanized team. Of special interest in his account is the parallel development of the command and control mechanisms and procedures necessary to orchestrate the employment of combined arms on the modern battlefield. Throughout the analysis Captain House underscores the significance of recurring problems and themes, including the difficulties of air-ground cooperation, equipment design and acquisition, and inter-service and intra-service rivalries. Many if not all of these issues are relevant to contemporary discussions on doctrinal development.

Toward Combined Arms Warfare is also a primer in force design. By tracing general trends in division organization within the armed forces of various powers, including the United States Army, Captain House provides force developers with useful historical perspective on many key issues. Some of the more salient include questions related to the balance of arms within an organization, the level at which arms should be integrated, and complications that stem from task organizing units by attaching nonorganic elements. If "the past too may serve," then an examination of these and other problems within their historical context affords valuable insight into concerns of enduring importance for both theoreticians and practitioners.

DAVE R. PALMER
Major General, USA
Deputy Commandant

ABOUT THE AUTHOR

Captain Jonathan M. House

Captain Jonathan M. House earned a bachelor's degree at Hamilton College and a master's and doctorate in European and Military History at the University of Michigan. He has since completed courses at the U.S. Army Armor School, the U.S. Army Intelligence Center and School, and the U.S. Army Command and General Staff College.

Captain House has taught at the University of Michigan, the Armor School, the Intelligence Center and School, and the Command and General Staff College. He has also served as a tactical intelligence officer in both the United States and the Republic of Korea. He wrote this survey while serving as a research fellow in the Combat Studies Institute of the Command and General Staff College.

COMBAT STUDIES INSTITUTE
Mission

The Combat Studies Institute was established on 18 June 1979 as a separate, department-level activity within the U.S. Army Command and General Staff College, Fort Leavenworth, Kansas, for the purpose of accomplishing the following missions:

1. Conduct research on historical topics pertinent to the current doctrinal concerns of the Army and publish and distribute the results of such research in a variety of formats to the Active Army and Reserve components.

2. Prepare and present instruction in military history at CGSC and assist other CGSC departments in integrating applicable military history materials into their resident and nonresident instruction.

3. Serves as the TRADOC executive agent for the development and coordination of an integrated, progressive program of military history instruction in the TRADOC service school system.

4. Direct the CAC Historical Program.

5. Supervise the Fort Leavenworth Museum.

INTRODUCTION

> We have gotten into the fashion of talking of cavalry tactics, artillery tactics, and infantry tactics. This distinction is nothing but a mere abstraction. There is but one art, and that is the tactics of the combined arms. The tactics of a body of mounted troops composed of the three arms is subject to the same established principles as is that of a mixed force in which foot soldiers bulk largely. The only difference is one of mobility.
>
> -Major Gerald Gilbert, British Army, 1907[1]

The concept of "Combined Arms" has existed for centuries, but the nature of the combination and the organizational level at which it occurred have varied greatly. Prior to the seventeenth century, for example, there was often no need to combine infantry, artillery, and cavalry at the small-unit level. Each branch served a specific function on the battlefield, and only the senior commanders present needed to coordinate the effects of the different arms. In succeeding centuries, the general trend has been to combine the arms at progressively lower levels of organization. The concern of commanders has gone from coordinating the separate actions of separate arms, to gaining greater cooperation between them, and finally to combining their actions to maximize the effect of their various properties.

At the time that Gilbert made his plea, many officers paid lip service to "combined arms," but few understood the need to achieve such cooperation or combination between the branches at the small-unit level. Since then, twentieth century warfare and especially mechanized warfare have developed to the point at which some form of combined arms is essential for survival, let alone victory, on the battlefield. Yet the very complexity of this warfare leads to specialization in both training and maintenance, a specialization that is currently reflected in the formation of companies and battalions consisting of one or at most three different major weapons systems. A mechanized infantry battalion, for example, normally includes direct-fire infantry weapons, antitank weapons, and limited indirect-fire support in the form of mortars and grenade launchers. Such a battalion has little or no organic capability in the areas of armor, air defense, engineers, long-range indirect fire, or air support. A tank or artillery battalion is even more specialized and restricted in its equipment.

Although these units are task organized and cross attached for field operations, the demands of specialization, unit identity, and maintenance naturally cause many soldiers to concentrate on the use of one weapon or arm to defeat the corresponding weapon or arm of the enemy. Such a narrow view has frequently characterized professional soldiers, who wish naturally to conserve techniques that seem effective. This simplistic approach is perhaps less common among senior commanders and within infantry or reconnaissance (armored cavalry) units, where the different weapons are integrated on a more frequent basis than in some other organizations. Still, at least some tank crews train primarily to fight enemy tanks, tactical fighter units seek air superiority over enemy fighters, and engineers concentrate on enhancing the mobility of their own forces while impeding the mobility and countermobility efforts of enemy engineers. All of these tasks are essential for combat success, but none by itself will ensure proper interaction between the different arms and weapons. Indeed, almost by definition a particular arm or weapon system has most of the same strengths and weaknesses of its enemy counterpart, and thus may not provide the best means of defeating that enemy.

The very term "combined arms" often means different things to different people, or is left undefined and vague. As a minimum, however, this term includes at least three related elements:

1. The combined arms <u>concept</u> is the basic idea that different arms and weapons systems must be used in concert to maximize the survival and combat effectiveness of each other. The strengths of one system must be used to compensate for the weaknesses of others. Exactly which arms and weapons are included in this concept varies greatly between armies and over time. Today, however, the list of combined arms would include at least the following: infantry (mechanized, motorized, airborne, air assault, light, and special or unconventional operations forces), armor, cavalry/reconnaissance, artillery, antitank forces, air defense, combat engineers, attack helicopters, and some form of close air support. Under certain circumstances, this list may also include electronic warfare and, when authorized, nuclear and chemical fires. Beyond this basic list, all the combat support and service support elements are equally important if the force is to fight in a coordinated and sustained manner. In the interests of brevity, however, logistical aspects of combined arms will be discussed only briefly in this study.

2. Combined arms <u>organization</u>, at whatever level (company, battalion, brigade/regiment, etc.), brings these

different arms and weapons systems together for combat. This may include both fixed, peacetime tables of organization and ad hoc or task-organized combinations of elements in wartime.

       3. Combined arms <u>tactics and operations</u> are the actual roles performed and techniques applied by these different arms and weapons in supporting each other once they have been organized into integrated teams. This is the area that is of most concern to professional soldiers, yet it is precisely this area where historical records and tactical manuals often neglect important details. Moreover, combined arms tactics and techniques at the level of battalion or below are the most difficult aspects about which to generalize historically, because they are most subject to frequent changes in technology.

      A short study such as this cannot possibly consider all the complexities that these three elements bring to recent military history. What it can do is trace some recurring themes or problems in the recent conduct of combined arms warfare in the British, French, German, Soviet, and United States armies. At various times, each of these armies has led the world in the development of tactics and doctrine. For the period since 1948, the Israeli Defense Force (IDF) must be added to this list, because the Israeli experience has had a major influence on weapons and doctrine elsewhere. In particular, this paper will identify general trends in the development of tactical and organizational concepts for integrating the different arms and weapons systems at division level and below. This does not mean describing the thousands of minute changes that have occurred in divisional structure in these armies since the division became a fixed table of organization. Yet, the trends in terms of proportions of different arms and levels at which those arms were integrated can be illustrated with a limited number of line and block charts. Such trends should provide an historical framework and background for readers who are developing their own more detailed concepts of how to organize and employ the combined arms today.

      This study is a tentative overview rather than an exhaustive analysis. My hope is that it will prompt others to develop or even contest the trends described in these pages, thereby advancing the study of a central issue in land combat.

      Before proceeding to specific historical developments, some basic comments on the combined arms concept are in order. Most of these comments are self-evident, but they may assist readers in placing the following chapters into context.

      In the abstract, tactical warfare may be considered as a combination of three elements: mobility, protection, and offensive power.[2] Mobility means not only the ability to maneuver and concentrate forces over terrain, but also the ability to move men and units when exposed to the fire of the enemy. Mobility is not an absolute, but must be measured relative to the difficulty of the terrain and to the mobility of other friendly or enemy forces. For a combined arms team, the least mobile element may determine the mobility of the entire force. Without mobility, the principles of mass, maneuver, and offensive cannot be applied, and surprise becomes very difficult. Protection means both security against enemy surprise attack and protection to allow offensive maneuver or defense on the battlefield. This battlefield protection may be accomplished by using terrain defilade and defensive fortifications, or by employing artificial means such as armor. Offensive or fire power is necessary in order to impose one's will on the enemy, to overcome his protection.

These three elements have interacted continuously throughout military history. In particular, the past century has been characterized by a vast increase in weapons power, an increase that can be overcome only with great difficulty by a carefully designed combination of protected mobility and other firepower. The most obvious example of this is the defensive system of World War I. That combination of firepower and protection had to be countered by close coordination of infantry (mobility), fire support (offensive power), and armor (which theoretically combined all three elements). Even this explanation of World War I is simplistic, but the three basic elements of mobility, protection, and offensive power are present in most tactical equations.

At a more practical level, these three elements are combined technically in the design and employment of individual weapons and tactically in the combination of different weapons and arms. The 1982 edition of Field Manual 100-5, Operations, divides the concept and practice of combined arms into two procedures: supplementary or reinforcing combined arms, and complementary combined arms. As the name implies, supplementary combined arms means increasing the effect of one weapons system or arm with the similar effects of other weapons and arms. For example, the effects of mortars and artillery may reinforce or supplement each other in an integrated fire plan. Engineers may enhance the protection of armored vehicles by digging in those vehicles with engineer equipment. Complementary combined arms, by contrast, have different effects or characteristics, so that together they pose a more complicated threat, a dilemma for the enemy. The defender may place a minefield so that it halts an enemy force at a point where observed artillery or antitank fires can attack that enemy as he clears the minefield. The defender has thus integrated the different weapons to provide a much greater effect

4

than any one by itself could achieve. The resulting dilemma forces the enemy to accept casualties while clearing the mines, or to seek a passage elsewhere.

It is not sufficient, however, to develop a doctrine for combining the different arms and services. In order to practice, refine, and employ this doctrine, at least five other elements are necessary. First, an army must design and procure weapons with the characteristics required by the doctrine and must stay abreast of technical changes that may invalidate or modify those weapons and doctrine.

Second, the doctrine must be effectively explained and disseminated to the commanders who are expected to use it. Third, the commanders must believe that the doctrine can be effective with the organizations, weapons, and troops available. Dissemination and acceptance are hampered by the fact that soldiers naturally rely on past experience, so that a colonel may unconsciously expect platoons to function as they did when he was a lieutenant, years or even decades before. Experience is a priceless asset to any army, but it naturally retards or distorts the application of changes in technology and doctrine that may render parts of that experience obsolete.

Fourth, in the eyes of the commander, his unit must have the training and morale to implement the doctrine. A recurring theme of this study will be that professional soldiers tend to overestimate the amount and quality of training necessary for the rank and file to perform effectively in war. There is no substitute for good training, but historically leaders with high standards have rejected or modified doctrine that their troops seemed incapable of executing. On the other hand, training may genuinely be an obstacle to a particular doctrine or organization. If company commanders are, on the average, capable of coordinating only eighty men and two types of weapons systems, it would be useless to design 170-man companies with ten different weapons systems. Training officers to handle these larger, more complex units may be prohibitively expensive in peacetime.

Finally, a combined arms system cannot work without effective command and control to integrate and direct that system. Indeed, factors that improve span of control, speed of decision making, and leadership ability can be as important as the weapons themselves.

Successful commanders throughout history have instinctively understood these requirements. One could argue that neither Gustavus Adolphus of Sweden, nor Frederick the Great of Prussia, nor Napoleon I of France actually developed major new doctrines and weapons for the combined arms. What they did well was to procure weapons, understand and disseminate doctrine, train their troops, and apply the results in battle. With the larger armies and technical complexity of weapons in this century, it may be beyond the capability of a single leader to fulfill all these requirements. This possibility further complicates a military reality in which, since 1914, the combination of different arms has become essential for survival rather than optional for improved combat power. The process of developing and institutionalizing the combined arms concept, organization, and tactics in this century is the focus of this study.

Jonathan M. House
Captain, Military Intelligence
Combat Studies Institute
U.S. Army Command & General
  Staff College

CHAPTER ONE

PROLOGUE TO 1914

In the 1690s, European armies developed and fielded the socket bayonet, a long spike-shaped blade that could be fixed on the end of a musket without obstructing the bore of the weapon during loading and firing.[1] This simple device allowed well-disciplined infantry to withstand horse cavalry charges without the aid of specialized weapons such as the pike. For the next 150 years, infantry units armed solely with smoothbore firearms and bayonets were the backbone of all Western armies. Skilled senior commanders understood how to coordinate this infantry with cavalry and with direct-fire smoothbore artillery, but such coordination was rarely important at the level of regiment or below, because these units were basically armed with a single type of weapon. The need to maximize the firepower of inaccurate smoothbore weapons led to extremely linear deployments on the battlefield. The infantry maneuvered into long formations of two or three ranks, with the artillery located between or slightly behind the infantry battalions. The limited effect of even such carefully arrayed firepower made it possible, if dangerous, for dense masses of cavalry and infantry to attack at a specific point and break the thin lines of the defender. Fire-support coordination was simple, because the infantry and artillery unit commanders had face-to-face contact or used hand signals to designate targets.

The fundamentals of weaponry, technology, and small-unit tactics were refined but remained basically unchanged until the mid-1800s. Stability made professional soldiers skeptical of innovations even when they came from serious students of tactics.

Technology and Manpower

During the period 1827-1870, the first of two waves of technological change in the nineteenth century revolutionized the battlefield. The most important innovation of this first wave was the development of rifled, breech-loading firearms. The muzzle-loading rifle with a bullet-shaped projectile initially replaced the smoothbore musket. Rifling and an improved seal between bullet and bore increased the velocity and accuracy of small arms fire out to an effective range of nearly 500 meters.[2] During the American Civil War of 1861-1865, dense infantry formations in daylight provided lucrative targets for defenders armed with rifles. Both sides learned to spread out into skirmish lines when attacking. Defenders, for their part, had to dig in to reduce their own vulnerability to the attackers' rifle fire.

The muzzle-loading rifles used by most soldiers during the Civil War were already obsolescent, the result of the Prussian Army's development of the breech-loading rifle.[3] Unlike muzzle-loaders, breech-loaders could be reloaded in a prone position, allowing infantry to remain under cover while firing repeatedly. Soon fixed, metallic-cased ammunition made loading even faster. By the time of the Franco-Prussian War in 1870-1871, most armies had adopted breech-loading artillery as well as rifles.

The first wave of technological change also included the introduction of the railroad and the telegraph. These inventions greatly increased the speed of communication, mobilization, and troop movement at the strategic and operational levels. At the tactical level, though, troops still maneuvered on foot or on horseback.

The second wave of technological change came in the 1880s and 1890s. Smokeless gunpowder, magazine-fed repeating rifles, recoiling and quick-firing artillery, improved artillery fuzes, machine guns, and internal combustion engines appeared in rapid succession. With the exception of the engine, these developments all increased the volume, range, and accuracy of fire, placing the soldier in the open at a tremendous disadvantage compared to the soldier in prepared positions. General staffs were created to mobilize and deploy enormous armies using these new weapons. Although radiotelegraphs existed in the armies of 1914, the radio had not yet improved to the point where staffs could follow and direct events on the battlefield.

The cumulative effect of these two waves was to make cooperation and coordination between different units and arms absolutely essential. Anything less than total coordination in the attack might well result in defeat by defensive firepower. Conversely, an uncoordinated defense invited disaster.

The American Civil War and the Wars of German Unification (1864-1871) gave professional soldiers many opportunities to evaluate the first wave of technological change. That technology, in combination with an effective reserve component system, provided the tools of victory in Prussia's struggles to unite Germany. When World War I began, however, professional soldiers had not yet digested and agreed upon the effects of the second wave of change. As will be seen below, most tactical doctrines in 1914 showed a healthy respect for the effects of firepower, but such doctrines had not solved the resulting problems on the battlefield.

Quite apart from changes in weaponry, the Prussian example of large cadre and reservist forces overwhelming professional armies convinced other European governments that they must develop mass armies of reservists. European general staffs therefore produced elaborate plans to mobilize and deploy such reserves by railroad at the outbreak of war. As a result of these efforts, by 1900, Germany had only 545,000 men on active duty but a total wartime strength of 3,013,000; France had 544,450 men in peacetime and 4,660,000 in war; and Russia could mobilize over 4,000,000 from a peacetime strength of 896,000.[4] In contrast, the British Army Expeditionary Force of 1914 consisted essentially of regulars and contained only a limited percentage of reservists who had previously served on active duty.

The Prussian reserve and militia (Landwehr) formations of the 1860s were successful partly because they were filled with the veterans of previous Prussian wars. By 1914, however, a long period of peace had deprived most armies of such experienced reservists. Every continental army had to develop its own system of reserve training and organization, and every army had to decide what percentage of reservists could be absorbed into an active duty unit on mobilization. Many officers distrusted the competence of their citizen-soldiers. The absence of reservists from regular army formations during most of the year meant that units were well below authorized wartime strength and were in effect skeleton formations, thus making realistic training for both officers and conscripts difficult.

Organization and Doctrine

Pre-1914 armies organized the different combat arms into divisions and corps that bore a superficial resemblance to those of today. The most obvious difference was the absence of the vehicles and electronics associated with modern combat. By the end of the Napoleonic Wars, European armies had accepted the division as the wartime unit for combining infantry and artillery, although most cavalry was concentrated into separate brigades, divisions, or even corps.[5] As in so many other areas, the Prussian example had produced considerable agreement by 1914 on the basic organization of an infantry division. Most divisions contained twelve battalions of infantry, each with two machine guns either assigned or in direct support (see Figures 1 and 2).[6] Battalions were usually grouped into four regiments and two brigades, although the British regimental headquarters no longer had a tactical command function and therefore remained in garrison. Divisional cavalry was universally very small, because most functions of screening and reconnaissance were assigned to the separate cavalry brigades or divisions. These large cavalry

9

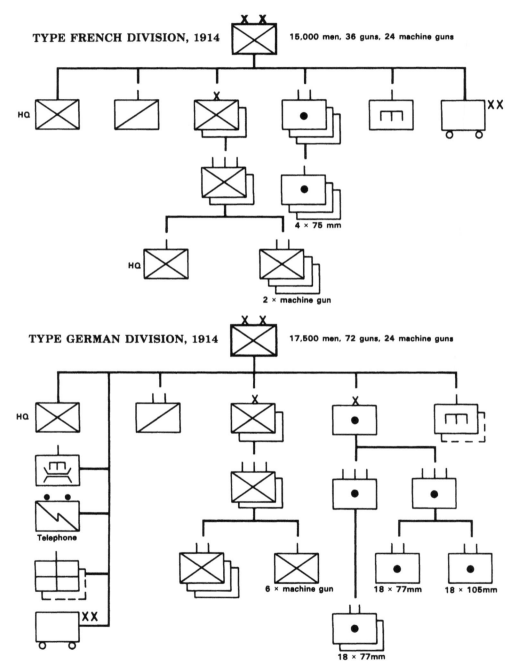

TYPE FRENCH DIVISION, 1914   15,000 men, 36 guns, 24 machine guns

HQ

4 × 75 mm

HQ

2 × machine gun

TYPE GERMAN DIVISION, 1914   17,500 men, 72 guns, 24 machine guns

HQ

Telephone

6 × machine gun

18 × 77mm   18 × 105mm

18 × 77mm

Figure 1. Type French and German Divisions, 1914

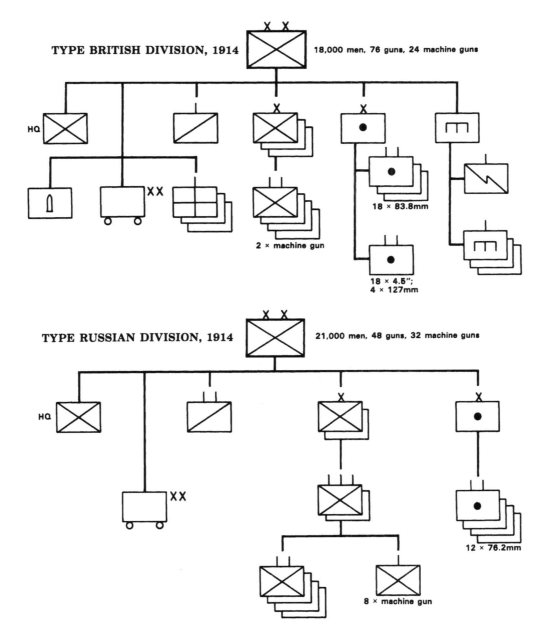

Figure 2. Type British and Russian Divisions, 1914.

formations were almost pure cavalry, with a few horse artillery batteries attached. Not until 1913-14, for example, did the Germans add company-sized elements of mounted engineers and bicycle-equipped infantry to their cavalry divisions.[7]

Where the armies differed most markedly was in the proportion and calibers of artillery included in the infantry divisions. Divisional artillery varied from as few as thirty-six light guns of 75-mm in the French division to as many as seventy-six artillery pieces, including eighteen 4.5-inch (114.5-mm) howitzers and four 127-mm guns, in the British division. These variations in structure reflected profound confusion and disagreement over the role of artillery and the importance of combined arms.

In order to understand the doctrinal interrelationships of the different arms before World War I, some consideration of each arm is in order. Cavalry and engineers may be discussed briefly; infantry and artillery deserve a more detailed explanation. Because the U.S. division was only just developing during the period 1911-17, it is omitted from this discussion.

Cavalry had the greatest mobility in the days before automobiles and was therefore closely associated with functions requiring such mobility. Traditionally, cavalry had three missions: reconnaissance and security before the battle, shock action on the battlefield, and pursuit after the battle. The increases in firepower during the later 1800s led many tacticians to suggest that shock action was no longer a feasible role except under rare circumstances. They argued that, because the charge seemed almost obsolete, cavalry should be reequipped as dragoons or mounted infantry. This would enable the mounted arm to continue its reconnaissance or security mission, while also functioning as highly mobile infantry that dismounted to fight after making contact with the enemy. Cavalry actually operated in this manner during the American Civil War, the Boer War (1899-1902), and the Russo-Japanese War (1904-05). By 1914, the British and German armies had equipped their cavalry with machine guns and trained them to fight dismounted when necessary.

Yet the desire to retain cavalry's operational mobility in reconnaissance, security, and pursuit caused many cavalrymen to prefer mounted fighting whenever possible, despite the large target a horse and rider presented to the enemy. Another factor, social conservatism, also helped preserve the traditional cavalry of lanoes and sabers in most armies. In addition, defenders of cavalry shock action justified their views by citing one cavalry charge of the Franco-Prussian War, an action appropriately known as "Von Bredow's death ride." At the battle of Vionville-Mars-la-Tour on 16 August 1870, Maj. Gen. von Bredow led his Prussian cavalry brigade down a depression to within a few hundred meters of the left flank of the French VI Corps. The French had already suffered from artillery fire and were not entrenched when von Bredow charged out of the smoke. The charge achieved its objective. Yet during an attack that took less than five minutes and produced only a momentary tactical advantage, 380 out of 800 German cavalrymen were killed or wounded.[8]

Of the four combat arms, engineers were the most neglected in doctrine. They generally operated in very small units, performing technical tasks and maintaining weapons or equipment in addition to their mobility and countermobility missions. Because of these missions, engineers were often the only troops trained in the detailed construction and destruction of obstacles and field fortifications.[9]

With respect to infantry, a rifle battalion before 1914 was just that--four companies of rifle-armed infantry plus, in most cases, two heavy machine guns. Such battalions lacked the variety of grenades, mortars, and similar short-range, indirect-fire weapons that we today associate with "infantry." To some extent, armies neglected these weapons because of the specialized training they required, or because, in the case of the heavy machine gun and mortar, the pieces were too heavy to keep pace with advancing infantry. Machine guns were usually cast in an economy-of-force role, such as protecting an open flank. Moreover, once an infantry battalion detrained and advanced to contact, it was neither more mobile nor more protected than infantry in the eighteenth or nineteenth century. The firepower of breech-loading, magazine-fed rifles and machine guns had greatly outstripped the mobility and survivability of foot-mobile infantry. As everyone discovered in the fall of 1914, the only immediate remedy was to entrench. All professional soldiers were aware of this problem before the war, but they regarded defensive firepower as a costly obstacle that had to be overcome by a highly motivated attacker. Attacking infantry was expected to forego protection in order to maximize its own firepower and mobility.

In order to understand this belief, we must consider the war that professional soldiers expected to fight in 1914. The Wars of German Unification had provided models of short wars won by decisive offensive action. Over and over during the summer of 1870, the better-trained and better-armed French infantry had taken up carefully selected defensive positions, only to be outflanked and driven back by determined and costly German attacks.[10] Thus, many soldiers concluded that standing on the defensive was a sure road to defeat. In any event, no one believed that a war that mobilized the entire manpower of a nation could go on for more than a few months. War in 1914 meant that an entire economy halted while the reserves mobilized and fought. Under such circumstances, societies and economies would collapse if the war dragged on.

This belief in a short war determined many of the tactical expectations of European soldiers. With few exceptions, they did not anticipate assaulting prepared fortifications across open ground. Instead, most soldiers envisaged a series of meeting engagements or encounter battles.[11] Each commander hoped that his cavalry screen or his infantry advance guard would find a weak point which he would attack immediately to develop the situation, and force that enemy onto the defensive. The attacker's artillery would then act to pin down and isolate the enemy defender, preventing reinforcement or serious entrenchment.

Meanwhile, the attacking infantry would approach the hastily entrenched enemy, preferably by maneuvering to an open flank. The goal was to infiltrate to within 400-800 meters of the defender by using all available cover and concealment. During the Balkan Wars of 1912-13, Serbian and Bulgarian infantry had infiltrated to within 200 meters of the enemy before opening fire. Most soldiers considered this to be an exceptionally successful movement.[12] Once the defender engaged the advancing infantry, the attacker would deploy into a series of skirmish lines. The desired density of these skirmish lines varied between armies and over time, but soldiers generally moved one to three meters apart. Because of the recognized strength of the defender's firepower, skirmishers would advance by fire and movement, one group providing covering fire while another group rushed forward for a short distance. The size of each group and the distance covered at one rush would both become smaller as the attacker closed with his opponent. Enemy fire would intensify while the attacker found cover more sparse. Casualties were expected, but supporting troops would replenish the attacking skirmish line. The defender would be outnumbered and isolated. Prewar machine guns were too heavy to accompany the advancing skirmishers, so these guns were usually deployed to provide fire support from the rear. Eventually, the attacker expected to get within a short distance of the defender, establish fire superiority with infantry rifles, and assault with the bayonet.

With certain variations, most armies shared this doctrine before 1914. It had a number of problems that are obvious in retrospect, but were not so evident at the time. First, the attacker assumed that he would have local numerical superiority over the defender, whereas the numbers of troops fielded in 1914 were so similar that numerical superiority, even at specific points, was difficult to achieve. Second, this scenario assumed, perhaps unconsciously, that the enemy and friendly forces were operating in a vacuum, moving to contact against each other with their flanks open for envelopment. In practice, however, the density of forces along the French, German, and Belgian frontiers in 1914 was so great that anyone seeking to maneuver to the flank was likely to encounter another unit, either friendly or enemy. Open flanks did occur, notably in the battles of the Marne and Tannenberg at the end of August, but these were exceptions caused by faulty command decisions on a battlefield that was still fluid.[13]

The most significant problem with prewar doctrine was that many professional soldiers considered their subordinates incapable of executing the tactics required. The kind of battle envisioned seemed to depend on two things: high morale and firm control. Officers, especially in the French, Austrian, and Russian armies, continually emphasized the psychological advantage of the attacker. Yet most professionals recognized that discipline and control would be extremely difficult to maintain under intense direct fire. The problem was compounded by the fact that, with the partial exceptions of the British and German armies, most European units had a large number of reservists and untrained draftees. A French first-line infantry company, for example, had a wartime authorized strength of 225 enlisted personnel, of which 65 percent were reservists or first-year conscripts.[14] According to many observers of peacetime maneuvers, these reservists and conscripts demonstrated that they lacked the training and discipline necessary to conduct dispersed fire-and-movement tactics under heavy enemy fire. Professional soldiers argued that these troops would never stand up and advance if they were allowed to take cover. This belief, correct or not, led French, Russian, Austrian, and other officers to attack standing up in relatively dense formations. These officers recognized the risk they were taking, but felt that there was no other way to achieve the necessary rapid victory with undertrained personnel.[15]

Because the British Expeditionary Force of 1914 was a phenomenally well trained body of regulars and some reservists, the British did not face this training problem at the outbreak of war. The German Army minimized the same problem by a three-tiered system of units, consisting of twenty regular army corps with a relatively low proportion of well-trained recent reservists, fourteen reserve corps composed of regular cadres and large numbers of reservists, and numerous smaller Landwehr or militia formations. By carefully focusing on training before the war, the German Army not only reduced the problem in first-line units, but became the only European army to produce fairly effective reserve component units. Indeed, one of the great surprises for France in 1914 was the German willingness to use

15

these cadred formations in the line of battle immediately. Prewar French estimates of enemy strength had ignored these reserve units.[16] Both the British and German armies, however, suffered heavy casualties in the initial campaigns. They had to form new divisions from half-trained, patriotic volunteers during the fall of 1914, and these volunteers were then used in rigid attacks that repeated the suicidal French tactics of August-September.

Given the emphasis in all armies on the meeting engagement and the hasty attack, prewar training often neglected the defense. The Germans constructed field fortifications for their annual maneuvers, but their defensive doctrine focused on rigidly holding a single, densely occupied trench. French defensive doctrine, as reflected in prewar engineer manuals, planned for a defense-in-depth, with an advanced position to delay the enemy, a main line of resistance, and a second position to limit a successful enemy penetration.[17] Ironically, these doctrines had been reversed by 1915, with the French and British defending well forward in a rigid structure, while the Germans were beginning to develop a defense-in-depth.

If infantry had difficulty adjusting to the requirements of the new firepower, artillery was even slower to react. The traditional tactic for artillery, as perfected by Napoleon, was to concentrate the guns in a direct-fire role, placing them between or a few hundred meters behind the infantry units they were supporting. This tradition of direct-fire support meant that by 1914 all armies had standardized on relatively light, highly maneuverable field guns with flat trajectories, even after advances in technology had made accurate indirect fire possible. The French 75-mm, the German 77-mm, the American and Russian 3-inch (76.2-mm), and the British 18-pounder (83.8-mm) were all designed for this role. Larger weapons were too heavy for a standard team of six horses to move across country. These guns were too small to have much effect against even hasty field fortifications, and they lacked the high trajectory necessary for indirect fire in rough terrain. This was perfectly satisfactory to the French. In preparation for an infantry attack, French commanders relied upon an extremely rapid rate of direct fire to suppress temporarily, rather than to destroy, a defending enemy.[18] The volume of such fire was intended to force the enemy to remain under cover, unable to provide effective aimed fire, even if he were not wounded by the French shells. The colonial wars of the nineteenth century had encouraged the British to believe in a similar suppressive function. That same experience had also led the British Army to maintain a much higher proportion of artillery than in French divisions, because British infantry had discovered the value of such fire support.[19]   Artillerymen knew about indirect-fire techniques but rarely practiced them because they seemed complicated and unnecessary.

The Boer War, and even more the Russo-Japanese War, provided a glimpse into the future, with trench systems and the skillful use, particularly by the Japanese, of indirect-fire artillery. Many professional soldiers dismissed these conflicts as minor wars fought at the end of long supply lines and having no useful lessons for a future war in Europe. Yet observers of the Russo-Japanese War, especially those from the German Army and British Royal Artillery, were impressed with the necessity for indirect fire, if only to protect the gun crews from enemy counterbattery fire. The rest of the British Army, however, insisted upon having close direct-fire support and believed simplistically that massed firepower was accomplished only by massing guns well forward on the ground. Thus, the British in 1914 fell between two chairs: they possessed an assortment of weapons but no clear doctrine.[20]   The German Army, by contrast, conducted a serious study of indirect-fire techniques and equipment.   Beginning in 1909, the Germans increased their indirect-fire capability by converting one battalion in each division to 105-mm howitzers and by adding a battalion of 150-mm howitzers to each corps artillery.   These weapons had an effective range of 7.5 kilometers, as opposed to the French 75-mm with a four kilometer range.[21]   By 1914, Germany had 3,500 medium and heavy pieces, including many howitzers and large siege mortars, while France had only 300 modern guns larger than 75-mm.[22]   A few of the German heavy weapons had been developed to reduce Belgian fortresses, but they were still available for field use.

The small caliber and limited number of guns involved in most of the lesser wars at the end of the 1800s meant that no one was prepared for the devastating effects of massed, large-caliber artillery fire on the battlefield.   To complicate matters further, in the nine years between the Russo-Japanese War and the start of World War I, a final technological change occurred in the explosive charges contained in artillery rounds.   The experiments of Alfred Nobel and others gave all armies high explosive rounds that were much more destructive than the artillery shells of the nineteenth century.[23]

Thus, at the outbreak of World War I, cavalry and artillery in most armies had not fully adjusted to the new technology, while infantry commanders doubted their ability to execute the relatively sophisticated fire-and-movement tactics of the day. Perhaps most significantly, none of the combat arms had trained for really close cooperation with the others, an oversight that proved disastrous in 1914. The most obvious example of this mind-set was the standard method of describing the size of an army in the field. Instead of counting combined arms divisions, or even single arm regiments, the average professional officer described any force in terms of the numbers of rifles, sabers, and guns--the separate weapons of the three principal arms.

CHAPTER TWO

WORLD WAR I

The defensive power of indirect artillery and machine guns dominated the battlefields of 1914. From the very first contacts, commanders had to restrain the "impetuosity" of their troops and insist upon careful engineer preparation in the defense and artillery preparation in the offense.[1] The French and British were shocked by the vulnerability of their exposed troops and guns to carefully sited German machine guns and artillery. The Germans, in turn, were surprised by the accuracy and rapidity of British and French guns. By the end of 1914, this firepower had resulted in the creation of a continuous line of foxholes and hasty trenches from Switzerland to the North Sea. Thereafter, every attack was of necessity a frontal attack on these trenches.

The stereotype of trench warfare did not appear overnight. On both the Eastern and Western fronts, the battles of August-September 1914 were characterized by a great deal of fluidity and maneuver. Prewar infantry tactics appeared to work under the right circumstances. At 0430 on 8 September, for example, the infantry of the Prussian Guard Corps infiltrated forward and, in a surprise attack without artillery preparation, overran the positions of the French XI Corps.[2] On the Eastern Front, the German Eighth Army surrounded and destroyed an entire Russian army by a double envelopment. In fact, the Eastern Front was never as immobile as the Western, because of the greater frontages involved. Yet, this fluidity produced indecisive results until first the Russians and then the Austro-Hungarians became exhausted and demoralized by attrition.

Given these examples of maneuver, many commanders regarded the thin line of 1914 entrenchments as an unnatural and temporary pause in the war. British and French commanders spent most of the war seeking the means of penetrating and disrupting the enemy defenses in order to restore the war of maneuver. Because the Germans concentrated most of their efforts on the Eastern Front during 1914-1916, they conducted an economy-of-force defense with relatively few attacks in the West. In order to understand the nature of World War I tactics, therefore, we need to examine the problems of Allied attacks and, then, the development of German defensive doctrine. The solutions to both problems involved greater cooperation than had previously been established on either side; in some cases they also involved the combination of the different arms.

Artillery and Coordination

Once the infantry attacks failed and trench warfare because the reality of combat, the most obvious means of creating a penetration was massed artillery fire. Indeed, the British and French rapidly gave up any idea of combining artillery fire with infantry maneuver and concentrated instead on achieving overwhelming destruction in the preparatory fires. Although higher-level planners still saw a role for infantry, many tactical commanders interpreted the new techniques as "the artillery conquers, the infantry occupies."[3]

Artillery conquest was not easy. Everyone had expected a short war, and thus few armies had sufficient supplies of ammunition and heavy artillery to conduct the massive preparations necessary to demolish even temporary field fortifications. In both Britain and Russia, scandals arose over the long delays necessary to produce more ammunition and guns. Even when France began to produce more guns, the first models of medium and heavy artillery had extremely slow rates of fire, while the more rapid 75-mm gun had such a short range that it had to move well forward and displace frequently behind the advancing troops in order to destroy any defenses-in-depth.[4]

Adding to the problem was the fact that most gunners had little experience in precision indirect fire. Many of the procedures that are commonplace to artillerymen today were developed painfully during the period 1914-1917: establishing forward observer techniques, measuring and compensating for the effects of weather and worn barrels, and using ammunition from the same production lot to ensure that successive volleys fell in the same general area. The first French regulation describing such procedures was not published until November 1915. The British Royal Artillery needed new maps of the entire area of Northeastern France before it could establish a grid system for surveying battery locations and adjusting indirect fire. The fledgling air services of the belligerents had to provide aircraft for photographic mapping and both aircraft and balloons for adjusting indirect fire. Finally, improved radiotelegraphs allowed aerial observers to talk to the artillery fire controllers.[5] Such developments took most of the war to reach perfection.

Quite apart from the technical problems of indirect fire, there was the even greater problem of coordinating the infantry and artillery in an attack. The first deliberate attacks conducted by the British and French during late 1914 and early 1915 were particularly difficult to control, because both artillerymen and commanders lacked experience in indirect fire. The easiest procedure seemed to be the establishment of a series of phase lines, with artillery firing on the far side of a phase line while all infantry remained on the friendly side. Once the commander directed artillery fires to shift forward past a new phase line, the troops could advance in relative safety.

Such phase lines encouraged commanders to ignore the terrain contours to their front and the possibilities for maneuver, and to favor instead simple advances by all units on line. This in turn discouraged massing of artillery or infantry at critical points. More importantly, there were no effective communications procedures that would allow the leading infantry units to talk to their supporting artillery. During the Champagne campaign of 1915, the French went to the extreme of sewing white cloths on the backs of their soldiers to help observers determine the forward progress of troops, but casualties from friendly fire still occurred. The Germans experimented with colored flares and signal lamps to communicate between infantry and artillery, but such signals were often difficult to recognize amidst the destruction of battle.[6]

Beginning with the battle of the Somme in July 1916, artillery was able to provide a rolling barrage of shrapnel that could advance at a steady rate of speed. The use of shrapnel instead of high explosive made it safer for the infantry to advance close behind the artillery barrage (about 100 meters), because the explosive effect of shrapnel was focused forward along the line of flight. Shrapnel, however, had almost no effect against well-prepared positions--the best it could do was force the defender to stay under cover during the assault. In addition, there was still no way for the infantry to adjust the rate at which the rolling barrage moved forward. The rigid forward movement of artillery fire often outran the heavily laden infantryman struggling across the shell-pocked battlefield, allowing the defender time to leave his shelter and engage the attacker after the barrage had passed over a trench.

This problem of infantry-artillery coordination was only one aspect of the greater problems of command, control, and communications that plagued a World War I commander. The huge scope of offensives and the scarcity of trained staff officers at junior headquarters meant that most operations were planned at the level of field army or higher. Given the crude nature of artillery procedures in the early stage of the war, artillery planning and control were also centralized at a high level. This meant that each time the advancing infantry reached an objective or phase line they had to stop and request permission to continue the advance or to commit reserves. A messenger had to hand-carry the request under fire back to the lowest headquarters (usually brigade, regiment, or division) where the field telephone circuits had survived enemy counterfire. These circuits then relayed the request through the different levels of headquarters in order to obtain a decision from the senior commander in charge of operations. Once a staff estimate had been made and the commander's decision announced, this communications process had to operate in reverse before the troops could advance. For example, at the battle of Neuve Chapelle on 10 March 1915, one of the first concentrated artillery preparations of the war destroyed most of the shallow German defenses. The forward British troops, however, had to wait at a phase line for seven hours before they received authorization from their corps commanders to continue the advance. During this delay, the Germans were able to move in reserves and reestablish a defense in the very path of the British advance.[7] Once the momentum of an attack was lost, it was very difficult to organize a renewed advance.

To some extent, these communications problems were a product of the technology of the time. A senior commander could not command close to the front even if he wished to. He was tied to the field telephone system that brought all information to him and conducted all orders forward. Although radios did exist, they were bulky, unreliable, and generally suspect because of the possibility of enemy signals intelligence. These limitations, plus the difficulty of direct communication between infantry and artillery, made subordinate initiative and rapid exploitation potentially disastrous. The attacking troops might well fall prey to their own artillery support if they did not coordinate with higher headquarters.

By 1918, improvements in artillery techniques and communications made such initiative much more practical. The Australian general Sir John Monash, for example, developed an elaborate system to determine the forward progress of his forces. Advancing troops carried specially colored flares, while a detachment of aircraft did nothing but spot the location of these flares, write out reports based on the locations, and airdrop the results to Monash's headquarters. This gave a corps commander the forward trace of his forces with a delay of twenty or fewer minutes, provided he had local air superiority.[8]

The Problem of Penetration

The problems of indirect artillery fire and of command and control were only two aspects of the basic tactical question of how to achieve and exploit a penetration more rapidly than the defender could redeploy to prevent or seal off a penetration.

Consider the accompanying abstract diagram (Figure 3) of a fully developed trench system. In order to advance, one side had to begin by neutralizing the defensive fire of the enemy's

22

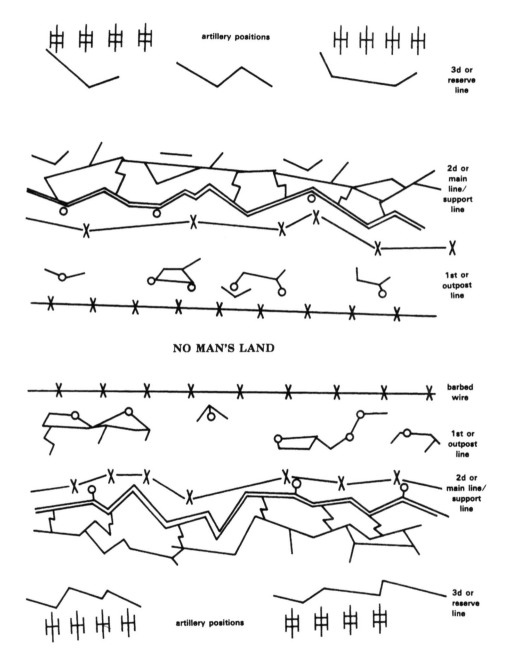

artillery positions

3d or
reserve
line

2d or
main
line/
support
line

1st or
outpost
line

NO MAN'S LAND

barbed
wire

1st or
outpost
line

2d or
main line/
support
line

3d or
reserve
line

artillery positions

Figure 3. Trench System, World War I.

trenches and artillery batteries. As early as the battle of Neuve Chapelle in 1915, the British had demonstrated the possibility of achieving such a penetration by concentrated or prolonged artillery fire. Eliminating the barbed wire and similar obstacles in front of the enemy trenches was somewhat more difficult. Shrapnel had very little effect against wire; nor would prewar fuzes for high explosive rounds detonate against the very slight resistance they encountered when passing through barbed wire. By 1917 the British had developed the instantaneous model 106 fuze that would detonate high explosive rapidly enough to destroy wire.[9] Indeed, even the Germans conceded that artillery and infantry together could always capture the first and even the second trench lines, especially if a short artillery bombardment and good operational security maintained surprise.

The problem came when the attacker tried to displace forward to develop and exploit the resulting partial penetration. The infantry that had made the initial assault would be exhausted and in many cases decimated, while the artillery would need to move forward in order to continue its fires on the enemy third line and artillery positions. Even after a senior commander learned of success, decided to exploit, and communicated his decision forward, all of his troops, guns, and supplies had to move across the intervening No Man's Land and captured enemy trenches, an area that usually was a sea of mud and shellholes. In most cases, by the time the attacker had completed this displacement, the defender had been able to bring up reserves and establish new trench lines in front of the attacker. The defender's role was much easier, because his reserves could move by railroad and motor truck while the attacker's forces toiled forward over the broken ground. Moreover, the defender could easily counterattack and pinch off any penetration that did not occur on a broad frontage, because the newly captured area would be exposed to concentrated defensive artillery fire.

Even if the attacker moved faster than the defender and actually penetrated through existing trenches and gun positions, the second echelon infantry would again be tired, out of the range of artillery support and communications, and essentially restricted to foot mobility. Thus, another passage of lines would be required. In theory, this was the stage when horse cavalry could use its greater mobility to exploit, although in practice a few machine guns could delay such exploitation significantly.

Thus, the timing of the decision to exploit and the problems of mobility across No Man's Land remained major obstacles for any attacker. Various solutions were tried. Some artillery batteries secretly moved forward prior to the battle and camouflaged themselves just behind the friendly first-line trenches, allowing sustained artillery support to a slightly deeper range. Attacking brigades or regiments developed a system of leapfrogging, with second-echelon battalions passing through the attacking battalions to sustain the advance. Ultimately, however, the point would be reached where the attacker's advantages of artillery preparation and, if possible, surprise were cancelled out by the defender's advantages of depth, terrain, and operational mobility.

Of course, these problems could be minimized if the attacker did not try to achieve a complete penetration in any one attack, but settled for capturing a limited objective. Meticulous planning and preparation would allow such a surprise attack to succeed within the limits of artillery range and command and control capabilities, after which a new defense would be organized to halt the inevitable counterattack. French commanders such as Philippe Pétain were particularly noted for using this technique during 1917-18, after the French morale had been shattered by too many blind frontal attacks. Such a set-piece battle certainly improved morale and could achieve a limited victory at low cost; it could not, however, break the stalemate and win the war. Ultimately, a combination of attrition, new weapons, and new infantry tactics were required to achieve the elusive victory.

Flexible Defense

While the British, French, and later the Americans sought to solve the mystery of the penetration, the Germans gradually perfected their defenses against such a penetration. This evolution of German defensive doctrine was by no means rapid or easy, but the result was a system of flexible defense-in-depth that not only hindered attack but developed the capabilities of the German infantry.

At the beginning of the war, senior commanders on both sides emphasized a rigid defense of forward trenches. As the cost of taking ground increased, it seemed treasonous to surrender voluntarily even one foot of precious soil to an enemy attack. Moreover, many commanders believed that creating defenses-in-depth and allowing units to withdraw under pressure would encourage cowardice, as troops expecting a retreat would defend their positions only half-heartedly.[10] Only gradually did German leaders realize that massing their forces in the forward trenches was suicidal; the artillery bombardment before a French or British attack eliminated many of the defenders in those trenches, increasing the possibility of enemy penetration. This was most obvious at the battle of Neuve Chapelle, when the single line of German trenches disappeared under the weight of a British bombardment, leaving nothing but a string of concrete pillboxes behind the lines to block the British advance until reinforcements arrived.

Beginning with the shock of Neuve Chapelle, Germany gradually evolved a system that by 1917 included up to five successive defensive lines, one behind the other, in critical sectors. The first two or three lines were sited on reverse slopes wherever the terrain permitted. This not only complicated the task of adjusting enemy fire on those trenches, but meant that the attacking British and French infantry were out of sight and therefore out of communication with their own forces when they reached the German defenses. At the same time, if a German trench on a reverse slope were captured, it would be fully exposed to fire and counterattack from the German rear positions. The rearward trenches were beyond the range of enemy light and medium artillery, making them more difficult to reduce.

Quite apart from the choice of terrain, the German defensive system emphasized three principles: flexibility, decentralized control, and counterattack. In terms of flexibility, the forward German trenches most exposed to bombardment contained few troops, with perhaps one battalion out of every four in the first two trenches. By contrast, the French put two-thirds of every regiment in these forward lines, with orders to hold at all costs. By 1916, the Germans had gone even further and had decided that trench lines were useful shelters only during quiet periods. Once a bombardment began, the rearward German troops moved into deep bunkers, while the forward outposts moved out of the trenches, taking cover in nearby shellholes. The British and French artillery bombarded the deserted trenches until their barrage passed and their infantry began to advance. At that point the Germans would come out of the shelters and open fire from the shellholes or from the remains of the trenches.

The second aspect of the German system was decentralized control. Squad and platoon leaders had considerable independence and might defend or delay anywhere forward of the third, or main, defense line. The forward or "Front Battalion Commander" frequently directed the entire defense of a regimental sector. In the mature system of 1917-18, this battalion commander had the authority to commit the remaining two or three battalions of his regiment in a counterattack at the moment he judged most appropriate. This only exaggerated the difference in decision cycles: while the British and French attackers had to seek orders and reinforcements from their corps or army commander located miles to the rear, the defending German battalion commander could direct a regimental counterattack on the spot.[11]

This, in fact, pertains to the third element of the German defensive tactics: counterattacks at every echelon to retake lost ground before the attacker could consolidate. In those areas that seemed most vulnerable to attack, a second-echelon division was located behind every one or two front divisions,

26

ready to counterattack if needed. Whenever a major offensive began, the German defenders sought to contain the flanks of the penetration by blocking positions; counterattacks would then eliminate the resulting salient.

Such tactics did not evolve overnight. Many German commanders bitterly opposed the flexibility and decentralized control of the elastic defense. For example, at Passchendaele in July-August 1917, the local commander ordered all outposts to hold in place while awaiting the counterattack. The result was disaster, with many outposts being cut off. There is some evidence that the British incorrectly decided that this costly experiment was the real key to German defenses, leading to the rigid forward British defense that collapsed in March 1918.[12]

The combination of flexibility, decentralized control, and counterattack at every echelon made the German defensive system almost invincible until attrition and demoralization gave the Allies an overwhelming numerical superiority.

The Allies, by contrast, received fewer attacks from the Germans and therefore took longer to arrive at the same conclusions. A French directive of 8 July 1915 did require commanders to hold the majority of their troops in the rear for counterattack, but this order was frequently ignored. Not until the five German offensives of 1918 did French field commanders learn to array their forces in depth and accept the loss of lightly defended forward positions.[13]

Technological Change

Like all major wars, World War I accelerated the development of new technology. In addition to changes in artillery and communications, a number of new weapons appeared as the result of efforts to solve the penetration problem. None of these efforts was entirely successful, but they all represented additional weapons or tools to be combined with the traditional arms.

Gas warfare was the first attempt to break the trench defense. Although the French had experimented with various noxious gases on a small scale at the end of 1914, it was the Germans who first conducted major gas attacks. The first German test of gas took place in January 1915, at Łódź on the Russian front. Much of the chemical, however, failed to vaporize because of low temperatures. The first use on the Western Front was on 22 April 1915 at the Ypres salient. There a surprise attack routed French colonial troops on a five-mile front, but the Germans were not prepared to exploit their success. They had no significant reserves available to advance before the French sealed the breach. Thereafter, each side found that primitive gas masks and uncertain weather conditions made the existing nonpersistent and early persistent agents difficult to employ successfully. When the British first used gas at Loos on 25 September 1915, the wind conditions were extremely calm, so that the gas moved too slowly or in the wrong direction along most of the front. The British troops advanced into their own gas, suffering more casualties than their opponents. The Germans, for their part, had problems with chemical warfare on the Western Front because the prevailing winds came from the west, often blowing gases back in their faces. Gas warfare became only an adjunct, useful to degrade enemy effectiveness but not to achieve a penetration by itself. By 1917-18, the most common use of gas was to mix chemical and high explosive artillery shells during a preparatory fire, in hopes of forcing the enemy out of his deep shelters where the gas settled.[14]

World War 1 was also the first conflict to have significant air action. Military aviation developed at a tremendous rate during the war, but was still in its infancy in 1918. All of the publicity went to fighter pilots, whose primary mission was to achieve local air superiority. This condition allowed the primitive aircraft of the time to conduct their more basic functions of reconnaissance and artillery fire adjustment. Not until 1917 did the British and Germans officially recognize the possibility of ground attack by fighters in the forward area, and both sides considered the main effect of such an attack to be demoralization rather than destruction.[15] By 1918, the first bombers with significant payloads appeared, but in most cases reconnaissance and not bombardment was the critical contribution of air power.

The military motor vehicle also developed from a few primitive cars in 1914 to thousands of large trucks by 1916. Although not a tactical weapon, the truck allowed the rapid movement of troops and supplies between widely separated points. As such, it increased operational mobility as significantly as had the railroad in previous generations. This made it possible to mass suddenly and conduct a surprise attack at an unexpected point, or to move reserves to blunt a penetration. Trucks were also essential for stockpiling the ammunition and materiel needed for major offensives.

The tank was originally designed as a special weapon to solve an unusual tactical situation, the stalemate of the trenches. Basically, the tank was intended to bring the firepower of artillery and machine guns across the morass of No Man's Land while providing more protection than a purely infantry unit could carry. The sole purpose of this weapon was to assist the infantry in creating a penetration so that the cavalry, which had been waiting for the opportunity since 1914, could exploit into the German rear.

This purpose must be remembered in order to understand the shortcomings of early tanks. British and especially French heavy tanks had slow speeds, poor mechanical reliability, and great vulnerability to direct-fire artillery once the initial surprise wore off. After all, these new weapons had to advance only a few miles and then turn the battle over to the cavalry. Moreover, the great secrecy surrounding tank development, coupled with the skepticism of infantry commanders, often meant that infantry had little training to cooperate with tanks. As a result, the infantry would become separated from the tanks, allowing the German infantry to defeat the two arms separately. Generally speaking, infantry that had the opportunity to train with tanks before battle and to work with tanks in battle swore by them, while infantry that was thrown into battle without prior tank training swore at them.

Small, local attacks, beginning at Flers on the Somme on 15 September 1916, dissipated the initial surprise of the tank. Not until 20 November 1917, at Cambrai, did the British Tank Corps get the conditions it needed for success. Using new survey techniques, the British guns moved into position without firing ranging shots prior to the attack. The tanks then began to move forward at the start of a very short artillery bombardment, with the infantry following in the lee of the tanks. The elimination of a long artillery preparation not only achieved surprise, but also left the ground more trafficable. Four hundred seventy-four heavy tanks in three brigades had practiced extensively with five of the six infantry divisions they accompanied. Tanks operated in sections of three: one tank used machine gun fire and its treads to suppress the defending infantry, while the other two tanks, accompanied by British infantry, crossed the trenches. These tactics worked well except at Flésquières Ridge, in the center of the Cambrai sector. Here the commander of the 51st Highland Division, believing that German fire would be focused on the armor, had forbidden his infantry to come within 100 yards of their tanks. Furthermore, the Royal Flying Corps erroneously reported that it had driven off the German artillery in the area, whereas one enemy battery had moved onto the reverse slope of the ridge. As a result, the British tanks were unsupported when they slowly topped the ridge. Direct-fire German artillery knocked out sixteen unmaneuverable tanks in a few minutes.[16] This incident convinced many people that armor could not survive when separated from infantry, an attitude that persisted after 1918, even when tank speed and maneuverability improved. In any event, the available tanks were distributed evenly across the Cambrai front, leaving no reserve to exploit the greatest success. Moreover, because of the attrition battles of 1916-17, the British had few infantry reserves to commit at Cambrai--they had regarded it as a raid rather than another attempt to penetrate.

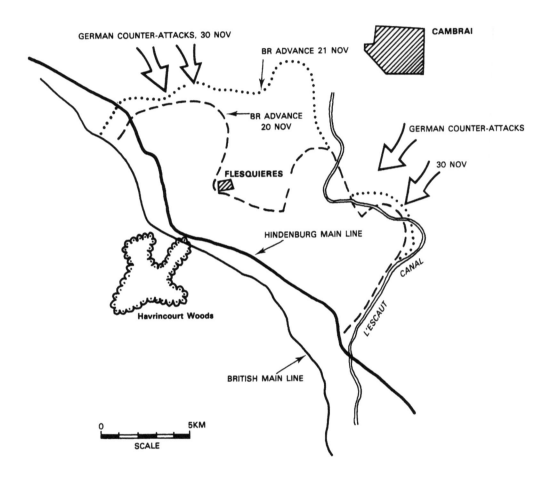

GERMAN COUNTER-ATTACKS, 30 NOV

BR ADVANCE 21 NOV

CAMBRAI

BR ADVANCE
20 NOV

GERMAN COUNTER-ATTACKS

30 NOV

FLESQUIERES

HINDENBURG MAIN LINE

L'ESCAUT CANAL

Havrincourt Woods

BRITISH MAIN LINE

0   5KM

SCALE

Map 1. Battle of Cambrai, 20—30 November 1917.

The usual problems of Allied generals commanding from the rear meant that the Germans rebuilt their defenses before the British cavalry moved forward to exploit. Ten days after the British offensive at Cambrai, the Germans counterattacked and restored the original front. In its own way, this counterattack also reflected the latest developments of the war: surprise, colored flares to shift artillery at phase lines, and multiple attacking waves to clear out British strongpoints bypassed by the first wave.

Even before Cambrai, the Germans had begun to develop an antitank doctrine. In marked contrast to the beliefs of British armor commanders, the German commanders were more concerned by the psychological effect of tank attacks than by the limited firepower and armor of the tanks themselves. Psychological effect rather than infantry support was the point emphasized by postwar German theorists. In 1917-18, however, the Germans lacked the resources to compete in tank production. Instead, they relied upon obstacle plans combined with existing light artillery pieces (the 77-mm guns) and some armor-piercing rounds for infantry weapons. These rounds were effective against early British tanks, and by 1918 the Germans had developed oversized antitank rifles against later British models. To combat the terror of tanks, German troops received training on how to defeat them. Where possible, German infantry would wait until the attacking tank had passed, engage the accompanying British infantry, and throw bundles of grenades to disable a tank tread.[17]

By 1918, tanks were extremely vulnerable unless accompanied by infantry and ground-attack aircraft, both of which worked to locate and suppress antitank defenses. During the first three days of the battle of Bapaume in August 1918, German antitank defenses or mechanical failures immobilized 81 percent of the attacking tanks.[18] Any tank that broke down on the battlefield was almost certain to be knocked out by antitank fire in a few minutes. Again, such experiences shaped perceptions of tank capabilities and roles long after technological change had restored the tank's initial advantage.

The French, British, and (with French equipment) Americans organized light tank units in 1918. The British "Whippet" tank was faster (7.5 miles per hour versus four miles per hour) than most heavy tanks, but was still hardly a vehicle for rapid exploitation. Light tanks were much easier to redeploy in secret from one sector to another, because they could be loaded onto trucks instead of moved by rail.

Although the Royal Tank Corps experimented with special armored vehicles in which to transport radios, supplies, and even machine guns, all tank units in World War I were just that--pure tank formations of up to brigade size, intended for attachment to infantry units rather than for independent combined arms mechanized operations of their own.

Gas warfare, aviation, motor transport, and tanks had two effects, other than those derived from their individual tactical characteristics, on the positional battlefield of World War I. On the one hand, their development made the problem of combining different weapons for attack or defense much more complicated. This reinforced the tendency for detailed planning and centralized control at a time when infantry-artillery cooperation was still being developed. On the other hand, the army that succeeded in this orchestration had a much better chance of eventually defeating its opponent by attrition, even if penetration was never achieved.

The Resurgence of Infantry

Most of the developments in artillery, gas warfare, aircraft, and armor were based on the supposed inability of 1914 infantry to advance under fire. During the course of World War I, however, the infantry gradually evolved to a point where it had recovered some of its original ability to take and hold terrain on its own. In the process, modern infantry organization was developed.

The 1914 infantry battalion was almost exclusively armed with rifles, plus a few heavy and almost immobile machine guns. As soon as the effects of firepower became evident on the battlefield, however, the infantry of various armies sought to increase their own firepower in return. The first such effort was the trench mortar. Mortars had existed as a form of heavy artillery for centuries, but in 1914 the German Army introduced a limited number of small, cheap, portable minenwerfers, which were breech-loading, low-trajectory mortars. Other armies quickly copied the minenwerfer, and in March 1915, the English engineer Wilfred Stokes developed the grandfather of all current infantry mortars, the 3-inch muzzle-loading Stokes mortar.[19] This weapon was much simpler to manufacture than artillery and therefore was employed extensively in all armies during the war. However, larger caliber mortars were often classified as weapons for artillerymen or, in the German Army, for engineers, and thus placed in batteries and battalions separated from the infantry.

As early as 1915 the French began to issue other new weapons to the infantry, notably the light automatic rifle and the rifle grenade launcher. These, plus ordinary hand grenades, gave the

French infantry more mobile automatic firepower and short-range (up to 150 meters) indirect-fire capability. On 27 September 1916, France reorganized the infantry company to consist of a headquarters, which included communications and pioneer (combat engineer) personnel, plus four platoons of two sections each. Within these twelve-men sections, hand grenadiers, rifle grenadiers, and riflemen were organized around the automatic rifleman as the base of fire. Three of these infantry companies, plus a company of eight heavy machine guns and a 37-mm gun in the headquarters, made up an infantry battalion that modern infantrymen can recognize as such. Other armies adopted similar armament and organizations, although the Germans delayed until 1917. The German preoccupation with accuracy of fire by heavy machine guns made them reluctant to accept the relatively inaccurate light machine guns and automatic rifles, until in desperation the frontline German infantry began to use captured French automatic rifles.[20]

The resulting changes in infantry tactics were slow to take root. In May 1915, an obscure French captain named André Laffargue privately published a pamphlet that suggested a variety of innovations, including not only trench mortars but so-called skirmisher or sharpshooter groups. These groups, armed with light machine guns, rifle grenades, and hand grenades, would precede the main assault wave by fifty meters. Their mission was to provide covering fire for the main attack and, if possible, to infiltrate through the forward German positions to suppress and outflank German machine gun posts. The French government distributed but did not endorse this pamphlet; the British largely ignored it and were among the last to give up the linear advance. Not until 1916 did the French officially reduce the density of their skirmish lines to one man every two, and later every five, paces, as opposed to every pace, and integrate the new weapons fully into infantry organization. Meanwhile, the Germans captured a copy of Laffargue's pamphlet during the summer of 1916 and may have adapted parts of it to their own tactical doctrine.[21]

The evolution of German offensive tactics during World War I was slower than that of the elastic defense. Although the Germans as early as Verdun in 1916 used small groups of riflemen, machine gunners, and engineers to infiltrate past the French outposts at the start of an attack, their new infiltration tactics actually evolved in 1917 on the Russian and Italian fronts, in the battles of Riga and Caporetto. These tactics are sometimes called, probably erroneously, "Hutier tactics." Gen. Oskar von Hutier commanded such attacks on the Russian and Italian fronts during 1917 before directing one of the field armies in the German spring offensive of 1918, but he did not invent the concepts. Some German officers have since denied the very existence of the "infiltration" or "soft-spot" tactics, and in fact the victories of 1918 were probably the result of the intelligent application of lessons learned against the Russians and Italians, rather than any sudden innovation in tactics. It is clear, however, that the German Chief of Staff, Erich von Ludendorff, issued a set of offensive instructions dated 8 February 1918, which directed infantry to attack on its own using machine guns, rifles, grenades, light mortars, and accompanying direct-fire artillery pieces. During early 1918 as many as seventy divisions rotated through a special training course in the new offensive tactics.[22]

The result was the astonishing German success of March and April 1918. The tactics involved represented the culmination of German developments in combined arms during World War I. The spirit behind these tactics, when combined with armored equipment, had much to do with the later German blitzkrieg.

The Return Of Mobility, 1918

The German infiltration tactics of 1918 can be summarized under four headings: Bruckmüller artillery preparation; the combined arms assault or storm battalion; rejection of the linear advance in favor of bypassing enemy centers of resistance; and attacks to disorganize the enemy rear area.

Col. Georg Bruckmüller, an obscure officer retired for nervous problems in 1913 but recalled to duty for the war, developed German artillery techniques to a fine art. The essence of the Bruckmüller artillery preparation was a carefully orchestrated, short but intense bombardment designed to isolate, demoralize, and disorganize enemy defenders. Before each of the great offensives, Bruckmuller and his assistants held classes for junior leaders of both artillery and infantry, explaining what would take place. The result was not only unprecedented understanding and cooperation, but a much greater confidence on the part of the infantry. Next, Bruckmüller allocated different weapons against different specific targets. For example, each trench mortar was given only twenty-five to thirty meters of enemy front to engage, while each artillery battery was assigned to suppress a specific enemy battery or to attack 100 to 150 meters of enemy positions.[23] Bruckmüller avoided area targets, concentrating on such key points as artillery observation posts, command posts, radio and telephone centers, rearward troop concentrations, bridges, and major approach routes. He carefully pinpointed all these targets on aerial photographs. The result was to cut enemy communications and isolate forward units. The effect was increased by surprise. Using the survey techniques developed in all armies during 1916-17, Bruckmüller was able to position and range his batteries in secret from points immediately behind the forward infantry trenches.

At the start of the German offensive on 21 March 1918, Bruckmüller began his bombardment with ten minutes of gas shells to force the British to mask, followed by four hours and twenty-five minutes of mixed gas and high explosives.[24] The preparatory fires shifted back and forth, so that the British did not know when the artillery was actually lifting for the infantry advance. Meanwhile, automatic rifle teams moved as close as possible to the British positions during the bombardment.[25] When the Germans did advance, they moved behind a rolling barrage, further enhanced by intense fog. The combination of surprise, brevity, intensity, and carefully selected targets was unique.

The combined arms assault or storm battalion was a union of all the weapons available after years of trench warfare, weapons which could be focused by a battalion commander. A typical assault battalion task force consisted of:

    3-4 infantry companies
      1 trench mortar company
      1 accompanying artillery battery or half-battery of 77-mm guns
      1 flamethrower section
      1 signal detachment
      1 pioneer (combat engineer) section

The regimental commander might attach additional machine gun units and bicyclists. The accompanying artillery pieces did not participate in the artillery preparation, but waited behind the infantry, ready to move immediately. One of the principal tasks of the pioneers was to assist in the movement of the guns across obstacles and shellholes. Upon encountering a center of resistance, the infantry provided suppressive fire, while the guns, mortars, and flamethrowers attempted to eliminate that resistance. Despite a specially constructed low carriage on some 77-mm guns, the result was a very high casualty rate among the exposed crews, although the disorganized state of British defenses made such situations relatively rare.[26]

The essence of the German tactics was for the first echelon of assault units to bypass centers of resistance, seeking to penetrate into the enemy positions in columns or squad groups, down defiles or between outposts. Some skirmishers had to precede these dispersed columns, but skirmish lines and linear tactics were avoided. The local commander had authority to continue the advance through gaps in the enemy defenses without regard for events on his flanks. A second echelon, again equipped with light artillery and pioneers, was responsible for eliminating bypassed enemy positions. This system of decentralized "soft-spot" advances was second nature to the Germans because of their flexible defensive experience. At the battle of Caporetto in 1917, the young Erwin Rommel used such tactics to bypass forward defenses and capture an Italian infantry regiment with only a few German companies.[27]

The final aspect of the German infiltration tactics was the effort to disorganize the enemy rear. The artillery preparation began by destroying communications and command centers; the infiltrating infantry also attacked such centers, as well as artillery positions. The British defenders who opposed the first German offensive of 1918 lost all organization and retreated thirty-eight kilometers in four days. Col. J.F.C. Fuller, one of the foremost British tank tacticians, observed that the British seemed to collapse and retreat from the rear forward. Major British headquarters learned of multiple German attacks on forward units just before losing contact with some of those units. The higher British commanders then ordered their remaining forces, which were often successfully defending their bypassed positions, to withdraw in order to restore a conventional linear front.[28]

The German spring offensives ultimately failed for a variety of reasons, including lack of mobility to exploit initial successes and lack of clear strategic objectives. As a result, Ludendorff dissipated his forces in a series of attacks that achieved tactical success but no operational or strategic decision.

In other words, the German offensive of 1918 used tactics and organization that could be described as a blitzkrieg without tanks, disorganizing and demoralizing rather than systematically destroying the defender. This was especially easy to do against a World War I army, where the static nature of deployments and telephone communications had combined with the elaborate planning necessary for a set-piece battle to produce a defender who had great difficulty reacting to sudden changes. Both sides found that their soldiers no longer knew how to fight in open terrain, but dug in immediately whenever they broke through the enemy defensive system.

The German spring offensives of 1918 were the most obvious example of mobility returning to the battlefield, but in fact all armies in 1918 were better able to attack than they had been in the preceding three years. Beginning on 15 July 1918, the British, French, and Americans launched a sustained series of attacks that combined all the Allied innovations made during the war. Infantry units used renewed mobility and firepower, plus tanks to precede them and suppress enemy strongpoints. Airpower provided limited ground-attack capability plus reconnaissance both before and during the battle. This air reconnaissance focused on antitank threats to the advancing forces. Artillery had become much more sophisticated and effective than in 1914. Most important of all, the different weapons and arms had learned to cooperate closely, at least in carefully planned set-piece operations. Commanders could no longer rely on one or even two arms, but had to coordinate every available means to overcome the stalemate of the trenches.

Despite all this, the 1918 offensives in France never achieved a decisive result on the battlefield, and the Germans were defeated more by sustained attrition and demoralization than by any decisive penetration and exploitation.[29] One of the few cases in which a 1918 army penetrated a prepared defense and then exploited with conclusive results occurred in Palestine rather than France, where the British defeated Germany's ally, Turkey. This victory is known as the second battle of Armageddon or Megiddo (Map 2), because it was fought in the same area as the original battle of 1479 B.C.[30]

The British commander, Sir Edmund Allenby, had steadily advanced from Egypt through Palestine against a Turkish army with a German commander, Liman von Sanders, and a few German units. The Turkish government had diverted its resources elsewhere, so that in 1918 the British outnumbered the Turks two to one. Allenby further increased his advantage by a detailed deception plan that convinced the Turks that the British would attack at the eastern end of the front, in the Jordan Valley. The actual attack was then conducted in the west, near the seacoast. The fact that the British possessed a tremendous numerical advantage does not detract from the significance of the second battle of Armageddon in terms of its tactical methods and strategic objectives.

Allenby used all available elements, beginning with irregular troops in the enemy rear areas. On 17 September 1918, two days before the planned offensive, the famous T. E. Lawrence and Prince Feisal of Arabia conducted a wave of attacks on Turkish rail lines in order to divert attention and isolate the battlefront. The Royal Air Force also harassed Turkish lines of communications for days. At 0430 on 19 September, the British infantry began to move forward behind a fifteen-minute artillery barrage. This short preparation achieved surprise and avoided tearing up the ground. Moreover, the long delays in assembling troops and supplies prior to the offensive had enabled the British and Commonwealth infantry to train to high standards of flexibility. Unlike the campaigns in France, exploitation forces

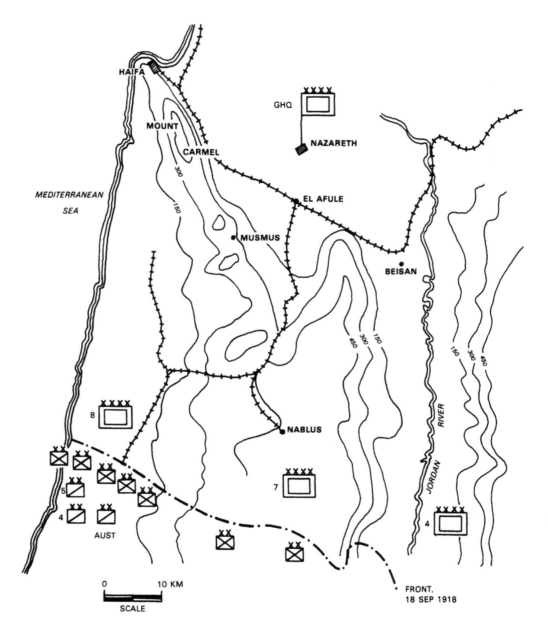

HAIFA

GHQ

MOUNT

CARMEL

NAZARETH

300

150

EL AFULE

MEDITERRANEAN
SEA

MUSMUS

BEISAN

450

300

150

150

300

450

JORDAN RIVER

8

NABLUS

XXXX

XXXX

7

4

5

4

AUST

0   10 KM

SCALE

FRONT,
18 SEP 1918

Contour Interval 150 meters

Map 2. Second Battle of Armageddon, 19—24 September 1918

did not have to wait for authority to engage. Instead, one Australian and two British cavalry divisions began the battle closed up tightly behind the assaulting infantry, with exploitation objectives already designated. Because of this decentralized control, the 4th Cavalry Division had completed its passage of lines and had begun the exploitation within four hours of the initial assault.

The primary objectives of the campaign were the railroad junctions at El Afule and Beisan, forty miles behind the front; a secondary objective was Nazareth, the German-Turkish headquarters. Seizure of these points would cut off the forward Turkish units from their supplies, commanders, and route of retreat. The key was to move cavalry through the passes of the Mount Carmel heights so rapidly that the Turks could not react to block the passes. This was accomplished on the evening of the first day. The next morning, a brigade of the 4th Cavalry Division encountered a reinforced Turkish infantry battalion marching forward in a belated effort to block the pass at Musmus. A combination of armored car machine gun fire and horse cavalry lances captured this battalion before it ever deployed. Twenty-five hours after the offensive began, another British cavalry brigade surrounded Nazareth, which had been isolated and harassed by air attacks. Although the German commander escaped in the confusion, the British captured all the documents in the enemy headquarters. The Turkish Seventh and Eighth Armies, except for a few hundred stragglers, surrendered in mass, and only the November armistice ended the British pursuit.

The significance of Second Armageddon was threefold. First, it represented a rare ability to make a transition from penetration to exploitation and pursuit before the defender could react. The key to this success, apart from numerical superiority, was the fact that the exploitation force did not wait for permission from higher headquarters, but was committed on the decision of division commanders and in execution of a previously arranged plan. Second, Allenby used all his weapons and units in a flexible and integrated manner that was matched in World War I only by the Germans. Finally, Second Armageddon influenced an entire generation of British cavalry officers, who considered it the model of a mobile, deep battle. After the frustrations of trench stalemate in France, the exploitation in Palestine seemed a dream come true. When these cavalry officers became armor commanders, they stressed the need for mobile, lightly armored vehicles. As a result, one-half of the British armored force in 1939 was equipped with inadequate guns and armor and was not prepared to cooperate with the other combat arms.

Organizational Results

In addition to the changes in infantry battalion structure, the rapid development of weapons and tactics during World War 1 significantly changed tactical organizations. The number of automatic weapons in an infantry division rose from a norm of twenty-four heavy machine guns in 1914 to the following totals in 1918:

> Germany: 144 automatic rifles and 54-108 machine guns
> France: 216 automatic rifles and 72-108 machine guns
> Britain: 192 automatic rifles and 64 machine guns
> Italy: 288 automatic rifles and 72 machine guns
> United States: 768 automatic rifles and 260 machine guns[31]

Artillery developed almost as dramatically, although most of the additional guns were concentrated in nondivisional units whose numbers varied depending on the mission of the division being supported. As Gen. Wilhelm von Balck, a major German tactician both before and after the war, remarked:

> The question as to the proportion of the artillery is no longer: 'How many guns for each thousand men should be provided?,' but far rather: 'How much infantry will be required to utilize the success of the fire of the artillery?' . . .there are no longer principal arms. Each arms has its use, all are necessary.[32]

More complex problems drove other organizational changes. For example, both the French and the Germans found that the square division structure, with two brigades each of two regiments, was unsuited to positional warfare. Given the broad frontages involved in this type of war, no European power had enough manpower and units to deploy divisions with two regiments in first line and two in second. If, on the other hand, three regiments were in the first line and the fourth regiment served as a general reserve, one of the two infantry brigade commanders was superfluous. So the Germans left one brigade commander in control of all infantry, and by 1916 both the French and the Germans had reduced the number of infantry regiments in a division from four to three (Figure 4). The British had entered the war with a three-brigade structure, which they retained, but they eventually followed suit by reducing the brigade from four infantry battalions to three when manpower shortages became acute. This had the added advantage of increasing the proportion of artillery and other branches to infantry, although the Germans moved part of their artillery into nondivisional units. Thus, a

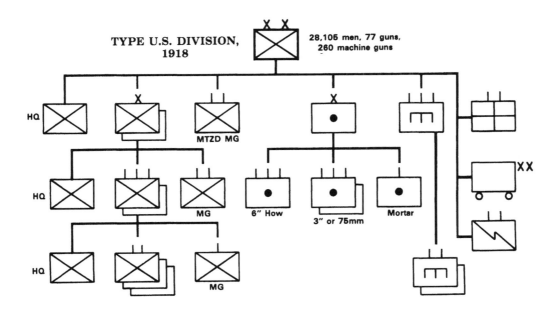

TYPE U.S. DIVISION,
1918

28,105 men, 77 guns,
260 machine guns

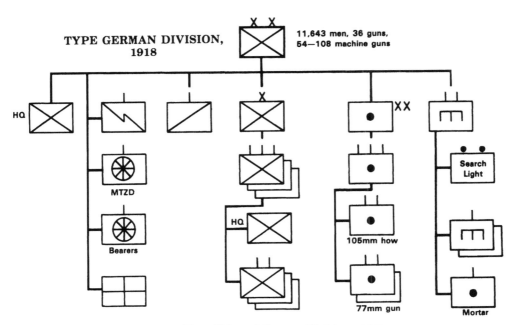

TYPE GERMAN DIVISION,
1918

11,643 men, 36 guns,
54—108 machine guns

Figure 4. Type U.S. and German Divisions, 1918

1914 French infantry division consisted of 87 percent infantry, 10 percent artillery, and 3 percent support elements, while the 1918 version had a proportion of 65 percent infantry, 27 percent artillery, and 8 percent support.33

The one exception to this trend was the United States Army, which not only insisted upon a four-regiment structure, but actually increased the size of rifle companies during 1917 (see figure 4). The result was a division that varied in size from 24,000 to over 28,000 men, a giant considering the average strength of a European division was down to 8,000 men or fewer. In fact, the French and British commanders who controlled American divisions refused to use them according to their design and, instead, pushed them into line with three regiments forward and the fourth either in second echelon or in corps reserve. In one instance, the 42d U.S. Infantry Division assumed the defense of a sector previously occupied by an entire French corps of three divisions.34 In principle, however, the American design was intended to provide for sustained offensive and defensive operations despite the high casualties of trench warfare. The apparent intent was that an American brigade commander, with one regiment in contact and the second behind it, could leapfrog his regiments to sustain an offensive almost indefinitely, thereby cutting the decision cycle time necessary to relieve exhausted assault troops. Unlike all higher commanders on the Allied side, this colonel or brigadier general had only a few aides and was free to command from forward locations. The only reserve available to the division commander was the two-battalion combat engineer regiment, which was frequently pressed into service as infantry.

Even though the Americans differed with their allies about many details, all participants came away from World War 1 with certain impressions in common: the tremendous problems of logistics and manpower; the necessity for detailed planning and coordination; and the difficulty of advancing even when all arms worked closely together. Under carefully planned and controlled circumstances, the Allies had been able to combine all weapons systems to maximize the effects of each. Of all the belligerent systems for achieving this combination, the German proved to be most adaptable to new weapons and tactics.

CHAPTER THREE

THE INTERWAR PERIOD

The conventional image of military affairs and doctrine between the two world wars depicts most armies as rigidly committed to a repetition of the positional warfare of 1914-18. According to this view, only Hitler's Germany listened to the advocates of mechanized warfare, with the result that between 1939 and 1941 the German blitzkrieg achieved almost bloodless victories over the outdated Polish, French, and British armies.

The reality was much more varied and complex. No major army entered World War II with the same doctrine and weapons that it had used twenty years before. During the interwar period, the majority of professional soldiers recognized that some change was necessary if they were to perform better the battlefield functions of penetration and exploitation that had proven so difficult during World War I. Yet armies differed markedly in their solutions to these problems. Instead of a simple choice between trench warfare and blitzkrieg, each army was faced with a variety of possible changes, a series of degrees of modernization between the two extremes. In many cases, the choice was determined by social, economic, and political factors more than by the tactical concepts of senior officers. Even in Germany, the advocates of mechanized warfare did not have a free hand. In a real sense, the German forces and doctrine of 1939 were not so much the perfect solution as they were simply a solution that was closer to the problems of the moment than were the organizations and doctrine of Germany's early opponents.

Because of this tactical variety between the world wars, the doctrine and organization of each of the major powers must be considered up to the point at which that nation entered World War II. Before reviewing these armies, however, it is necessary to examine some common factors that hampered military change in most nations.

The first of these factors was a general revulsion against warfare and all things military. After decades of peacetime preparation and years of incredible bloodshed, few people in Europe or America were interested in further military expenditures or experiments with new weapons and tactics. Particularly in France, firepower seemed so great that few soldiers foresaw any type of offensive success against prepared enemy positions without the combination of a mass army with tanks, artillery, and attrition tactics, the means that had succeeded in 1918. Even after most armies concluded that trench warfare was a special kind of combat that would not necessarily recur, the general public and political leadership were unwilling to risk another war. In 1928, fifteen nations signed the Kellogg-Briand Pact, renouncing the use of war except in national self-defense. During the 1920s and early 1930s, a series of international conferences attempted to limit military and naval armaments. Although these conferences ultimately failed, it was difficult for professional soldiers to justify the purchase of new weapons such as tanks and aircraft in a social and political environment that might outlaw such weapons at any time.

During the first fifteen years of peace, extremely tight defense budgets reflected the public distaste for warfare. The victorious armies were saddled with huge stockpiles of 1918-model equipment and ammunition and had to use up these stockpiles at peacetime rates before major new expenditures could be justified. Thus, during the early 1930s the U.S. Army spent more money researching means to preserve ammunition than to develop new weapons.[1] Just as the stockpiles were consumed or worn out, the Great Depression caused even tighter defense budgets, which hampered development and procurement of tanks, aircraft, and other new weapons. The Germans, by contrast, had been deprived of their weapons by the Versailles Peace Treaty of 1919 and could therefore start fresh. To some extent, the German tactical successes of 1939-42 were due not to any superiority in equipment quality or quantity, but rather to the fact that the German tanks and other vehicles were produced early enough to allow extensive experimentation and training before the war. In contrast, the British and French had few modern weapons with which to train until the very eve of World War II, when they mass-produced them on a crash basis. Nations with a smaller industrial base, such as Japan and Italy, could not fully compete in the arms race. The Japanese selectively built a few types of warships and aircraft of high quality. In land warfare, they relied upon training and morale to make up for weapons that they could not afford to mass-produce. Italy lacked not only production facilities, but equipment design capability and even public understanding of automobiles and other machinery. As a result, the Italians failed to produce any modern, well-designed weapons.[2]

A third factor was technology, which affected military change in two ways. On the one hand, rapid changes in technology made governments even more reluctant to invest in existing designs that would soon be outmoded. In 1938, for example, the Inspector-General of the French Air Force had to advise the French and British governments to avoid a showdown at Munich because he believed that the majority of French combat aircraft were suddenly obsolescent; new developments such as flush-riveted metal construction gave the German Luftwaffe the appearance of technical superiority.[3] On the other hand, it was often difficult to determine exactly how this new technology affected the tactics of 1918. Equipment designed to fulfill these tactics might be unsuitable for different functions and concepts, while new designs appeared without appropriate tactical concepts to accompany them.

There was also considerable confusion in terminology. Both advocates and opponents of mechanization often used the term "tank" loosely to mean not only an armored, tracked, turreted, gun-carrying fighting vehicle, but also any form of armored vehicle or mechanized unit. Such usage made it difficult for contemporaries or historians to determine whether a particular speaker was discussing pure tank forces, mechanized combined arms forces, or mechanization of infantry forces. Similar confusion existed about the term "mechanization." Strictly speaking, any use of the gasoline engine for warfare could be termed mechanization. However, this term is usually employed to describe the use of armored tracked combat vehicles. By contrast, "motorization" describes the use of motor vehicles that are not intended to go into combat, but which may improve logistics and mobility off the battlefield. No nation in the world could afford to mechanize fully in this sense, but all armies made some motions in the direction of motorization. Indeed, there was almost no choice about the matter. Prior to World War I, all nations relied on a pool of civilian horses as transportation in case of war. With the rise of motor vehicles during the 1920s, this supply of civilian animals declined to the point where armies had to base their transportation planning on motor vehicles.[4] Thus, motorization was often seen as an easier, cheaper, less revolutionary change than mechanization.

Fifth, advocates of change did not always speak persuasively or with one voice even when their terms were understood. Even those reformers with a clear vision of mechanized, combined arms war were often so extreme in their statements that they alienated the men they needed to convert, the commanders and politicians who set military policy. In the French and Soviet cases, political issues retarded the development of new mechanized formations. Moreover, proponents of strategic airpower such as William Mitchell and Emilio Douhet made exaggerated claims that retarded the development of the tactical combined arms team. Intent on achieving independence from army control, the airpower advocates vigorously opposed tactical air support and air-ground cooperation; they considered the targets involved to be too minor to justify risking aircraft. These air enthusiasts had a limited success as publicists, influencing politicians with an apparently cheap, efficient solution to defense needs. As a result, funds were diverted from valuable training or ground weapons development to build air forces that were not in proportion to their respective armies. This leads to the sixth and final common factor, the opposition of the more traditional combat arms. Many commentators have blamed such opposition for thwarting or retarding the development of mechanized warfare. There is some truth to this accusation, as will be seen below. Yet the tank and the aircraft were not the only weapons systems that developed between the world wars. The older branches had genuine needs that competed with new weapons for funding and for roles in the combined arms team. The infantry had legitimate requirements for increased organic firepower, for antitank and antiaircraft defenses, as well as for some form of armored support to assist it in the deliberate attack. The artillery needed the same mobility as the armored forces in order to support those forces in the breakthrough. Fast moving mechanized formations required more flexible communications and fire support. Combat engineers, which had become preoccupied with maintaining lines of communication during the positional warfare of 1914-18, were more important than ever when mechanized units increased the problems of mobility and countermobility on the battlefield. As a result, although much of this chapter will focus on the development of mechanized formations and tactics, such development must be viewed within the context of a more traditional mass army. Any nation that created a mechanized elite ran the risk of dividing its army, with catastrophic problems of coordination and morale.

Great Britain: "Hasten Slowly"[5]

In 1918, Great Britain led the world in both armored equipment and armored doctrine. At a time when most soldiers regarded the tank as a specialized infantry-support weapon for crossing trenches, a significant number of officers in the Royal Tank Corps had gone on to envision much broader roles for mechanized organizations. In May 1918, Col. J.F.C. Fuller had used the example of German infiltration tactics to refine what he called "Plan 1919." This was an elaborate concept for a large-scale armored offensive in 1919, an offensive that would not only produce multiple penetrations of the German forward defenses, but also totally disrupt the German command structure and rear organization. Fuller's expressed goal was to defeat the enemy by a "pistol shot to the brain" of enemy headquarters and communications, instead of by destroying the combat elements through systematic attrition. In order to attack German headquarters before they could displace, Fuller relied upon the Medium D tank. Potentially, the Medium D could drive at twenty miles per hour, a speed that would allow it to exploit the rupture of trenches caused by slower heavy tanks. In fact, the Medium D suffered the usual developmental problems of any radically new piece of equipment and might not have been available even if the war had continued into 1919. Moreover, then as later, Fuller was noteworthy for his neglect of infantry in the mechanized team. He could and did conceive of trucked infantry advancing after the tanks under certain circumstances, but not fighting in close coordination with armor except at the point of rupture in a deliberate attack.[6]

Despite the efforts of numerous innovators like Fuller, the British Army gradually lost its lead not only in armor but in most areas of tactical progress. In addition to the six common factors previously discussed, there were several special obstacles to continued British innovation.

The most commonly cited obstacle was traditionalism within the British Army. This institutional resistance has often been exaggerated, but certainly the strong unit identity of the British regimental system discouraged radical changes within the traditional arms and services. A related problem was that Great Britain was the first nation to create an independent air force. The Royal Air Force (RAF) was intent upon developing its own identity as a separate service and resisted any close relationship with the army. Like most other air services, the RAF was increasingly interested in interdiction and strategic bombing, but not ground support. In 1922, for example, the army requested that eight "Army Co-Operation Squadrons" be permanently assigned for liaison and reconnaissance duties with ground troops. The RAF would only provide three squadrons. During mechanized exercises in 1928, a number of RAF pilots practiced close air support for armored units, but after this display the Air Ministry formally requested that the army refrain from encouraging pilots to violate RAF doctrine.[7] This limitation was clearly reflected in British Army regulations from 1924 onward, where the RAF was described as providing only liaison and reconnaissance in the immediate proximity of ground units. Fighter aircraft could conduct strafing and other ground attacks "in exceptional circumstances," but only at the expense of their air superiority mission. Despite the efforts of many British armored theorists, close air support doctrine was not really developed in Britain until 1942.[8]

The problem of imperial defense also limited change. Since 1868, most British troop units stationed at home exchanged places with units overseas on a regular basis. In particular, a large portion of the British Army was always stationed in the Middle East and India. These overseas garrisons required large numbers of infantrymen to control civil disorders and made logistical support of elaborate equipment and weapons difficult. Consequently, a unit in the British Isles could not be motorized or mechanized without considering the effect of this change on that unit's performance in low intensity, imperial police operations. This did more than delay mechanization. It also meant that in designing armored fighting vehicles the British

47

were often thinking about the requirements of warfare against relatively unsophisticated opponents, and not against well-armed European forces.9

Despite these limitations on innovation, British doctrine did not stand still during the 1920s. A repetition of World War 1 seemed unthinkable, so positional warfare rapidly declined in British doctrine to the status of a special case. Instead, the British returned to the concepts of open, maneuver warfare that had been common before 1914, updating those concepts only to allow for the effects of firepower and motor vehicles. The 1924 Field Service Regulations considered infantry support to be the chief mission of tanks, but also recognized the possibility of tanks attacking the enemy flanks and rear to disorganize the opponent, as envisioned by Fuller. These regulations showed a serious and practical concern with the problems of antitank and antiaircraft defense of all arms, although actual weapons for these problems were slow to appear. By 1929, British regulations had abandoned the old belief in the primacy of infantry, which instead became "the arm which confirms the victory and holds the ground won" by a close cooperation of all arms. Still, this cooperation was apparently to be achieved by detailed, meticulous planning of the 1918 variety. Coordination in encounter battles was much more difficult.10

At the same time the British, despite significant budgetary restrictions, were able to motorize parts of their artillery and supply units and to continue development of the small Royal Tank Corps. In 1927-28, an Experimental Mechanized Force conducted brigade-level exercises in Britain. This force included a light tank battalion for reconnaissance, a medium tank battalion for assault, a machine gun battalion for security and limited infantry operations, five motorized or mechanized artillery batteries, and a motorized engineer company. Unfortunately, the equipment used varied greatly in its cross-country mobility and reliability. The vehicles were a mixture of tracked and wheeled, experimental and well-developed equipment that could not move together except at very slow speeds. As a result, some officers of the Royal Tank Corps decided that the other arms were incompatible with armored operations and focused their attention on almost pure tank formations.

The British War Office dissolved the Experimental Mechanized Force in 1928 for a variety of factors, including budgetary restrictions and the opposition of some military conservatives. This force did, however, provide the basis for Col. Charles Broad to produce a new regulation, Mechanized and Armoured Formations, in 1929. This regulation was a great advance in describing the roles and missions of separate armored formations, but it also reflected the pure-tank attitude that was becoming common in the Royal Tank Corps. Even when Broad proposed a Royal Armoured Corps that included tanks, mechanized cavalry, and mechanized infantry, he explicitly excluded artillery and engineers.[11] Still, Broad recognized different models of armored vehicle and different roles for them. In particular, the standard "mixed" tank battalion of an independent tank brigade was a combination of three different types of vehicle. Within each company, seven light tanks would reconnoiter the enemy positions and then provide fire support for five medium tanks that actually conducted the assault. In addition, two "close support tanks"--really self-propelled howitzers or mortars--would provide smoke and suppressive fire for the assault.[12] Since in practice the "light tanks" were often small armored personnel carriers, the parallel with more recent American armored cavalry should be obvious.

British armored theorists did not always agree with each other. Basil Liddell Hart, a noted publicist of armor, wanted a true combined arms force with a major role for mechanized infantry. Fuller, Broad, and other officers were more interested in a pure-tank role, in part because they experienced difficulty cooperating with the other arms. G. L. Martel, one of the most innovative theorists and tank designers of the period, was fascinated with the idea of using extremely small armored personnel carriers, capable of transporting one to three men and a machine gun, to assist the infantry in its attacks. Unfortunately, the machine gun carriers designed at Martel's instigation participated in experiments both as reconnaissance vehicles and infantry carriers, and proved inadequate for either function.[13] Not until the eve of World War II did the British develop a reliable machine gun carrier, and even then it was dispersed in small numbers within infantry battalions that attacked on foot.

Despite these differences of opinion, the next step in developing the role of armor was to form an independent mechanized force of division size. This was undertaken as an experiment in 1934, using Col. Percy Hobart's 1st Tank Brigade, a newly formed unit of the type envisaged by Broad, and Maj. Gen. George Lindsay's partially mechanized 7th Infantry Brigade. Unfortunately for the British, personality differences, lack of training, and artificial restrictions from the umpires turned the resulting exercise into a disaster. General Lindsay, one of the few senior officers who was genuinely committed to the development of a combined arms mechanized division, was so discredited by the fiasco that he ceased to have any influence over policy.[14]

Instead, the conservative Chief of the Imperial General
Staff, Gen. Sir Archibald Montgomery-Massingberd, chose to create
a permanent "Mobile Division" by mechanizing large portions of
the British cavalry. The Mobile Division authorized in December
1937 consisted of two armored cavalry brigades, each almost
entirely mounted in light tanks and armored cars, plus one tank
brigade, two mechanized infantry battalions, and limited amounts
of artillery, engineers, and support units. Such a formation was
quite appropriate for performing the functions of reconnaissance
and security, whether in the empire or on the continent. It did
not, however, integrate the different arms at a sufficiently low
level to fight in fluid operations as an armored formation
against a sophisticated enemy. In most cases, reconnaissance,
medium armor, infantry, and artillery were under separate
brigade-level commands. With various minor changes, this mobile
division became the 1st Armoured Division, which sacrificed
itself piecemeal in France in 1940.[15] A second mobile division
formed in Egypt, providing the basis for later British operations
there.

There were also problems with equipment. The Royal Tank
Corps had to make do with the same basic tanks from 1922 until
1938, despite frequent changes in design and technology. Almost
the only improvement came in the period 1930-32, when radio
communications changed markedly. Until this time, each vehicle
crew had to tune its radio by hand to a common frequency, and the
motion of a moving tank could easily throw the radio off that
frequency. Colonel Broad instigated a series of developments
that eventually provided crystal-controlled, preset frequencies.
The complexity and expense of such equipment, however, made
distribution of radios down to individual tanks very slow.[16]
Only such radios could allow a commander to control his rapidly
moving units while observing and leading from the front.

During the 1930s, the confusion about tank roles combined
with frequent changes in the defense bureaucratic structure to
thwart good armored vehicle design.[17] Generally speaking,
British armored vehicles tended to maximize either mobility or
protection. Both the cavalry and the Royal Tank Corps wanted
fast, lightly armored, mobile vehicles for reconnaissance and
raiding--the light and medium (or "cruiser") tanks. On the other
hand, the "army tank battalions" performing the traditional
infantry-support role required extremely heavy armored protection
in order to advance successfully against prepared enemy defenses
that included antitank guns.

As a consequence of these two doctrinal roles, firepower was
neglected in tank design. As late as 1937, the very thin armor
on most tanks of the world made armor-piercing machine guns, or
at most a 20-mm cannon, seem entirely adequate for antitank

50

defense. In fact, many soldiers believed that the tank was more vulnerable than ever because infantry had acquired some antitank training and equipment. Anticipating improvements in tank armor, the British standardized on a two-pounder (40-mm) antitank gun. This was also the standard weapon mounted in most British tanks well into World War II. Yet such a weapon could only penetrate German armor of 1939-42 design at 500 or fewer meters and was not designed to fire high explosive ammunition to suppress enemy infantry and towed antitank gun fire. Although Hobart called for a six-pounder (57-mm) tank gun in 1938, this was not stated as a formal requirement for tank design until after the fall of France in 1940.[18] Even then, most turrets designed for the two-pounder were too small to be upgunned.

While Britain drifted in the area of mechanization, developments in the more traditional arms were equally mixed. Cavalry, as already noted, in essence merged into the mechanization process, although too late to learn all the mechanical and tactical differences between horses and light armor. Infantry was saddled with inappropriate weapons throughout the 1920s. It had no useful antitank capability, and the Lewis machine gun was really too heavy to maneuver as a squad weapon. Between 1936 and 1939, new equipment and organization finally restored the firepower and mobility of British infantry, but at a price. The excellent Bren light machine gun, with its accompanying small armored carrier, was a significant advance. Each squad in a rifle platoon had a dismounted Bren gun, and the platoon had a two-inch smoke mortar and a caliber .55 Boyes antitank rifle. The battalion consisted of four rifle companies, plus a headquarters with platoons of Bren gun carriers, two-pounder antitank guns, three-inch mortars, and antiaircraft machine guns. Heavy machine guns and 4.1-inch mortars were centralized into separate support battalions. The result was that the infantry battalion was much lighter and more mobile than it had been, but it had a somewhat reduced firepower and only limited antitank capability. On the eve of World War II, the inadequacies of the Boyes rifle rapidly forced the artillery to assume primary responsibility for antitank defense.[19] The artillery had indeed developed excellent pieces that had an additional antitank capacity. In the process, however, the British had largely neglected the scientific procedures of indirect fire developed during World War I. Only the School of Artillery continued to teach these techniques, so that a few officers were familiar with them. In 1939, the prejudice of many artillerymen against artillery survey techniques led to a reorganization that briefly eliminated survey parties from artillery headquarters.[20]

51

Thus, by 1939 the British Army had lost much of its pioneering advantage in both equipment and technology. Outside of the infantry battalion, cooperation between different weapons systems and arms was little better than it had been in 1914.

Germany: "Strike Concentrated, Not Dispersed"[21]

France, Britain, and the United States, the victors of 1918, had a natural tendency to employ at least some of the materiel and doctrine of 1918 during the immediate postwar years. A defeated Germany, by contrast, had every reason to embrace new tactics and weapons.

Even if it wished to, Germany could not reproduce the mass armies and static defenses of 1914-18. The Treaty of Versailles limited the German Army to 100,000 long-tour professional soldiers, without reserves except for the paramilitary police forces. The same treaty forbade Germany to possess tanks, poison gas, combat aircraft, and heavy artillery. Paradoxically, for the Germans this prohibition may have been a blessing in disguise. The German defense budget and tactical thought were less restricted to, or dependent on, the technology of 1918 than were other budgets and armies. Instead, planners could study concepts and then develop the equipment to make those concepts reality. Doctrine led technological development, in contrast to the situation in other armies. In those instances where field trials had to be conducted, the Germans used mock-ups, or tested equipment and concepts in secret within the Soviet Union.* This is not to say that German planners started from scratch. No army can completely escape its past, but Germany certainly had an advantage over the victorious Allies.

Since the 1860s, the German tradition of tactics and operations had favored outflanking and encircling the enemy or, if that failed, breaking through to disrupt his organization. This was in contrast to the frontal battles of attrition that most of Germany's enemies had fought in World War I. This German tradition meant two things. First, unlike the French and British, who had learned to attack on a broad front in order to protect their flanks, the Germans believed in concentrating all their resources on a relatively narrow front for breakthrough.[22] Second, this concentration of forces required the careful integration of all weapons and arms at battalion

_____

*As the two outcast nations of Europe during the 1920s, Germany and the Soviet Union had much in common. Their secret exchange of military knowledge continued until Hitler came to power.

level or below to overcome the enemy's defenses. The infiltration tactics of 1917-18 reflected this viewpoint and were retained after the armistice. Despite the restrictions of the Versailles Treaty, the 1921 German Regulation on Command and Combat of the Combined Arms included not only the infantry assault battalion and the carefully planned artillery and preparations of 1918, but also close air support, gas warfare, and tanks in an infantry-support role.[23] Again, the Germans were free to develop doctrine on the basis of their experience but without being restricted to specific technology. Despite later manuals, this sophisticated regulation remained the basis of German doctrine between the wars.

Another part of the German military tradition was decentralized execution. German commanders moved forward to observe and make tactical decisions for themselves. This enabled them to communicate their decisions to subordinates much more rapidly than was possible from a command post in the rear. This decentralization was facilitated by a mutual understanding among German leaders, an understanding based on common doctrine such as the Command and Combat of the Combined Arms. Aware of both a commander's intention and the common doctrine, subordinate leaders could execute that intention in accordance with that doctrine and, thereby, reduce the need for detailed instructions from higher echelons. This decentralization and rapidity of decision making were ideally suited to any form of fluid combat, including mechanized operations.

In retrospect, it might seem inevitable that, once combined with the German experience of the psychological effects of tanks during World War I, the German infiltration tactics, the belief in massing on a narrow front, and decentralized execution would lead to blitzkrieg. In fact, however, the German Army did not wholeheartedly accept the concept of mechanized blitzkrieg until the defeat of France in 1940. Prior to that time, the majority of senior German commanders apparently regarded mechanization as a useful but very specialized tool that would not replace ordinary infantry divisions. In thinking this, they shared much of the traditional viewpoint that characterized their counterparts in Britain, France, and elsewhere.

Among the German proponents of mechanization, Gen. Heinz Guderian was probably the most influential. Like Percy Hobart in Great Britain, Guderian had considerable experience with the early military use of radio communications. This had two effects upon his later career. First, Guderian's 1914 service with radiotelegraphs in support of cavalry units led him to insist on a radio in every armored vehicle, a major advantage in command and control. By contrast, the French and others often had radios only for the command tanks and depended on hand signals or flags to maneuver small units. More generally, Guderian's early service taught him the difficulties of integrating new doctrine and equipment and then overcoming institutional resistance to that doctrine and equipment.[24] As a staff officer concerned with motorized transportation, Guderian gained further experience from his first studies of mobile warfare. The small size of the German Army in the 1920s forced it to increase its mobility in order to shift limited forces rapidly. Guderian was one of a group of officers who studied the use of motor vehicles to achieve this mobility. To a certain extent, the German theorists had to rely on British experience and regulations to learn about equipment that Germany did not possess in large numbers. Yet, the German concept of mechanized warfare developed almost independently of such trends in Britain. By 1929, when many British students of armor were tending towards a pure armor formation, Guderian had become convinced that it was useless to develop just tanks, or even to mechanize parts of the traditional arms. What was needed was an entirely new mechanized formation of all arms that would maximize the effects of the tank. Only such a formation could sustain mobile warfare, whether offensive or defensive.[25]

The general belief among military theoreticians that antitank defenses were becoming stronger did not deter Guderian. Unlike most advocates of armor, he considered antitank weapons to be an essential part of the mechanized combined arms team, rather than the defender of the traditional arms against the new weapons. Most early tanks were too small and unstable to carry accurate, high-velocity antitank guns. By contrast, the towed antitank gun was specially designed for maximum effectiveness against armor, and its small silhouette made it difficult to detect and engage. The German armored units trained to avoid fighting other tanks or antitank guns, and instead to exploit in areas of little or no resistance. In the event of tank-versus-tank combat, the German tanks might withdraw temporarily, luring the enemy into a hidden screen of antitank weapons that had deployed behind the German spearhead. To do this, tanks needed reconnaissance units to lead the way and screen the flanks of the advance, with combat engineers to sustain the mobility of the mechanized force. Motorized or mechanized infantry and artillery were necessary to reduce bypassed centers of resistance, to support tanks in the attack, and to hold areas seized by such attacks. The entire force required support units that could keep up with a rapid advance.

In 1931, Guderian became commander of the 3rd Motor Transport Battalion. Using dummy equipment because of the limitations of the Versailles Treaty, this battalion was actually an experimental "mechanized" force consisting of one company each of motorcycles, armored cars, tanks, and antitank guns. A similar small-scale demonstration, using some of the first light tanks produced in Germany, impressed Hitler in 1934.[26] That same year, experimental maneuvers for a full panzer division took place, and in 1935 Hitler formed the first three such divisions on a permanent basis (see Figure 5). As in the other armies, Germany's first effort at armored organization included a tremendous number of tanks (561 per division).[27] Otherwise, this organization showed considerable balance in numbers and types of weapons. Moreover, regardless of the paper organization, the brigade and regimental headquarters were trained to control cross-attached units and weapons systems. Such a system required considerable training and put great stress on the maintenance and logistical support of the cross-attached elements, but it enabled the panzer division to combine different weapons systems as needed.

Guderian did not, however, succeed without opposition and difficulties. The other branches of the German Army resisted the creation of this new arm and demanded a share of mechanization and motorization for themselves. During the later 1930s, the Chief of the German General Staff directed the motorization of all antitank units and one engineer company in all infantry divisions, plus complete motorization of four selected infantry divisions, at a time when the panzer divisions were still short of transportation. In 1937-38, two separate tank brigades were formed for infantry support, isolated from the other arms. At the same time, four "Light Divisions," based on cavalry units in most cases, absorbed more motorized and mechanized equipment. The actual composition of these units varied, but the most common pattern was an armored reconnaissance regiment, two motorized infantry regiments, one light tank battalion, and two towed howitzer battalions. A frustrated Guderian found himself shunted aside as "Chief of Mobile Troops," with little or no control over the motorized infantry and light divisions.

Nor were the German tanks up to the standards of Guderian's concept. Despite Hitler's support for panzer units, those units had to compete for production capacity and new weapons not only with the rest of the expanding German Army, but also with the German Air Force. Hitler placed first priority on the Luftwaffe because of the intimidation value that air power gave him when dealing with the rest of Europe. Under the circumstances, Guderian had to settle for tanks that were not completely battleworthy. The Mark I was really a machine gun-armed tankette, derived from the British Carden-Loyd personnel carrier. The Mark II did have a 20-mm cannon, but little armor protection. These two vehicles made up the bulk of panzer units until 1940.[29] Their value lay not so much in their armor and armament, but in the fact that they were available early, in considerable numbers, and with radio communications. This

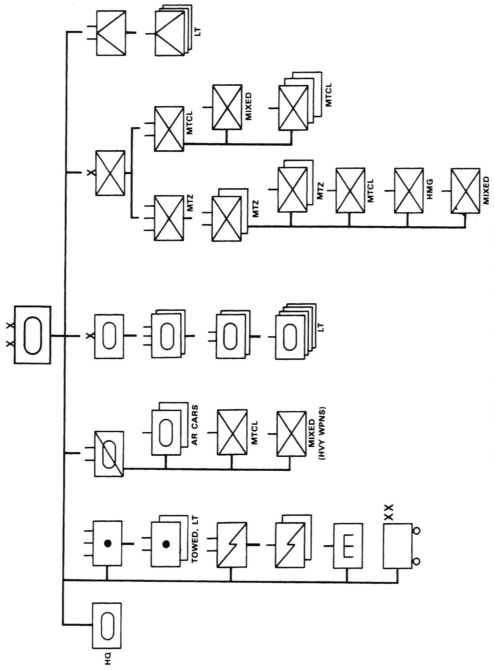

Figure 5. Type German Panzer Division. 1935.

84-3330

allowed the new panzer force to conduct extensive training, establish battle procedures, identify and solve problems, and develop changes in organization and equipment. By 1939, the panzer divisions were not completely ready, but they had gone through their first, most necessary stages of organization and training. Such an advantage was denied to most of Germany's opponents.

Another German advantage was in the field of close air support of ground operations. When the Luftwaffe was established in 1933, most of the higher commanders were World War 1 aviators and others who had served in the ranks of the 100,000-man army imposed by the Versailles Treaty. Initially, the Luftwaffe, like other air services, favored missions such as strategic bombing and air superiority to the neglect of supporting ground forces. The experience of the Spanish Civil War (1936-39) changed priorities to some extent. The German force sent to aid Franco used a limited number of obsolete fighters in a ground-attack role, with considerable effect. These experiences provided the impetus for Germany to create five ground-attack aviation groups in the fall of 1938. Ernst Udet, the chief of the Luftwaffe's development branch after 1936, persuaded his superiors to produce a limited number of close support dive-bombers patterned after the U.S. Navy's Curtiss Helldiver. The resulting JU-87 Stuka dive-bombers equipped four of the five ground-attack groups during 1939. Dive-bombers were extremely accurate and demoralized ground defenders rapidly. In addition, in both Spain and Poland a very small number of air liaison detachments were attached to the infantry corps and armored division headquarters making the main attack. These detachments could pass air-support requests directly to the Luftwaffe and could monitor in-flight reconnaissance reports. They could not, however, actually guide the aircraft onto targets without departing the ground headquarters to which they were attached, nor did they have training for such a role. In any event, the handful of dive-bomber groups and air liaison detachments was available only to the army units at the point of main effort; all other army headquarters had to submit preplanned requests that might or might not be honored. In 1939, on-call air support against targets of opportunity was well in the future for most of the German Army.[30]

Thus the tradition of combined arms integration was continued and updated in the German Army between the world wars. Guderian was tactically incorrect when he denied the need to provide armor and motorized equipment for the other elements of an army that remained essentially foot-mobile and horse-drawn. His determined opposition, however, did enable Germany to keep the majority of its mechanized assets concentrated in combined arms mechanized

57

units, despite the equipment given to other branches. In September 1939, twenty-four out of thirty-three tank battalions and 1,944 out of 3,195 tanks were concentrated in the six panzer divisions.[31] The contrast with other countries, where large numbers of tanks were dedicated to infantry support and cavalry roles, is striking.

France

The existence of a 100,000-man professional German Army forced the French to develop plans to counter a sudden invasion by that army. The postwar French Army was huge, but ill prepared to stop a surprise attack by even the small German force. It was basically a cadre for reservists, who required weeks or even months to mobilize. After 1918, French war weariness eliminated the highly developed mobilization system of 1914 and, in 1928, reduced conscripted service to a bare twelve months of training.

To protect itself from a sudden attack by the small German Army, France chose to construct a sophisticated version of the defenses that had apparently worked so well at Verdun. The Maginot Line (Map 3) was a string of self-contained concrete forts with gun turrets. It was built between 1930 and 1936 in Northeastern France; its function was to protect the land regained in 1918 and to force any German invasion to pass through Belgian territory before reaching France. This extra distance would give France time to mobilize.

The Maginot Line has frequently been criticized because, in retrospect, it appeared child's play for the Germans to outflank these fortifications. Yet, quite apart from the political reality that France could not abandon Belgium by building a major wall between the two countries, the Maginot Line concept was much less defensive than popular wisdom suggests. In addition to providing security during mobilization and protecting critical areas near the French frontier, the Maginot Line was a secure anchor, a base around which the mobile field forces of the French Army would maneuver.[32] More specifically, in the later 1930s both France and Britain expected that any future war with Germany would be a repetition of 1914, with Germany advancing through all of Belgium and possibly the Netherlands as well. Because Belgium was neutral, France and Britain could not enter that country to help defend it until the Germans had already invaded. Thus, the majority of French and British mobile forces planned to make a headlong rush into Belgium. The surprise to the Allies in 1940 was the German penetration through Luxembourg towards Sedan, a penetration that cut the hinge between the mobile forces and the Maginot Line.

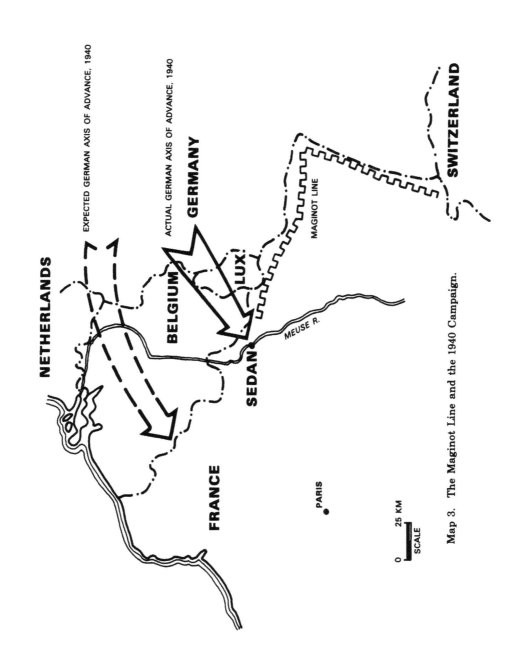

NETHERLANDS

EXPECTED GERMAN AXIS OF ADVANCE, 1940

ACTUAL GERMAN AXIS OF ADVANCE, 1940

GERMANY

BELGIUM

LUX

MAGINOT LINE

SWITZERLAND

MEUSE R.

SEDAN

FRANCE

PARIS

0   25 KM
SCALE

Map 3.   The Maginot Line and the 1940 Campaign.

Moreover, despite the intent of the Maginot Line, its practical effects were much less positive for French defense. The tremendous expense of fortress construction restricted the depth of the fortifications and even the size of armament of those forts. Only a few positions included the lavishly constructed works shown in contemporary photographs. In case of war the line had to be supplemented by field fortifications and troops deployed between the fixed positions. More importantly, once built the Maginot Line had a negative psychological effect on the politicians, if not on the commanders. The apparently invincible defensive strength of the Maginot Line reinforced the general left-wing political belief that France should avoid any aggressive actions and be content to defend its frontiers.

This defensive orientation influenced not only national budgets but French military doctrine, at least immediately after 1918. More than any other participant in the First World War, France retained the positional warfare concept in its postwar regulations. Under the influence of Marshal Philippe Pétain, the French Army produced the <u>Provisional Instructions for the Tactical Employment of Larger Units (1921)</u>. This regulation was not entirely defense-oriented, but to minimize casualties it did insist on careful, methodical preparations before attacking. Within the carefully coordinated circumstances of a set-piece offensive, battle would involve all arms to assist the infantry:

> The infantry is charged with the principal mission in combat. Preceded, protected, and accompanied by artillery fire, aided where possible by tanks and aviation, it conquers, occupies, organizes, and holds the terrain.[33]

This conception had two flaws. First, such a meticulously planned, centrally controlled operation was unable to react to sudden changes. The German offensives of 1918 had already demonstrated that any enemy action that disrupted the defender's linear deployments and lockstep planning would catch the French headquarters off guard, unable to reorganize a defense against a highly mobile attacker.

More generally, the French doctrine viewed combined arms as a process by which all other weapons systems assisted the infantry in its forward progress. Tanks were considered to be "a sort of armored infantry," subordinated to the infantry branch.[34] This at least had the advantage that armor was not restricted purely to tanks. The French cavalry experimented extensively during the 1920s with armored cars and ultimately half-tracks. These half-tracks sometimes formed combat teams with armored cars, towed artillery, motorcycles, and light tanks carried on trucks until contact was made.[35] In fact, the French half-tracks may well have been the models for later German and American infantry carriers. Still, the subordination of tanks to infantry impeded the development of roles for armor other than close infantry support. Moreover, while half-tracks might be useful in colonial wars or for reconnaissance tasks, infantry still walked in the deliberate assault. Armor was tied to the rate of advance of foot-mobile infantry. The alternative of finding ways to increase the mobility and protection of the infantry in order to keep pace with the tanks was rarely considered. The slow speed of the World War 1 vintage FT tank, which equipped most French armor units throughout the 1920s, reinforced this attitude.

Not all Frenchmen held this view. Gen. Jean-Baptiste Estienne, commander of the World War 1 French tank corps before it was disbanded, was quite farsighted in his concept of mechanized warfare. In 1919, Estienne submitted a "Study of the Missions of Tanks in the Field" to Petain's headquarters. This remarkable document explained the need to provide armored, tracked vehicles not only for tanks, but also for reconnaissance, infantry, artillery, and even battlefield recovery teams. Estienne's vision of this massed force, supported by air bombardment and attacking in-depth against a narrow enemy front, closely resembled the best mechanized ideal of World War 11. In 1920, Estienne proposed a 100,000-man armored army with 4,000 tanks and 8,000 other vehicles. Instead of rejecting the use of infantry, he argued that armored infantry would again be able to attack using its organic weapons.[37] Estienne's concept was not only radical militarily, but also seemed too offensively minded, too aggressive to be acceptable to French politicians. Nevertheless, Estienne remained Inspector of Tanks until his retirement in 1927.

Despite the restrictions imposed by the Great Depression and by the enormous cost of the Maginot Line, Chief of Staff Maxime Weygand took significant steps towards motorization and mechanization during the early 1930s. Five and ultimately seven infantry divisions became motorized, and one brigade in each of four light cavalry divisions was equipped with half-tracks and armored cars. In 1934, Weygand continued the trend towards armored cavalry by forming the first "light mechanized division" (Division Légère Mécanique, or DLM, shown in Figure 6). This division, with its combination of reconnaissance, light tanks, trucked infantry, and towed artillery, was remarkably similar to the German panzer division being developed at the same time. Because Weygand was a cavalryman, and because it was politically easier to justify a defensive covering force than an "offensive" armored unit, the four DLMs ultimately formed by France all received standard cavalry missions of reconnaissance and security, rather than mechanized main battle tasks.[38]

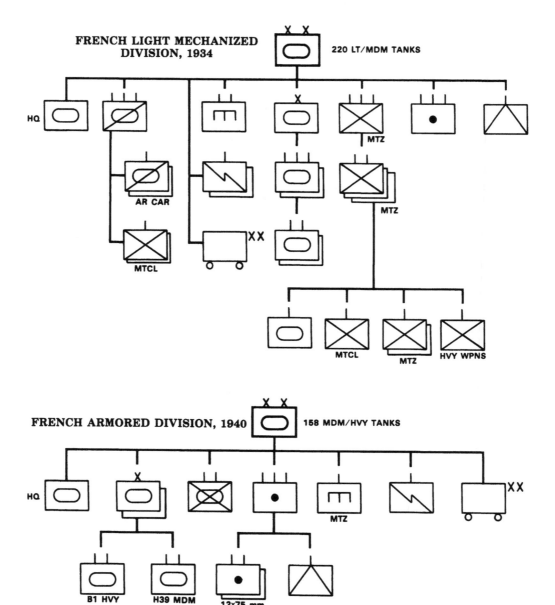

FRENCH LIGHT MECHANIZED DIVISION, 1934

220 LT/MDM TANKS

HQ

AR CAR

MTCL

MTZ

MTZ

MTCL   MTZ   HVY WPNS

FRENCH ARMORED DIVISION, 1940

158 MDM/HVY TANKS

HQ

MTZ

B1 HVY   H39 MDM   12×75 mm

Figure 6. French Light Mechanized Division, 1934, and Armored Division, 1940.

Just as the French Army was cautiously moving forward in the area of mechanization, its development was almost aborted by the writings of Charles de Gaulle. In 1934, Lieutenant Colonel de Gaulle published Towards the Professional Army. This call for a 100,000-man armored army was based heavily on Estienne's work. De Gaulle's book was hardly innovative in terms of doctrine and organization in that it envisioned a pure armor brigade operating in linear formation, followed by a motorized infantry force for mopping-up operations. The real problem was political. In a nation that was extremely pacifistic and dedicated to the doctrine of the citizen soldier, de Gaulle was advocating an aggressive, professional standing army of technicians. His "instrument of repressive and preventive maneuver"[39] might well be used to start an offensive war with Germany or to support a military coup d'etat in republican France.

De Gaulle's sensational book not only jeopardized the more gradual efforts of Weygand, but also set extremely high standards for what constituted an armored division. In 1936, France belatedly decided to produce armor and other equipment in larger quantities, including 385 B-1 bis tanks. The B-1 bis, developed by Estienne in the early 1920s, was still one of the best tank designs in the world fifteen years later. It had sixty millimeters of frontal armor in a carefully cast hull, hydromatic transmission, and other advanced features. It was limited by the small size of its turret, where one man had to be both tank commander and gunner for a 47-mm gun, but a lower-velocity 75-mm gun was mounted in the hull. The B-1 bis was an excellent weapon that caused the Germans much difficulty in 1940. Yet, given the fine craftsmanship involved in B-1 bis production and the weakened state of France's industry, it took years to produce sufficient tanks to organize an armored division on the pattern desired by Estienne and de Gaulle. Even after the war started, France could never produce more than fifty of these tanks per month, and the rate prior to 1939 was much lower.[40] As a result, France did not form its first two armored divisions (Division Cuirassée, or DCR, as shown in Figure 6) until after the war began and, even then, had to greatly reduce the authorized number of heavy tanks in each division. The resulting unit was primarily a collection of tanks for an armored breakthrough; it lacked sufficient reconnaissance, antitank, infantry, artillery, and engineer support. Similar problems plagued the production of other tanks and military equipment, so that French troops rarely had the time for realistic training and experimentation that the Germans had achieved before 1939. The French regulation for large armored unit tactics was not issued until March 1940, a few weeks before the German invasion of France.[41]

Despite such limitations, France slowly modernized during the 1930s. The 1921 <u>Provisional Instructions</u> gave way to a much more sophisticated regulation in 1936. The new <u>Instructions</u> recognized the major changes in warfare, including fortified fronts such as the Maginot Line, motorized and mechanized units, antitank weapons, increased air and antiaircraft involvement in combat, and improved communications. The regulation no longer classified tanks by size, but rather designated the particular mission they would perform at any given time. Tanks could either accompany infantry, precede infantry by bounds to the next terrain feature, or operate independently, especially after the enemy's defenses had already been disorganized. The 1936 regulation, however, still insisted on the primacy of infantry, the careful organization of artillery, and the methodical advance of all elements in accordance with an elaborate plan. As in Britain, French air support to ground forces consisted primarily of reconnaissance in the battle area, with bombing only outside the range of artillery. The regulation repeatedly emphasized the need for "defense without thought of retreat," which tended to mean rigid orientation toward the terrain and the enemy to one's front, rather than toward maneuvering to deal with a threat to the flank or rear. References to antitank defense-in-depth also appeared frequently in this regulation, but France lacked the troops to establish such a defense in 1940. Finally, because of the possibility of enemy signals intelligence, radios were only to be used when no other means of communication were available. In any event, at least some French tank radios were meant only for short-range communications with dismounted infantry in a deliberate attack and were consequently useless in mobile operations. Thus, most of the French command and control still moved at the pace of communications in World War I.[42]

France entered World War II with a militia army that would require months to organize and train, and with new mechanized formations and modern equipment that had been fielded too late for proper testing, evaluation, and training. Like those of the British, French armored units were specialized either for cavalry missions or deliberate breakthrough attacks; they were not balanced for all types of mobile operations. Given these limitations, the French doctrine of slow, methodical offensive action appeared as the only course that would allow them to attack at all. Unfortunately, the Germans did not wait for the French to plan and execute such attacks.

The Soviet Union: "Deep Battle"[43]

The Soviet Union's military development after World War I differed from that of the rest of Europe for two reasons. First, the Red Army was created in 1918 after the Bolshevik revolution

64

and lacked the traditions and training of other major armies. Many of the new Red commanders had been noncommissioned or commissioned junior officers during World War I, but few trained senior officers of the Tsarist Army remained with the new regime. Even those who did remain were, with some exceptions, suspected of anti-Bolshevik sympathies. As a result, the Red Army was open to change, unhampered by excessive traditions or past habits. It was also subject to the blunders of ignorance. Second, the Russian Civil War of 1918-21 was markedly different from most of the European campaigns of World War I. Because of the vast distances and understrength armies involved in the Civil War, penetration and encirclement were no longer difficult, and fluid maneuver was the rule. The elite of the Red Army by the end of the Civil War was Marshal S.M. Budenny's 1st Cavalry Army, which had patterned its encirclements and pursuits after the best Tsarist cavalrymen. The veterans of this army received the patronage of Joseph Stalin, who had been the commissar of the next higher headquarters. As a result, many officers from this army rose to senior positions before and during World War II.[44]

Like Hitler's Germany, but unlike France and Britain, the Soviet Union was openly interested in offensive warfare as a means of spreading its political doctrines. As a practical matter, Stalin chose to concentrate on developing the Soviet Union before expanding into Europe. Still, the Red Army could expect that any future war would be offensive, using weapons that democratic societies abhorred as too aggressive. This offensive orientation was reinforced by the close relationship that existed between the Red Army and the German Army from 1923 to 1932. Soviet officers studied in Germany, while the Germans secretly manufactured and tested tanks, aircraft, and poison gas in European Russia. Soviet doctrine, however, appeared to be largely independent of similar developments in Germany; Soviet concepts were official policy long before Guderian gained even partial approval from his government.

During the course of the 1920s and early 1930s, a group of Soviet officers led by Marshal Mikhail Tukhachevsky developed a concept of "Deep Battle" to employ conventional infantry and cavalry divisions, mechanized formations, and aviation in concert. These efforts culminated in the Field Regulations of 1936. Instead of regarding the infantry as the premier combat arm, Tukhachevsky envisioned all available arms and weapons systems working together in a two-part battle. First, a massed, echeloned attack on a narrow front would rupture the defender's conventional infantry-artillery-antitank defense. The attacker's artillery and mortars would suppress defending artillery and especially defending antitank guns. Moving behind the artillery barrage and a few meters in front of the infantry, the tanks could safely crush wire, overrun machine gun posts, and reduce other centers of enemy resistance. Once the enemy's forward defenses were disrupted, accompanying tanks would not be tied strictly to the infantry rate of advance, but could take advantage of local opportunities to penetrate and attack enemy reserves, artillery, headquarters, and supply dumps. This action would duplicate on a smaller scale the second part of the battle, which was to disrupt and destroy the enemy by deep attacks. "Mobile Groups," composed of cavalry, mechanized formations, or both, would exploit their mobility advantage to outflank the enemy or develop a penetration in order to reach the enemy rear areas. The object was to attack the entire depth of the enemy defenses simultaneously, with conventional frontal attacks, long range artillery fires, deep penetrations by mobile forces, and bombing and parachute attacks of key points. Smoke and deception operations would distract the enemy from the attacker's real intentions.[45]

This remarkably sophisticated doctrine was backed up by a force structure that, by 1937, was well on its way to implementing Tukhachevsky's concepts. Using the expanded production facilities of the Soviet government's first Five Year Plan with design features taken in part from the American inventor Walter Christie, the Soviets produced 5,000 armored vehicles by 1934.[46] This wealth of equipment enabled the Red Army to create tank organizations for both infantry support and combined arms mechanized operations. Virtually all rifle divisions had a tank company or battalion attached to them, with an entire regiment of 190 or more tanks for each of the horse cavalry divisions. Beginning in 1930, the Red Army experimented with integrating all arms into mechanized functional groups at battalion, brigade, and higher levels. Although organizations changed frequently as equipment and tactical techniques evolved, the 1935 mechanized "corps" was typical of these developments (Figure 7). The four corps organized under this concept were really small armored divisions (the Soviets frequently used the terms "corps" and "brigade" to designate experimental units of division and regimental size, respectively). These mechanized corps were extremely armor-heavy, but nevertheless integrated the essential combat arms at a relatively low level. The trend during the later 1930s was for these corps, redesignated "tank corps" in 1938, to become increasingly large and armor-heavy.

This Soviet force structure had its problems, of course. To begin with, despite the massive industrial support of the Soviet Union, the armored force was so ambitious that not all units could be fully equipped. Soviet historians have criticized the separation of available equipment into infantry-support and independent formations under these circumstances.[47] More

66

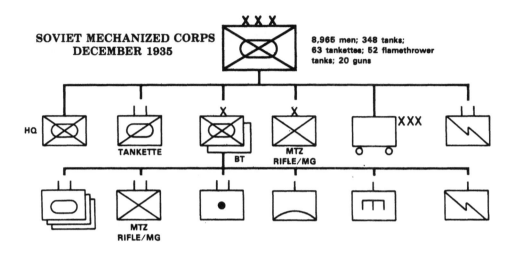

SOVIET MECHANIZED CORPS
DECEMBER 1935

8,965 men; 348 tanks;
63 tankettes; 52 flamethrower
tanks; 20 guns

HQ

TANKETTE

BT

MTZ
RIFLE/MG

MTZ
RIFLE/MG

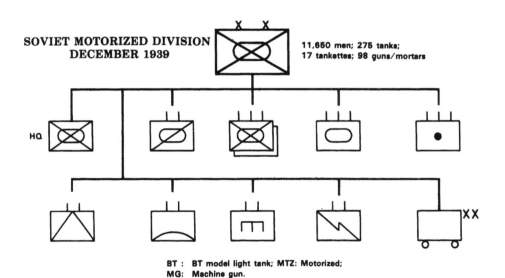

SOVIET MOTORIZED DIVISION
DECEMBER 1939

11,650 men; 275 tanks;
17 tankettes; 98 guns/mortars

HQ

BT : BT model light tank; MTZ: Motorized;
MG: Machine gun.

Figure 7. Soviet Mechanized Corps, December 1935, and Motorized Division, December 1939

specifically, the average Soviet citizen had little experience with motor vehicles, so that maintenance was often a problem, particularly as the vehicles wore out. Soviet radios were notoriously unreliable, making command and control of this mass of moving vehicles difficult. Despite frequent major exercises during the mid-1930s, the Soviet armored force needed several more years of experimentation and training before it could realize its full potential.

It never got that time. On 12 June 1937, the Soviet government executed Tukhachevsky and eight of his high-ranking assistants, as Stalin shifted his purge of Soviet society against the last power group that had the potential to threaten him, the Red Army. In the ensuing four years, the Soviet government imprisoned or executed at least 20 percent of the officer corps, including a majority of all commanders of units of regimental size or larger. Thus, at the same time the Red Army was expanding because of the threat from Nazi Germany and Imperial Japan, it was losing its most experienced planners and leaders. The politically reliable survivors were promoted into positions far above their previous training and experience, with disastrous effects on unit development and tactics.[48]

At the same time that Tukhachevsky's thought was under suspicion, the Soviet experience in the Spanish Civil War caused the Red Army to reassess mechanization. Dimitri Pavlov, chief of tank troops and one of the senior Soviet commanders to serve in Spain, came back with an extremely pessimistic attitude. The Soviet tanks were too lightly armored, their Russian crews could not communicate with the Spanish troops, and in combat the tanks tended to run away from the supporting infantry and artillery. Pavlov argued that the new mechanized formations were too unwieldy to control, too vulnerable to antitank fire, and would have great difficulty penetrating enemy defenses in order to conduct a deep battle. The fact that Pavlov had been able to use only fifty tanks without any chance of surprise at the battle of Esquivas (29 October 1936) apparently did not dissuade him from generalizing.[49] In any event, many observers from other armies reached the same conclusions based on the limited experience in Spain.

In July 1939, Gen. G.I. Kulik chaired a commission to review the question of tank force organization. With most of Tukhachevsky's followers dead or imprisoned, there were few advocates for large mechanized formations. The commission therefore directed the partial dismantling of such units, emphasizing the infantry-support role. The commission also created a new, more balanced organization, the motorized division of December 1939 (Figure 7). This continued support for the 1936 doctrine and force structure may have been in response to the

German armored success in Poland in September 1939, and the Soviet success that year against Japan (see below). Four of a planned fifteen motorized divisions were formed in early 1940, representing a better all-around organization than the tank corps they replaced.[50]

In spite of this reorganization, the Red Army was a shambles, unable to occupy Poland effectively in 1939 or to defeat Finland rapidly in 1939-40. These battlefield failures prompted a series of reforms in organization, leadership, and tactics that slowly began to improve Soviet military ability. The only successful Soviet campaign of this period was in the undeclared war against Japan. Stalin was apparently so concerned about Japanese expansion in northeast Asia that he gave one of Tukhachevsky's most able students, Gen. Georgi Zhukov, a free hand in commanding the Soviet forces there. The Red Army in Siberia was among the last to be affected by Stalin's purges, and so, with the exception of some reserve component units, the training and command structure of these forces were still intact when hostilities with the Japanese Army erupted in the summer of 1939 on the Khalkin-Gol River of Manchuria (Map 4). The Japanese decided to fight the Soviets in this remote area on the border between Japanese-occupied Manchuria and Soviet-dominated Outer Mongolia, believing that the Soviets would be unable to concentrate and supply a major force there. To the surprise of the Japanese, the Soviets massed 469 light tanks, 426 other armored vehicles, 679 guns and mortars, and over 500 aircraft, all supplied by thousands of trucks. Zhukov organized a classic double envelopment between 20 and 31 August 1939. First, a series of Soviet probing attacks in the center fixed the Japanese defenders, and Soviet artillery concentrated against strongpoints found by these probes. Then the two Soviet flanks pressed forward, encircling the Japanese 23rd Infantry Division and part of the 7th Infantry Division. The Soviet attacks used tank and machine gun direct fire, as well as coordinated artillery fire, to protect their advancing infantry. In some cases, the infantry rode on the outside of armored cars, reducing the time needed to close with the enemy, but exposing both vehicles and riders to concentrated enemy fire. On the other hand, some Soviet commanders were unimaginative in executing Zhukov's plan, making repeated frontal attacks instead of bypassing Japanese resistance.[51] Still, Khalkin-Gol provided an excellent trial of Soviet doctrine on the very eve of World War II. Zhukov and his subordinates naturally rose to prominence during that war.

United States

The U.S. Army, despite its unique division structure, was heavily under the influence of French tactical and staff doctrine in 1918. Of necessity, American officers had learned to do business in a manner compatible with the French units they dealt

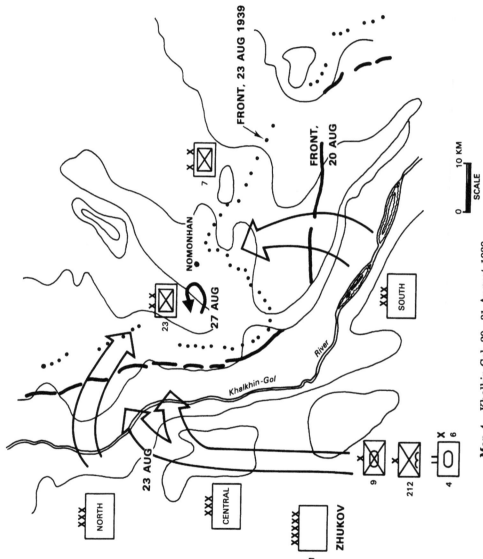

Map 4. Khalkin-Gol, 20—31 August 1939.

84-3330

—70—

with daily. To some extent, therefore, the immediate postwar doctrine of the U.S. Army paralleled that of the French Army. As in France, the United States subordinated tanks to the infantry branch. Initial postwar regulations reflected the French view of combined arms so faithfully that in 1923 the War Department drafted a Provisional Manual of Tactics for Large Units that did not even mention the fact that it was a direct translation of the 1921 French Provisional Instructions.[52] The same year, the revised version of the U.S. Field Service Regulations insisted that "No one arm wins battles. The combined employment of all arms is essential to success." In the next paragraph, however, it stated that the mission of the entire force "is that of the infantry."[53]

Still, this rigid view of combined arms did not affect all American soldiers, nor did it last for a long period of time. As early as 1920, staff officers such as Brig. Gen. Fox Conner had decided that the requirements of trench warfare were inappropriate for operations on the American continent, the expected arena of future American wars. Conner asked Gen. John J. Pershing, the U.S. wartime commander in France, to discard the square division structure because it was too immobile and unwieldy for such operations. Pershing recommended that the infantry division be reorganized along the lines of European triangular divisions and that units needed only for specialized operations be pooled at the level of corps and field army.[54] These principles eventually produced a comprehensive review of the fundamental relationships between the different arms and services.

Despite a number of boards reviewing the American experience in World War I, the square division's organization changed only slightly during the 1920s. By 1925, American officer education was focused on mobile warfare, with trench warfare relegated to the status of a special operation. However, financial restrictions and the general peacetime neglect of the U.S. Army prevented major changes in equipment and organization until the mid-1930s. Then the army was able to use public works funds allocated to restart the depression economy as a means of achieving limited improvements in equipment. These included partial motorization of active and National Guard divisions and production of different carriages with pneumatic tires for existing artillery pieces. Such carriages allowed the artillery to be towed by motor vehicles and, in the case of the French-designed 75-mm gun, to be used in a limited antiaircraft role.

In 1935, Gen. Malin Craig became Chief of Staff of the U.S. Army. Craig had apparently been influenced by Fox Conner and the other reformers of 1920, and he instigated a review of all combat organization and tactics.[55] Craig specifically suggested development of a smaller, more mobile division using mechanical power to replace human power wherever possible. A General Staff board drew up a proposed division structure that totalled only 13,552 men and closely paralleled European divisions of the same period. From 1936 through 1939, the 2d U.S. Infantry Division conducted extensive tests of this concept, reviewing such matters as the amount of firepower and frontage that should be allocated per man and per unit, the proportion of artillery and transportation that should support the infantry, and the echelon (platoon, company, battalion, or regiment) at which different infantry weapons should be pooled. One of the driving forces behind these tests was Brig. Gen. Lesley J. McNair, who later designed and trained the Army Ground Forces of World War II.

The resulting organization of infantry was remarkably close to the Pershing-Conner ideas of 1920. In essence, the machine gun and other specialized heavy weapons were integrated into the infantry rifle organization at every level. To avoid an excessive span of control, each commander had a headquarters, three subordinate rifle units, plus a weapons unit--three rifle platoons and a heavy weapon platoon in each company, with three such companies plus a heavy weapons company in each battalion. In practice, commanders might shift companies from one battalion to another, or even move entire battalions between regiments, but doctrinally all units operated with three subordinate maneuver units.

Each echelon also had a combination of flat-trajectory and high-angle weapons. Although the infantry received greater firepower in terms of automatic weapons and mortars, this firepower was echeloned so that it did not impede the mobility of the parent infantry unit. Thus, for example, the infantry platoon had nothing heavier than the Browning Automatic Rifle (BAR), while the company had nothing heavier than the 60-mm mortar.[56] It should be noted that this dedication to mobility, when combined with a continued faith in the individual rifleman, meant that an American army platoon had less firepower than its European counterparts--the BAR had a much lower rate of fire than most light machine guns found in European squads. This deficiency was only partially corrected by the rapid-fire ability of the M1 rifle. Since American tactics were based on the premise of establishing a base of fire and then maneuvering a light force in conjunction with that base, this organization left U.S. infantry at a disadvantage.

The same principle of weapons pooling was continued throughout the triangular division. Light antitank guns, heavy mortars, and machine guns were relegated to the heavy weapons company of each battalion. Specialized arms such as tanks, antiaircraft, and most antitank weapons were not authorized within the division, because McNair believed that such weapons should be held in a central mass and used only against a major enemy force. Similarly, the division received only one reconnaissance troop, with long-range reconnaissance being assigned to higher headquarters. The general result was an infantry force that was at once more mobile and more heavily armed than its predecessors, yet deficient compared to foreign armies. Its principal drawback, in addition to automatic weapons, was its limited capacity for antiaircraft and antitank defense. As remarked before, during the later 1930s heavy machine guns still seemed effective against aircraft and armored vehicles, so that these weapons, plus 37-mm antitank guns, appeared adequate for the triangular division. Once the German blitzkrieg demonstrated its psychological and physical effect on infantry, the U.S. Army realized that it had to add more antitank defenses.

The controversies about the triangular division tests included the proportions of engineers and artillery for the infantry component. The army was conditioned to regard the engineers only in their World War 1 role of road construction and limited fortification support. At one point, General Craig suggested eliminating all engineers from the division structure. In 1938, General McNair recommended an engineer company of 175 men, or 1.7 percent of the division, because he believed that only hasty road repair and limited roadblock construction would occur in the next war. The engineers had to campaign vigorously for their very existence in the division, arguing that an increasingly motorized and mechanized army had greater need for engineers to construct and reduce antitank defenses and other obstacles. Only the German use of combat engineers for such tasks in 1939-40 finally convinced the U.S. to retain an engineer battalion in each division.[57] Even this was a mixed blessing for the engineers, because they were frequently used as the division's infantry reserve force.

The 1935 division proposal had envisioned a division artillery consisting of three combined 75-mm gun/81-mm mortar battalions for direct support, with a 105-mm howitzer battalion for general support. All other artillery was to be nondivisional, attached as necessary. In actual testing, the artillery found that the 81-mm mortar was essentially an infantry weapon. In any event, McNair objected to this emphasis on dedicated support to the infantry, arguing that longer-range weapons with greater centralized control would lead to more flexible massed fires. No unit, he said, needed weapons whose

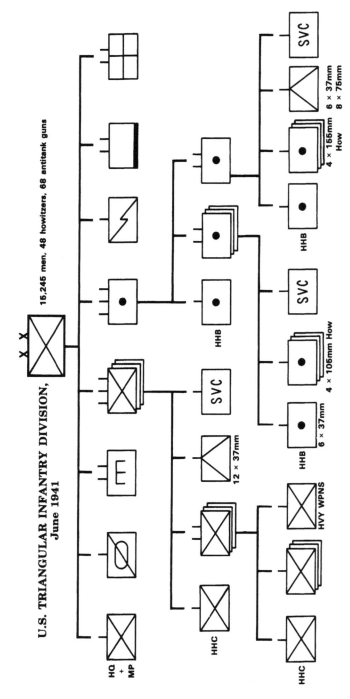

Figure 8. U. S. Triangular Infantry Division, June 1941.

range exceeded the parent unit's area of operations. Ultimately, the decision was made to have three battalions of 75-mm guns, to be replaced by 105-mm howitzers when they were produced, plus 155-mm general support artillery. The June 1941 organization (Figure 8) represented the final step prior to American entry into the war.

The debate over artillery in the division organization occurred at the same time that the U.S. Army Field Artillery School was developing the next major step in infantry-artillery fire coordination, the ability to mass fires on targets of opportunity. During World War I, massed fires were normally the result of carefully planned artillery concentrations, in which known targets were predesignated on maps or overlays. If the infantry needed artillery fire on an unexpected target of opportunity, however, it was difficult to bring more than one battery to bear on such a target. To begin with, a battery forward observer had both to see the target and to communicate with his battery, which meant in practical terms that he had to keep in field telephone contact with the battery. This reliance on landline communications greatly restricted his ability to accompany the infantry in the advance, although some forward observers managed this feat. Even if the forward observer could adjust his own battery onto a target, he had no accurate way of guiding other batteries, unless the target's map location was known precisely.

Between 1929 and 1941, a series of instructors at the Field Artillery School gradually developed a means of concentrating any amount of available artillery fire on a target of opportunity.[58] One obvious step in this process was to have observers use new, more reliable radios instead of field telephones to communicate. More importantly, the gunnery instructors developed forward observer procedures and a firing chart that together would allow a battalion headquarters to record adjustments in the impact of artillery shells as viewed from the observer's location, instead of the battery location. Graphic firing tables compensated for differences in the locations of different batteries, and one artillery piece in each battalion was ultimately surveyed in relation to a common reference point for all artillery in that division area. The resulting fire direction centers (FDCs) could provide infantry units with an entire battalion, or even multiple battalions, of field artillery firing on a target that only one observer could see. By contrast, throughout World War II German artillerymen had to use well-known terrain features to adjust on a target of opportunity; massed fires remained extremely difficult. Fire direction centers gave the U.S. Army a new and unprecedented degree of infantry-artillery integration. It also encouraged the

U.S. to maintain large amounts of nondivisional artillery to reinforce divisions as needed.

The United States was not nearly so advanced in the development of armored and mechanized forces.[59] As in France, the supply of slow World War I tanks and the subordination of tanks to the infantry branch impeded the development of any role other than direct infantry support. Yet the British experiments of the later 1920s, plus the persistent efforts of a cavalry officer named Adna Chaffee Jr., led to a series of limited steps in mechanization. In 1928 and again in 1929, an ad hoc Experimental Armored Force (EAF) was organized at the Tank School in Fort Meade, Maryland. Two battalions of obsolescent tanks, a battalion of infantry in trucks, an armored car troop, a field artillery battalion, plus small elements of engineers, signals, medical, ammunition, chemical warfare, and maintenance, formed the EAF. Despite frequent mechanical breakdowns, the experiments aroused sufficient interest for a more permanent force to be established at Fort Eustis in 1930. The continuing economic depression, however, caused the Army to disband this unit a year later for lack of funds. The Infantry School at Fort Benning absorbed the Tank School and remaining infantry tank units.

As Chief of Staff from 1930 to 1935, Douglas MacArthur wanted to advance motorization and mechanization throughout the army, rather than confining them to one branch. Restricted army budgets made this impossible, but Chaffee did persuade MacArthur to conduct limited mechanized experiments with cavalry units, because cavalry's existence was threatened by its apparent obsolescence. By law, "tanks" belonged to the infantry branch, so the cavalry gradually bought a group of "combat cars," lightly armored and armed tanks that were often indistinguishable from the newer infantry "tanks." In 1932 a one-squadron mechanized cavalry regiment moved to Camp Knox, Kentucky, to be followed by another regiment in late 1936. These units were the nucleus of the 7th Cavalry Brigade (Mechanized). A series of early armor advocates commanded this brigade, including Adna Chaffee himself in 1938-40. However, this force was plagued by the same difficulties as mechanized cavalry in Europe. It was too lightly armed and armored and was viewed generally as a raiding or pursuit force in the cavalry tradition. Despite all of Chaffee's efforts, the other arms only cooperated with the brigade on periodic exercises. Not until January 1940, for example, was a mechanized engineer troop authorized for the 7th Brigade.[60] At about the same time, the 6th Infantry Regiment joined the 7th Brigade, and a Provisional Tank Brigade grew out of the infantry tank units at Fort Benning.

The German armored attack on France in May 1940 gave further impetus to mechanized experiments already conducted in U.S. Army maneuvers. To avoid branch prejudices, Chaffee convinced the War Department to create an "Armored Force" outside of the traditional arms. In consequence, in July 1940 the 7th Cavalry Brigade and the Provisional Tank Brigade became the nuclei for the first two armored divisions. These divisions, like the first organizations of the European powers, were excessively tank heavy. Each was authorized six battalions of light tanks and two battalions of medium tanks (approximately 400 tanks total), but only two battalions of armored infantry and three battalions of artillery. The majority of light tanks reflected the cavalry heritage of this division. Such a structure left inadequate infantry to support the tanks and too many lightly armored vehicles to fight the heavier German tanks. Considerably more production and development was needed before the lopsided American armored units became a cohesive mechanized force.

Finally, close air support was also lacking in the American combat team. Despite the efforts of a few aviators such as Frank Lackland, the U.S. Army Air Corps was preoccupied with strategic bombing to the neglect of close air support.[61] As in France and Britain, American aviators argued that air power was best used in areas beyond the range of ground artillery. This apparently logical division of labor overlooked three aspects of ground combat: the psychological impact of close air attack, the necessity of massing all combat power to overcome the inherent advantages of the defender, and the need to achieve this mass rapidly in order to sustain mobile operations and deny the defender time to organize. Like Guderian, Chaffee hoped to use such techniques to avoid the delays and logistical buildup necessary for a deliberate, breakthrough attack. All three aspects argued in favor of close air support at the critical point, but in 1939-40 only the German Luftwaffe had made even limited preparations to provide such support.

The preceding discussion of five different armies appears to go in five different directions, and yet certain common threads are evident. First, anti-war sentiment, limited defense budgets, and similar restrictions hampered the development of new weapons and doctrine in every army except the pre-1937 Red Army. As a consequence, no nation was fully equipped with modern weapons when it entered World War II, although the Germans were several years ahead of their opponents and, therefore, had more experience and training with such weapons.

Second, even within the peacetime armies, the World War I traditions of infantry-artillery dominance delayed new developments designed to broaden the nature of the combined arms, although the Red Army was again an exception until 1937. In the British, French, and American armies, mechanization developed in two divergent directions. Heavy, almost armor-pure formations supported conventional infantry attacks, while highly mobile but poorly armed and protected light forces performed cavalry functions. For the British, the demands of imperial policing further restricted any move towards development of large mechanized units. Still, even the Germans and Soviets diverted some armor to specialized cavalry and infantry-support roles. During the 1930s, professional soldiers gradually broke free of traditional, 1918 views about the role of various arms. The Germans had the advantage in these new developments, certainly after the purges had shattered the Red high command. Thanks to Guderian and Hitler, the Germans funneled more of their assets into fewer Panzer units than did their opponents, who tended to modernize slightly a much larger part of their armies, and who therefore had no force trained and equipped for mechanized combat in 1939-41.

Finally, the air power advocates of all nations retarded the development of close air support for ground operations. Even the Germans had only the embryo of an air-ground command and control system when the war began.

Had World War II come in 1936 or 1937, Tukhachevsky's developments in the Red Army probably would have triumphed despite problems with materiel and training. Had the war begun in 1942 or later, the British, French, and Americans would all have had time to experiment with and adjust their mechanized organizations and doctrine. Germany's military success in 1939-41 was therefore the product of a very transitory set of advantages. The Germans had produced equipment and fielded mechanized units in the mid-1930s, so that this equipment was still usable and the units were well organized and trained when war began in 1939. In addition, Germany had two advantages that the other powers lacked: a primitive but developing close air-support system, and a command and control network that allowed for much more rapid maneuver than any opponent could achieve.

CHAPTER FOUR
WORLD WAR II: THE AXIS ADVANCE, 1939-1942

World War II did more than force armies to integrate all the available arms at every level into a mobile, flexible team. It also forced those armies to adjust to a variety of threats and terrain. Despite the vast scope of the struggle, some major trends are evident. First, the mechanized combined arms force came of age in this war. In 1939, most armies still thought of an armored division as a mass of tanks with relatively limited support from the other arms. By 1943, the same armies had evolved armored divisions that were a balance of different arms and services, each of which had to be as mobile and almost as protected as the tanks they accompanied. The Soviet, German, and American armies cannibalized infantry-support tank units to form more armored divisions. Second, this concentration of mechanized forces in a small number of mobile divisions left the ordinary infantry unit deficient in both antitank weapons for the defense and armor to accompany the deliberate attack. The German, Soviet, and American armies therefore developed a number of tank surrogates such as tank destroyers and assault guns to perform these functions in cooperation with the infantry. Third, one of the driving forces in both of the previous trends was the gradual development of the means to counter and control the blitzkrieg. During the period 1939 to 1941, conventional infantry units were unprepared psychologically and technologically to defeat a rapidly moving armored foe who broke into their rear areas to disrupt communications and organization. By 1943, those same infantry units had lost their paralyzing fear of armored penetration and had acquired a much greater antitank capability. Successful armored penetrations were still possible, as the Soviets demonstrated, but they were increasingly difficult. Finally, World War II represented the end of pure ground operations. Mechanized attack required air superiority and close air support, airborne landings required close coordination between air transport and ground forces, and amphibious landings developed as the most sophisticated and complicated form of combined arms and joint operations. Such joint service interaction was not achieved without operational errors and doctrinal arguments, but by the end of the war ground commanders had reached a temporary working compromise with the other services on most questions.

The best way to examine these developments is to consider the actions and reactions of the opposing armies during the course of the war. This chapter will begin with the reasons for the German success of 1939 and 1940, followed by British reactions and adjustments to that success. Turning to the next cycle of developments, the German victories in Russia during 1941-42 must be compared with Soviet efforts to adjust organization and tactics both before and after the German invasion. After reviewing American developments in organization, the next chapter will consider the many technological advances of the war, then survey the development of Allied antitank, mechanized, and close air support operations in the second half of the war. Specialized cases such as airborne, amphibious, and unconventional operations are discussed separately at the end of Chapter Five.

Poland, 1939

During the first seventeen days of September 1939, Germany overwhelmed Poland and occupied more than half of its territory. The western Allies, who were still mobilizing and training their reserve components, were unable to make more than a symbolic attack along the French-German border during this period. Yet the speed of the German conquest obscured a number of problems that the Germans encountered, problems that they attempted to solve during the winter of 1939-40. As a result, the Germans widened the gap of experience and experimentation that separated them from their future opponents, Great Britain and France.[1]

To begin with, the German higher commanders had not accepted Guderian's theories and did not employ their mobile divisions in mass for deep exploitation. The panzer and light divisions were parceled out among the various armies. The only exception was the German Tenth Army, which had two panzer, two motorized, and three light divisions in addition to its six conventional infantry divisions. In general, the mechanized and motorized forces were employed as the cutting edges of a more conventional advance on a broad front, with relatively shallow penetrations of the Polish defenses. Not until after organized Polish resistance collapsed did armored forces exploit into the rear for any distance.[2]

Although German tanks and motorized infantry had developed techniques for close interaction, the same was not true between these elements and their fire support. Within hours of the first attack, General Guderian was bracketed by his own artillery, which violated orders by firing blindly into the morning fog. The Luftwaffe concentrated on achieving air superiority and interdicting Polish lines of communication, rather than on supporting the ground troops directly. The complexity of close air support operations, the problems of coordinating and communicating between air and ground units, and the lack of training in such methods made it very difficult for the Luftwaffe and army to work together.

Many German tactical commanders were too cautious, allowing themselves to be halted by even minor Polish resistance. This was a natural response for an army that had not seen combat for years, but it was not appropriate to the situation. The Poles were probably doomed at the outset, because they had dispersed their forces along the entire Polish-German border in an effort to prevent any limited German grab for territory. Under the circumstances, German forces needed to punch through the thin Polish frontier defenses rapidly, rather than stopping to deploy whenever they made contact with Polish troops.

The German system of division and higher level commanders going forward to make on-the-spot decisions greatly increased the tempo of operations. However, the same system had several drawbacks that were evident even in this first campaign. The presence of a higher commander on the scene tended to inhibit the initiative of the battalion or regimental commander. This inhibition may have been partially responsible for the caution displayed by German units in Poland. Moreover, the senior commanders were extremely vulnerable to enemy attack while moving about in a fluid battle. For example, Guderian, a corps commander, was pinned down for hours by a few bypassed Polish troops. This was a recurring problem for leaders in many armies during World War II, especially for the more daring German commanders in North Africa. Ultimately some, like Rommel, organized ad hoc security task forces to travel with them. Yet such a security force reduced the combat power of subordinate units and at the same time increased the tendency for a senior commander to become involved personally in the small unit actions he saw when he visited the front. If he lost radio contact with his headquarters, the senior commander became isolated and even less effective.

Although no German unit advanced more than 250 kilometers into Poland, significant problems of supply and maintenance developed. All major tank repairs required evacuation to Germany, and forward maintenance units were unprepared for the new demands of active campaigning. By the end of the Polish campaign, the German mechanized force was almost immobilized for maintenance reasons.

A related problem was the unsuitability of German equipment. As noted in the previous chapter, the Germans had intended the Mark I tank for training rather than combat, and the Mark II was scarcely better. The use of such vehicles in Poland reflected two problems: Germany had begun the war before her mechanized forces had developed completely, and those forces still did not have priority for industrial production. During the month of September 1939, for example, the Germans lost 218 tanks in battle, approximately 10 percent of their entire force, while manufacturing only fifty-seven new ones. Even at the time of the invasion of France eight months later, the second generation Mark III and IV medium tanks constituted less than one-fourth of German tanks in field units.[3] The Polish campaign did accelerate the retirement of Mark Is by revealing their deficiencies and may have hastened the movement of Mark IIs into reconnaissance, engineer, and command units. As a result, the relatively few Mark III and IV tanks bore the brunt of the effort in 1940.

By contrast, other German equipment had unexpected uses. The half-tracks originally intended as prime movers for artillery proved to be so mobile that infantry units in panzer divisions sought to acquire them as armored personnel carriers. The vast majority of panzer grenadiers, however, continued to travel in trucks and motorcycles throughout the war; there were never enough half-tracks available. The 88-mm antiaircraft gun proved to be extremely useful in a ground-support role, foreshadowing its later use as the premier antitank weapon of the German Army.

A basic result of the German invasion of Poland was to begin the slow evolution of the German panzer division structure towards greater balance among the arms. At the time of the Polish campaign, the six panzer divisions averaged between 276 and 302 tanks each, organized into a panzer brigade of four battalions. Those same divisions had only three battalions of infantry and two of artillery. This tank-heavy force proved too unwieldy for some commanders, and in any event Hitler was interested in creating more panzer divisions. At the same time, the German "light divisions," built around two motorized infantry regiments and one tank battalion, proved to be too light for sustained operations, lacking the combat power of either a panzer division or a conventional infantry division. Given the limited number of tanks in the German inventory, the solution was obvious--tanks moved from the existing panzer divisions to the light divisions, three of which became panzer divisions during the winter of 1939-40. In addition, during the Polish campaign an ad hoc panzer division had formed around one of the infantry-support tank brigades created in 1938; this formation became the 10th Panzer Division. Thus, by the time of the French campaign, even more of the available German tanks were concentrated into panzer divisions, some of which were reduced from a four-battalion tank brigade to a three-battalion tank regiment, with a total of 160-200 tanks. This put the tank element in balance with the rest of the division, which normally consisted of three infantry battalions and two or three towed artillery battalions, an armored reconnaissance battalion, engineer battalion, and signals.[4] This trend towards a more balanced division would continue throughout the war.

Regardless of exact organization, all the panzer divisions were in the habit of task organizing for combat. The brigade, regimental, and battalion headquarters all practiced attaching and detaching elements of other arms in order to have a combination of tanks, infantry, artillery, engineers, and, on occasion, air defense. The balance between these arms varied with the mission, terrain, and enemy forces involved.

Beyond these organizational changes, German tactical concepts and structures seemed essentially sound. With the exception of a few technical problems with a particular machine gun design, the infantry divisions functioned well. The only other lesson of the Polish campaign was the predictable discovery that armored forces were at a disadvantage when fighting on urban terrain--fifty-seven tanks were lost in one day while attempting to seize Warsaw.[5] This experience only reinforced the need for a higher proportion of infantry to tanks, in order to provide close-in security for the tanks on urban terrain, where the tanks were vulnerable to short-range antitank attacks from nearby buildings.

The German Advance, 1940

Between the fall of Poland in 1939 and the beginning of the Belgian-French campaign in May 1940, another German operation unsettled Allied morale and foreshadowed the future complexity of joint operations. On 9 April 1940, an improvised German force used motor movements, small-scale airborne drops, and seaborne landings to occupy Denmark and Norway by surprise. Only one of the six German divisions sent to Norway was a fully trained, established organization, yet all units performed remarkably well. Despite the shoestring nature of the German operation, this "warfare in three dimensions" (land, air, and sea) caused a shift of Allied resources and planning away from the battlefields of France.[6] This shift meant further confusion and delays in the process of mobilizing and training the British and French troops.

The stunning operations in Denmark and Norway preceded another surprise when the main battle in France and Belgium was joined. On 10 May 1940, a small party of German glider troops landed on top of the elaborate concrete fortress of Eben Emael, the key to the Belgian defensive system. Using shaped-charge explosives* and the element of surprise, these Germans blinded and neutralized the huge fortress until ground troops arrived, thereby eliminating one of Belgium's main defenses.[7] This surprise, coming on the heels of the Norwegian invasion, caused many Allied military and civilian leaders to become excessively

---

*The "shaped charge" was a concept fully developed only during the 1930s. It allowed the user to focus the blast of a particular amount of explosive in order to achieve a much greater effect than the same explosive would produce if detonated normally. The essence of this shaping was to mold the explosive with a cone-shaped hollow on one end, so that the blast effect that centered within that hollow would produce a shock wave in one direction, towards the wide end of the cone.

concerned about the rear area threat posed by airborne and unconventional warfare forces. Such concern was the first step in creating the psychological uncertainty that was so critical to the success of the blitzkrieg.

Conquering Belgium and France required more than propaganda and a few paratroopers to create psychological paralysis. Contrary to frequent stereotypes, the western armies were remarkably well armed by 1940, having greatly increased their production during the later 1930s. One calculation indicates that Britain and France had a combined total of 4,340 tanks on the continent during the 1940 campaign, as compared to only 3,863 for Germany. Despite weaknesses such as lack of radio communications and crowded turrets, most of the Allied tanks were actually better armed and armored than their German counterparts. Only the light British cruiser tanks were more vulnerable. For instance, one obsolete French FCM tank took forty-two hits from German 37-mm antitank guns without being knocked out of action. The Germans had to bring up 88-mm antiaircraft guns or medium artillery to deal with the more heavily armored French B-1 bis and British infantry support tanks. Indeed, the Germans were disturbed by the general ineffectiveness of their antitank weapons. By contrast, the outnumbered French 25-mm and 47-mm antitank guns had much higher muzzle velocities and therefore greater armor penetration capacity than the German and British guns.[8]

Yet the Germans defeated the Allies so rapidly that they seemed to validate the concept of blitzkrieg in Germany and abroad, even when the details of this concept were not well understood. The true reasons for this success have already appeared in this study.

First, in contrast to their own performance in Poland and to the French dispositions in 1940, the Germans concentrated their available mechanized forces into a few large masses at critical points. Seven out of ten panzer divisions, with five motorized divisions following close behind them to mop up and protect the flanks, advanced through the Ardennes forest on a seventy-kilometer front. By contrast, the French Army dispersed thirty-six tank battalions evenly along its borders in support of infantry armies, even in the Maginot Line area. In most cases these battalions had never trained with the infantry and artillery to conduct a deliberate attack or counterattack. Much of the remaining French and British armor was in the extreme north, moving into Belgium in a direction away from the main German advance on Sedan. Four French armored divisions were still forming, but these were scattered at wide distances behind the front and were broken up in some cases when committed to battle.[9]

In addition, the western Allies had organized themselves for a linear defense, spreading their forces thinly across a wide front. The French command structure in particular was geared to methodical, set-piece battles, but lacked the forces to create a true defense-in-depth on the World War I model. By rushing through the Ardennes forest, the main German attack shattered this linear defense at one of its weakest points. By the fifth day of the campaign (14 May 1940), the German mobile forces were conducting the type of deep exploitation envisioned by many theorists during the 1930s. Such penetrations were psychologically unnerving to the defenders, who were suddenly faced by major enemy forces in the rear, but who lacked a procedure to redeploy units rapidly to meet and contain that threat. The rapid German advance disorganized French command and control and prevented any restoration of a cohesive defense.

Because there was so little resistance, the German commanders did not always lead with tanks. Instead, the armored reconnaissance battalions, plus in some cases engineers to clear obstacles, led the advance by up to a day's march, with the slower elements strung out in column behind. Commanders used armored vehicles or light aircraft for control during the pursuit. Of course, this advance in column made the Germans rather vulnerable if the defenders were able to mount a counterattack, as Erwin Rommel discovered when the British struck the flank of his panzer division at Arras on 21 May. Only the improvised use of 88-mm antiaircraft guns and 105-mm howitzers in an antitank role halted the heavy infantry-support tanks of the British 1st Army Tank Brigade. The British did not realize that the 88-mm gun was responsible for their defeat until they met the weapon again in North Africa. Even this unsuccessful British counterattack at Arras put some of the fear of tanks into the German higher commanders, causing German armor leaders to seek larger antitank weapons and higher velocity tank guns after Arras.[10]

At the tactical level, both the British and the French were at a distinct disadvantage in force structure and practice. German armored divisions were clearly better organized than those of France. The French Division Cuirassée was too tank-heavy, with four tank and only one infantry and two artillery battalions. When ordinary infantry or artillery units were attached to this division to correct the problem, the attached units had not trained to cooperate with tanks. French logistical support was too dependent on roads and rails to follow the all-terrain maneuver elements of these divisions. Finally, the inexperienced French commander of an armored division had to control most of his subordinate units directly; the "demi-brigade" headquarters that controlled his tank battalions were not trained or intended to integrate the other arms. By contrast, the German commanders had a number of subordinate headquarters, each of which had practiced the control of a combination of the various arms.

German training in combined arms was especially evident during the penetration of the Ardennes. The rapid German advance over a poor road network was made possible only by road repairs conducted by combat engineers. Anti-aircraft guns in the German columns decimated Allied air attacks. At the critical crossing of the Meuse River on 13 May, the German infantry and some engineers crossed the river under the covering fire of tanks, artillery, and tactical aircraft. Indeed, the Germans had relied on air support to limit the need for artillery units and ammunition resupply while moving through the Ardennes. Because close air support was still developing, however, the success at the Meuse River was a combination of good training and luck. In exercises before the campaign, Guderian had arranged for accurate air support from German dive-bombers, without which it would have been difficult to suppress the French defenses on the far side of the river. The day before the attack, the panzer group commander, General Ewald von Kleist, attempted to arrange high altitude saturation attacks by the less accurate medium bombers. This would have made crossing the Meuse during bombing attacks extremely dangerous for the Germans. Fortunately for them, the Luftwaffe did not honor von Kleist's air support request in time, while Guderian's prearranged dive-bombers did arrive.[11]

The fall of France demonstrated not only the importance of combined arms mechanized formations and blitzkrieg penetrations, but also the German advantage over the British and French in combined arms training and procedures. Yet the images of paratroops, tanks, and screaming Stukas tended to obscure the combined arms nature of blitzkrieg from many contemporary observers.

The British Response, 1940-42

The sudden collapse of France in 1940 caused professional soldiers in many armies to reassess their organizations as well as their offensive and defensive doctrine. As the only major belligerent still at war with Hitler, Great Britain had the most urgent need to reorganize its forces and reassess its doctrine in the months after Dunkirk. Unfortunately for the British, the period 1940-42 seems in retrospect to have witnessed the development of two British armies--the army at home, which gradually rebuilt and developed new doctrine and organization, and the field army in the Middle East, which after initial success against Italy found itself repeatedly outmaneuvered by the small forces of the German Afrika Korps. The British troops in North Africa were never able to reorganize and retrain as did the army at home. Yet these two armies were connected in doctrine if not in practice, and the British victories of 1942-45 owed a great deal to the quiet process of rebuilding forces at home.

Faced with the possibility of German invasion after France surrendered, the British felt that there was no time for major changes in organization, doctrine, or equipment. In a desperate effort to rearm the troops evacuated from Dunkirk, British industry continued to produce weapons whose designs were clearly obsolete. Cruiser tanks, armored cars, and two-pound antitank guns appeared by the hundred because there was no time to redesign and build better weapons.[12] Some British commanders became preoccupied with the material difficulties of obtaining trucks to motorize infantry elements within the newly formed armored divisions, thereby obscuring the more fundamental need for doctrine and techniques of infantry-armor cooperation. The British did develop some new weapons during this period, most notably a six-pound (57-mm) gun for use both as an antitank weapon and as the main gun on new tanks. Yet this gun did not appear in the field until 1942, and even then was too large to be mounted in the turrets of older model tanks.[13]

As the threat of invasion lessened, the British Army could emphasize training and reconsider its prewar doctrine in light of the experiences of 1940.[14] The General Staff published a series of notes from various theaters, identifying such points as the need for combined arms organization below division level and the German use of antitank weapons rather than tanks to defeat enemy tanks. Under the direction of Gen. Alan Brooke, Commander-in-Chief Home Forces and later Chief of the Imperial General Staff, the units of the expanded active and reserve (Territorial Army) forces conducted training at all levels. Some of this training was simply an improvement on prewar principles, such as the development of fire-and-movement battle drills for small infantry units. Col. H. J. Parham experimented with a single radio net to mass artillery on the basis of an estimated map reference; the results were rather inaccurate, but in the absence of the American fire direction center, Parham's ideas allowed the Royal Artillery to provide at least some response to targets of opportunity.

The most unusual feature of the period 1940-42 was the conduct of large-unit command post exercises and field maneuvers, with detailed study before and critiques after each step. Lt. Gen. Bernard L. Montgomery had pioneered such exercises as a division commander in France during 1939-40, enabling his division to move more rapidly and flexibly than most other British units. After Dunkirk, Montgomery applied the same training techniques as commander of two different corps and finally of an army-level force. He also acted as chief umpire for exercises involving other units in Britain. Similar if less elaborate training took place in the newly formed armored divisions under Lt. Gen. Giffard Martel, the Commander of the Royal Armoured Corps after December 1940.

Montgomery contended that few British officers had experience maneuvering any unit larger than a brigade, and certainly his exercises helped to produce commanders, staffs, and units that were capable of much more rapid changes in deployment and mission than those of World War I. More importantly, Montgomery and others developed a common conception of the interaction of different arms and of how to commit divisions and larger units to battle. For example, Montgomery argued that the decentralized nature of German mechanized pursuit and exploitation had caused many British commanders to lose sight of the necessity for centralized control in the deliberate attack and defense. Reconnaissance, artillery, tanks, infantry, engineers, and air power had to be "stage-managed" at the highest levels in order to concentrate combat power at any point where the enemy presented an organized defense or attack. Only in a fluid situation could commanders decentralize these arms and push them forward, so that subordinate leaders would have the different weapons readily available. Defense meant not a series of fixed lines on the terrain, but rather blocking positions in depth plus massive counterattacks of the kind Germany had used so well in World War I. All arms needed to employ night attacks to reduce the lethal effects of aimed enemy fire. Finally, Montgomery opposed the traditional British concept that tank units should maneuver like cavalry. Instead, he saw the armored division as a combined arms force that would seize key terrain in order to use the advantages of tactical defense when the enemy armor counterattacked. Infantry and antitank forces would follow the initial armored assault to mop up and hold terrain, releasing the armor to refit or attack again.[15]

In the Royal Armoured Corps, Martel developed these same concepts in a series of exercises, until in June 1942 the senior armor commanders in Britain agreed to an "RAC creed." This creed--a product of exercises and of a critical analysis of events in North Africa--began, "an armoured division is a formation of all arms. Each arm or branch of the service is a member of the team, and has its vital part to play." Like the Germans before them, British armor commanders concluded that antitank guns were the best means to defeat enemy tanks, although tank-tank combat might still occur. Motorized infantry and antitank weapons together would hold key terrain, around which the armored forces maneuvered.[16]

Changes in organization accompanied changes in doctrine. Immediately after Dunkirk, the pure tank brigades of the early armored divisions had given way to brigades composed of one motorized infantry and three tank battalions.* A 1940 British armored division therefore consisted of an armored car reconnaissance battalion, two armored brigades, and a support group, which included battalions of field, antitank, and light antiaircraft artillery, an additional infantry battalion, two engineer companies, and trains. Martel and his subordinates deliberately retained this organization until 1942 to avoid constant changes that would disrupt training.

By 1942, however, this structure was obviously too tank-heavy, and so the War Office removed one of the two armored brigades from the division (see Figure 9). The separate brigades that resulted from this removal could reinforce any division as needed for a particular mission. Moreover, the term "support group" had apparently caused the nonarmored elements of the division to be regarded as an afterthought to the tanks. A motorized infantry brigade plus a division artillery element therefore replaced the support group, with the intention that artillery, antitank, antiaircraft, engineer, and support elements would be centralized or attached to the armored or infantry brigade as needed. At the same time, the British created two different types of infantry division. The "division" per se, apparently intended for Asian operations, retained the traditional configuration of three infantry brigades of three battalions each. Conversely, the "infantry division" lost one brigade in favor of an infantry-support tank brigade. Martel and the new Commander-in-Chief Home Forces, Bernard Paget, strongly advocated this latter change in order to improve training and cooperation between infantry and supporting tanks.[17] Unfortunately, the British returned to a division of three infantry brigades by 1944. As a result, the quality of tank-infantry cooperation in 1944-45 varied widely between different divisions.

War in the Desert, 1940-42

The battles of North Africa did not always reflect the state of the British Army at home. In late 1940, the small force in the Middle East was the only British field army still trained to

---

*The British frequently used the term "regiment" to designate an armored force equivalent to an American battalion. American terminology and symbology are used here for simplicity.

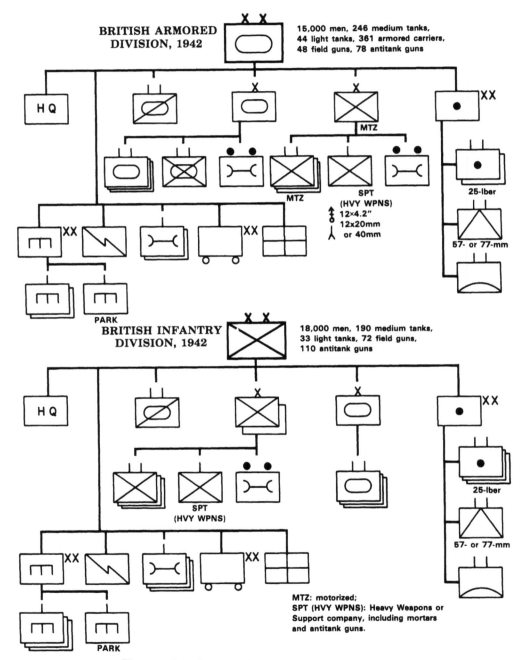

BRITISH ARMORED
DIVISION, 1942

15,000 men, 246 medium tanks,
44 light tanks, 361 armored carriers,
48 field guns, 78 antitank guns

HQ

MTZ

MTZ

SPT
(HVY WPNS)
12×4.2"
12x20mm
or 40mm

25-lber

57- or 77-mm

PARK

BRITISH INFANTRY
DIVISION, 1942

18,000 men, 190 medium tanks,
33 light tanks, 72 field guns,
110 antitank guns

HQ

SPT
(HVY WPNS)

25-lber

57- or 77-mm

MTZ: motorized;
SPT (HVY WPNS): Heavy Weapons or
Support company, including mortars
and antitank guns.

PARK

Figure 9. British Armored and Infantry Divisions, 1942.

84-3330

high prewar standards, although its equipment was little better than that found at home. Once Italy joined the war on Germany's side in mid-1940, Prime Minister Winston Churchill took a calculated risk and sent a portion of his scarce resources to defend Egypt against the threat from Libya, which was an Italian colony at the time. The shipment included a single battalion (7th Royal Tank Regiment) of heavily armored Mark II infantry support tanks. This battalion, in combination with the two understrength but well-trained divisions already in Egypt, was the basis for a classic demonstration of prewar British tactical doctrine (see Map 5).

In September 1940, Marshal Rudolfo Graziani's Italian army of ten divisions had advanced eastward from Italian Libya into British Egypt. Graziani was cautious, however, and in any event his force was largely foot mobile with poor logistical support. He therefore halted and established a series of widely scattered camps in the general area of Sīdī Barrāni, about eighty kilometers east of the Libyan frontier. Lt. Gen. Richard O'Connor, commander of the British Western Desert Force, used the infantry support tanks in conjunction with the 4th Indian Infantry Division to reduce these camps in a surprise advance on 8-10 December 1940. The tactics involved exemplified the best of interwar British practice.[18] Because the Italian camps were protected by minefields and obstacles, the British passed between these camps and attacked them from the far (western) side, aiming at the unmined entrance road to each camp. Artillery and mortar fire pinned the defenders down and distracted attention from the unexpected assault. Then two companies of the slow infantry tanks moved forward, with platoons of Bren gun carriers following behind and to the outside flanks, providing flank security and machine gun fire for the tanks. As soon as the British tanks broke into the enemy positions and came to close quarters, infantry moved up as closely as possible in trucks, dismounted, and accompanied the tanks in mopping-up operations.

After the tank-artillery-infantry team had reduced the enemy defensive system, the 7th British Armoured Division used its light, mobile armored vehicles to conduct a high-speed pursuit. The retreating Italians lacked effective tanks or antitank weapons and were tied to the single road that paralleled the Mediterranean Sea. The 7th Armoured Division therefore made a series of wide flanking movements south of the road, repeatedly turning north to the coast in order to intercept the Italian retreat. This Italian disaster led to the introduction of German forces in North Africa.

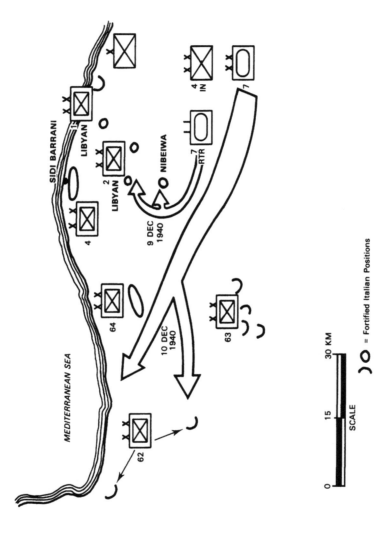

MEDITERRANEAN SEA

SIDI BARRANI

1 LIBYAN

2 LIBYAN

4

64

62

63

7 RTR

NIBEIWA

4 IN

7

9 DEC 1940

10 DEC 1940

SCALE

0   15   30 KM

) O = Fortified Italian Positions

Map 5, Sidi Barrani, December 1940.

The roots of the British victory lay in advantages of superior training, mobility, and equipment. German intervention negated these assets. In early 1941 and again a year later, the British reduced their forces in Egypt in favor of needs elsewhere--first in Greece and, then, after Japan entered the war, in Southeast Asia. As a result, when the German Afrika Korps attacked in March 1941, it met only partly trained British troops equipped with worn out and inferior equipment. Thereafter, German victories and London's repeated demands for British counteroffensives meant that the British desert forces had little time to analyze their mistakes and to train to correct them. With few exceptions, the senior British commanders did not stay in office long enough to learn and apply the lessons of the desert war. The Germans had arrived in Africa with a system of combined arms battlegroups, flexible commanders, and variable tactics to mass combat power on the basis of battle drills. By contrast, the British units had rarely studied combined arms tactics. Newly arrived units from Britain might be better trained, but were often squandered piecemeal before they had become acclimated to the desert.

The Germans also had a considerable technological advantage in equipment.[19] After their shocking encounter with British infantry-support tanks in France, the Germans had experimented with the 88-mm antiaircraft gun to test its effectiveness as an antitank weapon against captured British equipment. The German divisions sent to Africa had a number of organizational modifications, such as less field but more antitank artillery, including a small number of 88-mm guns. In addition, the German tanks in Africa were largely Mark III and IV medium tanks, with Mark II tanks in reconnaissance and command elements. These medium tanks were considerably better armed and armored than the British cruiser and light tanks.

During the course of 1941, a 50-mm medium-velocity main gun replaced the 37-mm on most Mark IIIs. Then in mid-1942, the Germans installed an even higher velocity 50-mm on some Mark IIIs, giving them the same penetration power as the 50-mm towed antitank gun that had already replaced the ineffective German 37-mm. This new 50-mm tank gun had improved sights and fired special "arrowhead" ammunition (an early form of Armor Piercing Discarding Sabot) capable of penetrating even thickly armored infantry support tanks at short ranges. By contrast, the Germans had designed the Mark IV to provide area fire support for other tanks, suppressing enemy antitank defenses while the Mark IIIs closed in the attack. As such, the Mark IV's original armament was a 75-mm low-velocity gun capable of damaging British tracks and roadwheels at 1000 meters, but not of penetrating thick armor. Again during 1942, the continuing German quest for gunpower caused some Mark IVs to receive a higher velocity 75-mm gun. All of these weapons outclassed the British two-pound tank and antitank gun. As late as May 1942, the British forces had only 100 six-pound antitank guns and were just receiving their first American Grant tanks with 75-mm guns. Considering that the frontal armor on German tanks was face-hardened, while that on British tanks was not, the British had to close to almost suicidal ranges of 500 or fewer meters in order to penetrate the German vehicles. In many cases, the British had to hit a German tank twice--once to shatter the face hardening and a second time to penetrate the armor.

These equipment problems obscured the more basic British failure to coordinate and combine different weapons systems. Despite Martel's efforts, British tank battalions in Britain and North Africa found it difficult to resist the temptation to close with the enemy, even when they had not located the enemy's antitank guns. Because the basic German tactic for dealing with enemy armor was still the antitank gun line, this British tendency was disastrous. On 15 June 1941, for example, a few German tanks decoyed the 16th Royal Tank Regiment into a screen of 50-mm antitank guns; the British lost 17 tanks in a matter of minutes.[20] Such bitter lessons rapidly convinced the British to value gun power above all other elements and to regard infantry as a liability in the desert. The armor's tendency to maneuver on its own often left the infantry exposed, and the resulting mistrust made any attempt at cooperation between these arms extremely difficult. In those cases where the British and Commonwealth infantry was able to entrench effectively, the commanders chose positions that were not mutually supporting, so that the Germans could concentrate all available firepower against one British unit at a time.

Early in the desert war, British commanders apparently grasped the German concept of combined arms task organization at the small-unit level, but did not always develop the tactics to complement that organization. As Montgomery was preaching in Great Britain, the tendency to form combined arms units of battalion and brigade size was not always appropriate or sufficient, and caused the divisions to fight as uncoordinated and dispersed collections of small units. The concentrated efforts of the German Afrika Korps often defeated these British task forces in detail.

The British tried to reverse this process. General Martel visited North Africa in early 1942, and the local armor commanders agreed to the newer concepts of a combined arms armored division. The local units, however, did not implement these changes in organization and tactics before the next German offensive, so the British again lost armored "brigade groups" piecemeal despite their intentions to employ divisions as unified forces. After losing most of their tanks, the British resorted to small motorized columns built around the few remaining effective field and antitank artillery units, with just enough motorized infantry to provide local security for those units. "Excess" infantry went to the rear.[21]

This was the situation when Montgomery took command of Eighth British Army in August 1942. Lt. Gen. Brian Horrocks, who had participated in Martel's training exercises as an armored division commander, arrived soon thereafter to command one of the corps. In effect, Montgomery had to retrain the Eighth Army from scratch, focusing upon the problems of centralized command and control for set-piece battles.

The British gained time by halting the Germans at Alam Halfa (31 August-5 September 1942). Having predicted the key terrain that the Germans would have to seize, British and Commonwealth defenders dug in to deny the enemy that terrain. The Royal Air Force attacked German armor while it was immobilized in British minefields. The main British defenses included Grant tank fire at long range, towed antitank guns at closer range, and finally massed artillery protective fires at short range. These successive defenses exhausted the German attacks.[22]

After Alam Halfa, Montgomery used an abbreviated form of his training program from Britain to prepare the Eighth Army for the deliberate attack known as the second battle of Alamein (October-November 1942). To ensure that the entire army attacked in a coordinated manner, Montgomery resorted to the elaborate planning and centralized direction characteristic of British attacks in World War I. Each corps directed its artillery, for example. Such procedures were more familiar to British staff officers than the fluid, improvisational tactics that they had attempted to copy from the Germans. Engineers, infantry, and artillery conducted a night penetration of the German-Italian defensive positions, seizing high ground on which to establish infantry-antitank defenses. Next, Montgomery planned to move armor forward under the protection of these antitank defenses, tempting the Germans to counterattack. In actual practice, the second battle of Alamein was an attrition contest in which Montgomery's plans changed frequently, largely because the armored units still had difficulty cooperating with the artillery and infantry. The ultimate British success clearly owed as much to Montgomery's methods of forcing combined arms cooperation upon his subordinates as to the British material superiority at the time. Historians have frequently criticized Montgomery for the cautious manner in which he conducted both deliberate attacks and more fluid exploitation and pursuits. Yet this caution enabled him to minimize or avoid the errors of his predecessors, errors caused in large part by an inability to coordinate the different arms.[23]

The German Advance in Russia, 1941

While Germany went from victory to victory in the period 1939-41, the Soviet Army stood nearly impotent, thanks in part to Stalin's purge of its officer corps. The administrative occupation of eastern Poland in the fall of 1939 strained Soviet logistics to the breaking point, and the disastrous Russo-Finnish War of 1939-40 demonstrated Soviet inability to coordinate units for a deliberate attack.[24] It is true that the Soviets eventually learned from their mistakes, redoubled their efforts, and forced the Finns to negotiate an armistice in March 1940. Nevertheless, the Red Army was a shambles.

In light of these experiences, during the period 1940-41 the Soviet government undertook massive reforms in military organization, equipment, command structure, and deployment. The Soviets mismanaged most of these changes, and none was complete by the time Germany attacked in June 1941. The Germans caught the Red Army in transition and ripped it apart.[25]

For our purposes the most noteworthy Soviet change before the German invasion was the reintroduction of large combined arms mechanized formations. In reaction to the German victories of 1940, the Soviet government ordered the creation of mechanized corps, each consisting of two tank and one motorized rifle division, for use as the exploitation forces in each field army. By January 1941, the Red Army had on paper twenty-nine of these huge corps, authorized 1,031 tanks each. Unfortunately, the Soviets had neither the men nor the equipment to implement their ambitious plan. By removing all tanks from infantry and cavalry support units, the Soviets collected approximately 17,000 tanks, but the new organizations called for a total of 29,899. Worse still, these tanks were almost entirely the lightly armed and armored variety produced in the mid-1930s. By 1941, such equipment was tactically obsolete and mechanically worn out. In late 1939, the Red Army had tentatively approved designs for new, second generation equipment, including the T-34 medium and KV-1 heavy tanks. Yet incompetent management prevented production of more than 1,475 of these outstanding new weapons before the German attack.[26] Similar managerial and bureaucratic problems deprived the Soviets of trucks to move infantry and artillery, of mines to stop tanks, and of modern fighters to contest German air superiority.

In contrast to Soviet disarray, the German Army that invaded on 22 June 1941 was at the top of its form. Hitler's continuing desire for more panzer divisions had unintentionally improved the balance of arms within those divisions. In order to assemble the tanks necessary for the additional divisions, the Germans had reduced all panzer divisions to an establishment of only two or three tank battalions of three companies each, for a total of 150-202 tanks per division. This action, plus an increase in infantry to a total of four trucked and one motorcycle battalion, meant that each division had six to nine tank companies, but fifteen motorized infantry companies; the other arms remained unchanged. Considering the high casualties and many demands for motorized infantry, this ratio was probably the most effective for all forms of mechanized combat.

Armored enthusiasts have frequently criticized Hitler for this reduction in tank strength, arguing that the resulting panzer division lacked the combat power for sustained advances of the type necessary in Russia.[27] It would be more accurate to argue that German planners geared the entire German Army for relatively limited distances and tied it to railroads and horsedrawn logistics. The problems in the German maintenance system, for example, had been evident even in the short Polish campaign of 1939. The Russian campaign involved much greater distances and longer operations. Under these circumstances, the German system of centralizing spare parts and evacuating most major repairs back to the factory was completely inadequate. In August 1941, the field commanders in Russia had to mount a major argument to convince Hitler to release 300 tank engines to replace those already worn out in the campaign. Every vehicle covered hundreds of miles over uneven and dusty roads, causing many breakdowns. If each panzer division had retained another tank battalion, those additional tanks would have worn out at the same rate as the rest of the division, leaving only a handful of additional vehicles still in the field by the time the division reached the gates of Moscow in December 1941. What the Germans needed was not so much more tanks as more trucks for resupply and a better field maintenance system to repair existing equipment.[28]

These problems, however, were not immediately evident. Operationally, the 1941 campaign was the heyday of German blitzkrieg and especially of the encirclement battle. The Soviet analysis and description of these encirclements offers the best summary (see Figure 10).[29]

First, the attacker had to penetrate or outflank the enemy's defenses. This was relatively easy in 1941, when the Germans caught the Soviets in their peacetime garrisons, unorganized for any coherent defense. Under these circumstances, the attacker

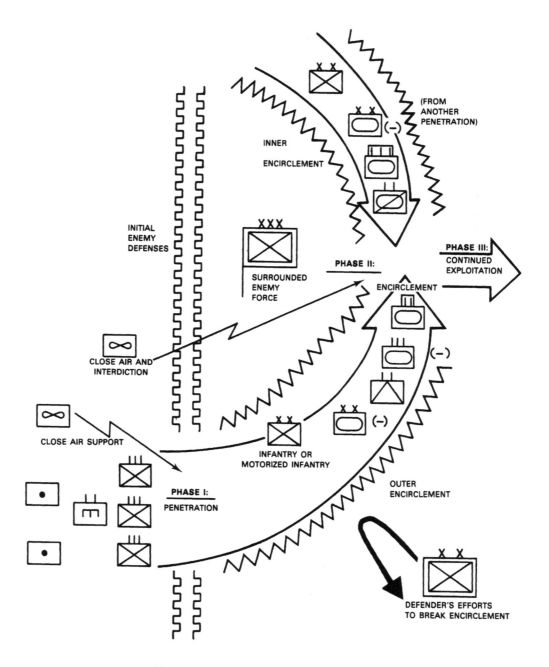

Figure 10. Schematic of Blitzkrieg Encirclement.

could exploit immediately with armored units. If a deliberate attack proved unavoidable, however, the Germans preferred to conduct the penetration with a conventional infantry force, supported by engineers to clear obstacles, with artillery and preplanned air strikes to suppress enemy defensive fires. As the war lengthened, such penetrations became increasingly difficult for all armies.

Next, once penetrations or flanking maneuvers had succeeded, the German armored forces sought to encircle the enemy in pincers. A combined arms battlegroup of battalion or regimental size usually led each pincer. After the jaws of the pincers closed, the attacker had to create two encirclements--one facing inward, to hold the surrounded force and gradually reduce it, and another facing outward, to ward off any efforts to relieve the encircled units. In order to establish these encirclements, the Germans tried to give each panzer corps one or more motorized infantry divisions to follow and support the two panzer divisions. In practice, the Germans never had enough force in a panzer corps to seal off the encirclements, so the process of holding and reducing encirclements had to wait upon the arrival of the foot-mobile infantry divisions. During the interim, surrounded Soviet soldiers and even entire Red Army units were able to infiltrate or break out of the loosely cordoned encirclement, escaping to join local partisans or to return to their own lines and fight again. This lag time also immobilized the panzer units, prevented further exploitation, and gave the defender time to reorganize his forces farther to the rear. Only when the infantry and logistics had caught up with the panzer units could the latter resume the exploitation and pursuit.

The Soviet Response, 1941-42

As the Germans advanced into European Russia, encircling one Soviet field army after another, the Soviet military took desperate measures to overcome their weaknesses. Two basic problems were immediately apparent. On the one hand, the average Soviet commander or staff officer lacked the skills necessary to orchestrate the different arms and weapons for an effective defense or counterattack. The general staff finally had to reprimand these commanders for continually deploying their forces evenly across the ground as if on a textbook exercise, without regard for the terrain or the high-speed avenues of approach that required antitank defenses-in-depth. On the other hand, the Red Army was seriously short of the specialized units and weapons that its commanders found so difficult to employ--engineers, tanks, antitank guns, and artillery.

99

The solution to both questions seemed obvious. Stavka (Supreme Headquarters) Circular 1, dated 15 July 1941, ordered the simplification of the commander's span of control by centralizing specialized units in pools at higher levels. This allowed more experienced commanders to mass them at the critical points. Specifically, the circular disestablished the rifle corps as a level of command. For the next two years, a Soviet field army consisted of only four to six divisions or separate brigades, plus specialized units such as artillery, tanks, and antitank weapons. Similarly, by the removal of tank and antitank units, and by a major reduction in artillery, the circular reduced the infantry division, which until that time closely resembled divisions in other European armies, from 14,483 men to only 10,859.[30] Much of this equipment only existed on paper in any case, and what was actually available was centralized at the level of field army or higher. The same order disestablished the huge mechanized corps of 1940-41. Some of the tank divisions within those corps were retained as separate formations, but in general the first German onslaught had already shattered the mechanized corps.

The remainder of 1941 was a desperate struggle for the Red Army, a struggle in which its traditional doctrines of deep battle and large mechanized units were inappropriate because of the German advantage in equipment and initiative. The few tanks coming off Soviet assembly lines were formed into small brigades used solely for infantry support.

Once the Red Army halted and threw the invaders back from Moscow in December 1941, the Soviet commanders began to revive their organization and doctrine.[31] Soviet factories made a phenomenal production effort in the spring of 1942, enabling Col.-Gen. Yakov Fedorenko, chief of the Armored Forces Administration, to begin construction of new tank corps in April. By July, these corps had settled on an organization of one rifle and three tank brigades, plus supporting arms--a fairly tank-heavy force that the Soviets intended to use as the mobile exploitation unit for a field army (Figure 11). In the fall of 1942, Fedorenko added mechanized corps, which were more infantry-heavy and therefore more expensive in manpower and trucks. Truck production was in fact a major problem throughout World War II, and the Soviets depended upon imported American wheeled vehicles to move and support their mobile formations.

Unlike those of 1940, these 1942 Soviet "corps" were actually of division size or smaller. To conduct the deep exploitations of 150 kilometers or more envisaged in the 1920s, the Red Army needed a larger formation, on the order of a German panzer corps or panzer army. In May 1942, the Commissariat of Defense took the next logical step, uniting the existing tank corps into tank armies. The 1942 tank armies, however, were merely improvised

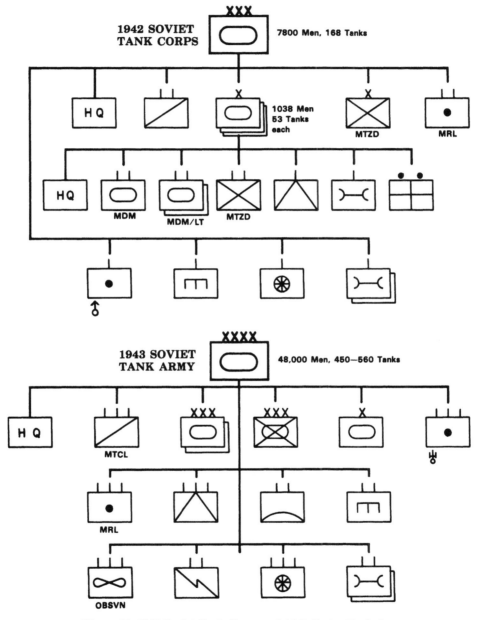

Figure 11. 1942 Soviet Tank Corps and 1943 Soviet Tank Army.

combinations of armored, cavalry, and infantry divisions, combinations that lacked a common rate of mobility and doctrine of employment. Moreover, these armies rushed into battle against the Germans during the summer of 1942 and were largely destroyed before they had even trained together.

Not until January 1943 did the Soviets finally produce a coherent tank army (Figure 11); the six tank armies formed in 1943 were the spearheads of all Soviet offensives for the remainder of World War II. Each of these new tank armies was actually a corps-sized formation in western terminology and, like the tank "corps," was extremely tank-heavy. This was probably an appropriate organization, both because of the open tank country of European Russia, and because of the high Soviet tank losses against the Germans. Given the inexperience of most tank crews and junior leaders in the Red Army of 1941-43, it was inevitable that the better trained German antitank and armor formations would inflict such disproportionate losses on the Reds. Thus, the Soviet Union's armored forces remained much more tank-heavy than those of other armies. Yet throughout the war, the Soviets also maintained corps-sized formation of horse cavalry, with limited tank and artillery support, for use in swamps, mountains, and other terrain that did not favor heavily mechanized forces.

The new mechanized formations must be understood in the context of their accompanying doctrine. During 1942, the Soviets digested the lessons of the first year of war and issued a series of orders to correct their errors. These orders greatly increased the effectiveness of the Soviet counteroffensive that encircled Stalingrad in November 1942. Senior Red commanders held conferences before Stalingrad to ensure that their subordinates understood the new doctrine.

The first problem was to penetrate the German defenses in order to conduct a counteroffensive. The initial Soviet counterattacks of December 1941-January 1942 had suffered from such dispersion that the German defenders often outnumbered their Soviet attackers. On 10 January 1942, Stavka Circular 3 directed the formation of "shock groups," concentrating combat power on a narrow frontage in order to break into the enemy defenses. Division and larger units were instructed to mass on narrow frontages in this manner. Stalin's Order 306, dated 8 October 1942, supplemented this directive by explicitly forbidding the echelonment of infantry forces in the attack. Given the continuing shortages of equipment and firepower, the Soviets decided to maximize their available force by putting almost all the infantry into one echelon. Thus, in a typical rifle division, as many as nineteen of the twenty-seven rifle companies would be on line for a deliberate attack.[32] The German defenses in 1942 were stretched so thin that this forward Soviet massing of infantry was more important than echelonment to sustain the attack. Later in the war, when both sides defended in greater depth, the Soviets tended to echelon their attack accordingly. Even in 1945, however, shallow German defenses prompted one-echelon Soviet attacks. Other orders in October 1942 governed the correct use of those tanks still assigned to assist the infantry assault. Because infantry commanders were still inexperienced, all such tank units were to be employed in mass under their own commanders.

Once the Soviets completed a penetration, their "mobile groups" would pass through for exploitation and encirclement operations, as described above. In effect, one such encirclement might include other, smaller encirclements within its pincers. Each field army attempted to use its own mobile group, composed of a tank, cavalry, or mechanized corps, to exploit penetrations to a relatively shallow depth of fifty or fewer kilometers, defeating the enemy reserves or linking up with a similar group from a neighboring army. Meanwhile, the tank armies acting as mobile groups for larger elements, such as a "Front" (army group), penetrated even deeper into the German rear areas. This, at least, was the theory. The first of these large, operational-level Soviet encirclements was in November 1942, when the German Sixth Army was surrounded at Stalingrad. In fact, the Soviet use of separate tank and mechanized corps in this battle may have been a test for the new tank army structure adopted two months later.

Thus, by late 1942, the German techniques for mechanized warfare had reached their peak, but were no longer meeting with the success of 1939-41. On the contrary, Great Britain and the Soviet Union had reorganized and retrained their own armies and were beginning to conduct their own successful mechanized offensives. Both German and British armored formations had become balanced structures where tanks no longer outnumbered the other arms. Moreover, all three armies were discovering the need for effective and mobile logistical support to make the mechanized offensives possible. The stage was set for a conflict in which logistics, technology, and defense-in-depth would determine as many battles as the armored division had decided in 1939-41.

CHAPTER FIVE

THE COMPLEXITY OF TOTAL WAR, 1942-1945

By deferring any consideration of the war in the Pacific, the previous chapter has reviewed the evolution of combined arms in World War II from the simple perspective of German advance and Allied response. The participation of the United States and the Soviet Union, however, made the war a much more complex affair, a war of production and technology as much as of battlefield maneuver. This chapter will identify those aspects of technology and tactics that affected the development of combined arms forces and doctrine during the second half of World War II. It will begin with the evolution of American force structure and doctrine, and then consider the changes in weapons design that made the latter half of the war so different from the first half. It will next survey the general trends in operational practice from 1943 to 1945 and conclude by examining the more complex and specialized questions of air-ground cooperation, airborne operations, amphibious landings, and special warfare units.

The American Response, 1941-44

Prior to the Japanese attack on Pearl Harbor in December 1941, the United States was an interested observer of World War II. Most of the U.S. Army did not become involved in major ground operations until the end of 1942 or even later. During the period 1941-42, however, the U.S. drew certain conclusions about the nature of weapons, organization, and tactics, and implemented those conclusions by continuing its evolution of the triangular infantry division and the 1940 armored division. Then, on the basis of maneuvers held in the U.S. and of initial combat experiences overseas, certain changes in American doctrine and organization occurred in the middle of the war. The resulting tactical system dominated American military thought into the 1950s.

In March 1942, Lt. Gen. Lesley McNair, one of the designers of the triangular division in the late 1930s, became head of Army Ground Forces, in charge of all unit training and organization. McNair continued to follow the concepts that had guided him in the 1930s, and thus the basic organization of the triangular division did not change significantly until after the war.[1]

First, McNair wanted each unit to have only the minimum essential forces that it needed to conduct offensive operations in fluid, maneuver warfare against relatively limited resistance. In the case of the triangular infantry division, this meant that the standard base of the division remained the three infantry regiments, four artillery battalions, reconnaissance troop, and engineer battalion developed in 1937-41.

On the other hand, a division did not need specialized units that were required only for specific situations or missions. This applied particularly to arms with an essentially defensive mission, such as antitank and antiaircraft artillery. These units that McNair "streamlined" out of the infantry division became a "pool" of specialized nondivisional companies and battalions, units that higher headquarters could attach to a division for a particular mission or else employ in mass at critical points on the battlefield. Thus the actual combat power of a division might change from day to day, depending upon requirements and missions. In December 1942, McNair extended this trend to form ad hoc task forces to nondivisional units by persuading the War Department to abolish all nondivisional regiments in favor of flexible groups. Nondivisional armor, antiaircraft, field artillery, mechanized cavalry, and combat engineer battalions all reported to group headquarters when not attached to divisions. Some group headquarters, notably those of mechanized cavalry, also acted as tactical control headquarters.[2] The number of battalions or companies subordinate to any group headquarters depended on the circumstances.

Another of McNair's principles was that staff and support elements must be as small as possible, in order to maximize the proportion of forces actually available for combat and to reduce paperwork and other organizational obstacles to rapid decision making and communication. Logisticians should bypass divisional and corps headquarters on routine supply matters in order to keep those headquarters small, mobile, and oriented on the tactical situation. Wherever possible, a specialist unit or person should have weapons to perform a secondary role as infantry or rear area security forces.

Finally, McNair sought to restrict as much as possible the amount of motor transportation in a unit in order to facilitate strategic deployment. The fewer vehicles that were organic to a division, the less shipping space that division would need when sent to Europe or the Pacific. For example, McNair sought to authorize only the number of trucks needed to shuttle necessary supplies and ammunition to the regiments during a twenty-four-hour period, rather than the number that could transport all necessary materials in one lift. Rifle units were not motorized, but could become so temporarily by the attachment of six truck companies to the division. Alternatively, if the division had attached elements such as a tank battalion, the infantry could mount the tanks and the organic trucks borrowed from the artillery, allowing short-range motor movements with some loss in logistical support.

When the U.S. Army finally employed these concepts overseas, they proved only partially successful. Regardless of the terrain or enemy involved, most divisions in Europe and many in the Pacific believed that they needed tank, antiaircraft, "tank destroyer" (antitank), and nondivisional engineer support in virtually all circumstances. Corps and field army commanders who followed doctrine by shifting these nondivisional units from division to division according to the situation found that they could maximize the use of such elements only at the cost of much confusion and inefficiency. Attachment to a different division meant dealing with a different set of procedures and personalities before the attached units could mesh smoothly with that division. Once such a smooth relationship was established, the division was reluctant to release its attachments as ordered. In many instances, tactical commanders found it expedient to leave the same nondivisional elements attached to the same divisions on an habitual basis that might last for months. A typical U.S. infantry division in France during 1944 normally had attached battalions of tanks, tank destroyers, antiaircraft automatic weapons, and corps engineers. In some cases the division also had attached 4.2-inch mortars, transportation, and logistical support from the pools at corps and field army level. Thus, the triangular division in combat was much larger, more rigid, and more motorized than McNair had envisioned. An augmented infantry division of this kind might well have the mobility and firepower of a motorized division or even an understrength armored division, which goes far to explain the superior mobility of American infantry units when compared with standard German infantry forces.

Many of these attached forces were subdivided and further attached to infantry regiments, as were the division's organic assets such as engineers and medical support. Minor changes in the regiment's organization in 1942 and 1943 had added six 105-mm howitzers, so that the regiment had its own artillery even without the direct-support field artillery battalion. In practice, a majority of infantry regiments normally operated as "regimental combat teams" (RCT). As a minimum, this meant that they had their share of the division's medical, engineer, and field artillery attached or in direct support. In addition, as noted above, many RCTs also had companies of tank destroyers, tanks, and self-propelled antiaircraft guns. Thus, the RCT was a combined arms force, a small division in itself.[3]

During the same period, the armored division underwent many more changes than the infantry division.[4] Of the six different changes in armored organization during the war, two were most significant. As described earlier, the 1940 American armored division was composed largely of light tanks that greatly outnumbered the medium tanks, infantry, and artillery; this division also had several fixed headquarters designed to control only one type of unit, including the headquarters for armored and infantry regiments. When Maj. Gen. (later General) Jacob Devers became chief of the Armored Force in August 1941, he sought to establish a more flexible, functional organization. His efforts culminated in the reorganization of 1 March 1942 (Figure 12). This reorganization eliminated the armored brigade headquarters and established two "Combat Commands," A and B, as headquarters that might control any mixture of subordinate battalions given them for a particular mission. This was an American way to institutionalize the battle group concept that the German panzer forces achieved by improvisation. The 1942 organization also reversed the ratio of medium and light tanks, leaving the armored division with two armored regiments, each consisting of two medium and one light tank battalion. The new structure still had six tank battalions, but only three armored infantry and three armored field artillery battalions. This imbalance existed in part because the Armored Force planned to create a large number of armored corps which, like the German panzer corps, would have two armored and one motorized infantry division each.

By early 1943, intelligence studies of the more balanced German and British armored divisions had reinforced General McNair's desires for a less cumbersome division structure. The one U.S. armored division used in the North African campaign never operated as a coherent division, but its dispersal into three or four different subgroups only illustrated the difficulties of controlling such a large formation. At the same time, the U.S. Army had dropped the concepts of an armored corps and motorized infantry division, making the imbalance of arms within the 1942 armored division structure even more significant. Technically, the U.S. light tanks had been no match for the increasingly well-armed and armored German vehicles, and therefore the U.S., like Britain before it, lost enthusiasm for the concept of deep raids by lightly armored vehicles.

As a result, in September 1943, the War Department announced a new, smaller armored division structure. This structure eliminated the regimental headquarters that had theoretically controlled only one type of battalion and reduced the tank component to only three tank battalions of four companies each. Thus, the 1943 structure had three battalions each of tanks, armored infantry, and armored field artillery, although in

108

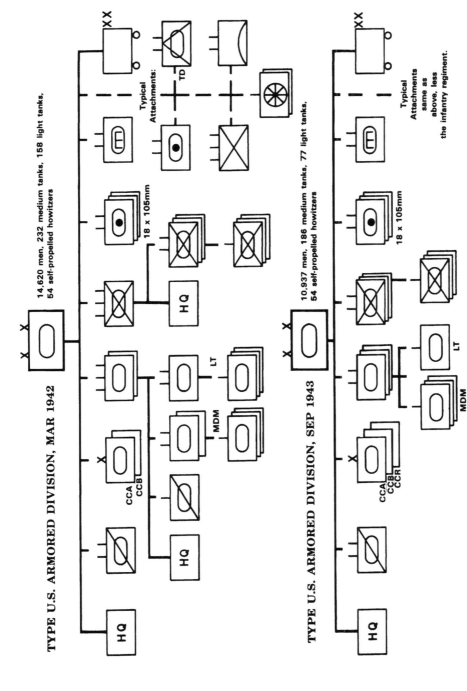

Figure 12. Type U.S. Armored Division, March 1942 and September 1943.

practice there were twelve tank companies to only nine infantry. A third, smaller combat command headquarters, designated reserve or R, was added to control units not subordinated to the other two combat commands. Some division commanders used this "CCR" as a tactical control element like CCA and CCB.

Two U.S. armored divisions, the 2d and 3d, continued under the heavier 1942 table of organization throughout the war. Corps or army headquarters frequently reinforced each of these divisions with an infantry regiment borrowed from an infantry division. As a result, the balance of tanks and infantry in American divisions, as in the German and British armored divisions, came to be approximately equal. Both types of U.S. armored division received attachments similar to those given to infantry divisions. In addition, virtually every American armored division habitually controlled two quartermaster truck companies capable of handling the great logistical requirements of a mobile division.[5]

The actual task organization within each of these divisions varied greatly, but a typical combat command within a 1943 (light) armored division usually had two task forces. The combat command headquarters created these by trading a medium tank company from a tank battalion for an armored infantry company from an infantry battalion, producing one task force of three tank companies and one armored infantry company, and one task force of two armored infantry companies and one tank company. These battalion task forces also had attached platoons of tank destroyers, armored engineers, and in some cases self-propelled antiaircraft guns. An armored artillery battalion could be either in direct support of the combat command, or attached to that command if the division were widely dispersed.

Antitank Technology

Effective force structure and tactics are intimately related to effective weapons design, and therefore any study of combined arms warfare must consider the major effects of technology. During World War II, one obvious influence of technology on tactics was related to the entire question of tank and antitank warfare. Even if defenders managed to overcome their psychological fear of deep mechanized penetration, the blitzkrieg would still succeed unless the defense acquired effective antitank weapons and doctrine.

Antitank ditches and similar obstacles may slow the movement of armored units or channelize those units into anti-armor kill zones, but ultimately there are only two ways to defeat armored vehicles.[6] Kinetic energy weapons penetrate armor plate by sheer momentum, as if they were "punching" through the metal, while chemical energy weapons use explosive blasts to destroy the armor. Until the middle years of World War II, chemical energy weapons were usually ineffective against armor. Antitank design therefore concentrated on the kinetic energy weapon. Mathematically, the energy of an object is equal to one-half the product of the object's mass times the square of its velocity ($1/2~MV^2$); therefore improving the armor penetration of a kinetic energy weapon required increasing either its mass or its velocity, or both. Greater mass meant larger caliber weapons or heavier, denser material in the projectile. Thus, basic physics explains the general trend towards larger caliber weapons during World War II, although an increase in caliber alone would reduce the projectile's velocity unless the designer also took other steps. Velocity, in turn, would be increased through changes such as longer gun barrels, more effective propellants, and a better seal within the breech so that all the propellant effect went to drive the projectile out of the gun tube.

In practical terms, World War II improvements in antitank guns had three consequences: first, the size and weight of those guns increased steadily as calibers increased, gun tubes lengthened, and stronger carriages were added to absorb the recoil of high-velocity weapons; second, tanks needed increased armor to protect themselves from improved antitank weapons; third, these antitank weapons were much more effective than those of the previous decade, but they were also more expensive and specialized. Such weapons formed the backbone of any antitank defense, yet no army could afford to have antitank weapons organic to every small unit that might need them. The kinetic energy antitank gun simply did not fulfill the battlefield requirement that every unit must have some protection when it suddenly encountered enemy armor.

The alternative means of defeating armor was the chemical energy weapon. The detonation of an explosive charge usually had little effect against armor, because unless it were focused against the armor plate it had to destroy, the blast effect dissipated in all directions equally. Ordinary explosive artillery rounds had to be quite large before they could do more than damage the tracks and roadwheels of a tank, and medium artillery, like antitank guns, was too large and specialized to be of general use. Moreover, using field artillery in an antitank role diverted it from its primary function of indirect fire. The solution was to concentrate the effects of a relatively small amount of explosive on one particular point of the enemy's armor--the shaped-charge principle described in Chapter Four. Because the blast and not the momentum of the shell caused the destruction, the high velocity and elaborate gun carriage of a kinetic energy weapon were unnecessary for a chemical energy weapon.

By April 1942, the U.S. Ordnance Department had developed the 2.36-inch "bazooka," which fired a shaped-charge warhead with a rocket motor. Later that same year, the Germans captured an American bazooka from the Soviets, and from it developed the larger and more effective Panzershrek antitank rocket launcher. The British PIAT (Projector, Infantry, Antitank) and the German Panzerfaust used the shaped charge propelled by a small conventional charge, similar to that of a grenade launcher. The same type of warhead enabled the Germans and Americans to develop experimental low-velocity recoilless rifles, which were light artillery pieces that eliminated the recoil by a controlled release of propellant blast behind the gun. Although recoilless rifles and rocket launchers lacked the long range and accuracy of conventional artillery, they gave the infantry, and indeed any unit, a much greater firepower and capability for organic short-range antitank defense.[7]

Tank Surrogates

Short-range antitank weapons were incapable of stopping a massed armor attack by themselves. Such weapons were most effective against the thinly armored flanks and rear of a tank that had already passed the defender. Towed antitank guns presented a small target for the enemy to detect and engage and could be maneuvered onto steep hills or river crossing sites where a self-propelled weapon could not go. The towed weapons, however, had very little armor; even if the enemy failed to score a direct hit on such an antitank weapon, a near-miss might cause casualties or at least disturb the gunner's aim. Many professional soldiers realized early in the war that the most effective antitank defense was a careful integration of obstacles, antitank mines, artillery, short-range antitank weapons, and some type of large caliber, longer-range antitank gun. This requirement for mobile, large-caliber antitank guns in the defense matched the continuing need for armor to support the infantry in the deliberate attack. Even if the nature of the enemy defenses did not always require tanks, the presence of tanks exerted a great psychological effect on both attacker and defender.

Armor experts in most armies, however, were determined to avoid being tied to the infantry, and in any event a tank was an extremely complicated, expensive, and therefore scarce weapon. The British persisted for much of the war on a dual track of development, retaining heavy tanks to support the infantry and lighter, more mobile tanks for independent armored formations. The Soviets similarly produced an entire series of heavy breakthrough tanks. Nevertheless, the widespread demand for tanks or tank-like vehicles outside of mechanized formations led to a number of tank surrogates, weapons designed to provide armored antitank defense, close support of the infantry attack, or both. In the latter case, the surrogate needed considerable frontal armor and a dual purpose (antitank and antipersonnel) main gun.

The most original of these tank surrogates was the American "tank destroyer." One particular source of controversy about General McNair's force structuring system was the question of antitank defense. McNair did not accept the extreme view, common in 1940-41, that the armored division had rendered the infantry division almost obsolete. Instead, McNair agreed with the German concept that the best means to halt the armored division was an antitank defense integrated with infantry units. McNair and Col. Andrew D. Bruce of the War Department staff sought highly mobile antitank guns that would end the psychological threat of blitzkrieg by aggressive action against the attacking armored forces. After the successful experiments during the 1941 maneuvers, Bruce became head of a Tank Destroyer Center that developed its own doctrine for these weapons.[8] While McNair had supported towed antitank guns on the conventional European model, Bruce wanted a high-velocity gun mounted on a mobile platform, sacrificing armor protection for speed and gunpower.

The 1942 tank destroyer battalions were combined arms forces in their own right, although they did not include a balance of all arms: each platoon had four self-propelled guns, an armored car section for security, and an antiaircraft section; in addition to three companies of such guns, the battalion included a reconnaissance company of three reconnaissance platoons plus a pioneer platoon. Ideally, when an armored penetration occurred, the tank destroyer battalions would mass to ambush the enemy tanks in the depth of the American defense. Within each tank destroyer battalion, the reconnaissance company selected likely anti-armor kill zones and emplaced minefields to impede the enemy advance through these areas. The gun companies would move to hull-down positions to reduce their vulnerability and then engage the enemy armor.

When the U.S. Army first encountered the Germans in Tunisia during 1942-43, the tank destroyers proved a dismal failure. Both tank destroyer doctrine and German armor design had outpaced the actual development of American tank destroyers, so that 1942 tank destroyers were little more than improvised guns mounted on half-tracks. The early tank destroyers lacked mobility and effective penetration power, the very characteristics that they were supposed to maximize. Moreover, most American units in North Africa were widely scattered, making it difficult to concentrate the tank destroyer forces according to doctrine. Finally, much of the North African terrain was too open for tank destroyer vehicles to find effective hull-down positions. As a consequence, American commanders in Africa tended to favor the British system of towed antitank weapons and specifically asked that one-half of all tank destroyer battalions slated for the 1944 invasion of France use towed rather than self-propelled weapons. Once in Normandy, however, the Americans discovered that the towed antitank gun was almost useless in the more restricted terrain of Western Europe. Towed guns were not only slow to move, but too close to the ground to shoot over hedgerows and other obstacles. Furthermore, between Africa and Normandy, the Tank Destroyer Center had procured much more effective, properly designed self-propelled guns. The M18 model with a 76-mm gun and especially the M36 with a 90-mm gun were excellent weapons, although even the 90-mm had less penetration capability than the German 88-mm. Also by 1944, improvements in German armor had rendered the standard 57-mm antitank gun of the American infantry regiment largely ineffective.

The original tank destroyer battalions had developed from divisional antitank battalions, which the 1944 divisions lacked. Tank destroyer units consequently became even more important for antitank defense. As a result, in July 1944 the U.S. Army began to reconvert all tank destroyer battalions to self-propelled weapons. These newly converted battalions did not mass in accordance with Bruce's doctrine. The limited nature of the German armor threat in the west prior to the Ardennes counteroffensive of December 1944 made massed antitank defense seem unimportant. Instead, commanders wanted a few effective antitank weapons distributed to every unit, where they could defeat the small German armored counterattacks that were common at the time. In most cases, therefore, corps and army commanders habitually attached a tank destroyer battalion to each infantry division, and in turn division commanders attached tank destroyer companies to infantry regiments. The regiments used the tank destroyers not only as antitank weapons, but also as accompanying artillery and as substitutes for tanks to support their infantry attacks.[9] Thus, the American tank destroyer units became a classic case of an arm that rarely functioned according to its doctrine, because that doctrine was never articulated clearly to field commanders.

In keeping with their doctrine of maneuver, U.S. tank destroyers usually had their guns mounted in turrets and, in fact, resembled tanks so much that they were often mistaken for such. In European armies, however, relatively few tank surrogates had turrets, because a turretless vehicle was much simpler and cheaper to produce. The absence of a turret gave German and Soviet tank surrogates a low profile that made them smaller targets on the flatter, open battlefields of Eastern Europe. This apparent advantage meant that the entire vehicle had to turn in order to traverse the gun more than a few degrees. Thus tank surrogates were at a disadvantage if they engaged tanks or infantry from anything except an ambush position.

The Germans actually developed two series of tank surrogates--assault guns to support the infantry in situations where tanks were not available, and "tank hunters" (Panzerjaeger) for the antitank role. Both were distinguished from self-propelled indirect-fire artillery by considerably thicker armor protection and by a flat trajectory gun intended for direct fire. Although armor purists criticized the expenditure of resources to produce these hybrids instead of true tanks, such weapons performed a necessary role, particularly as the German towed antitank guns became progressively less effective against Soviet armor. The armored self-propelled tank hunter was much more survivable and mobile than its towed predecessor. The one drawback of all such weapons was that, unlike the towed antitank guns, they had difficulty accompanying the infantry into inaccessible areas such as steep hills or bridgeheads across rivers.

The Soviet Union also produced outstanding, heavily armored assault guns during the second half of the war, but tended to use those guns as one component of a three-way team in the deliberate attack. Medium tanks led the assault, using their mobility wherever possible to turn the flanks of German defensive positions. Heavy tanks, operating in pairs, advanced slightly behind the medium tanks, supporting the Soviet infantry and eliminating German strongpoints. In the event of a German armored counterattack, the heavy tanks would move forward to engage the German tanks head on, while the less protected medium tanks maneuvered to the German flanks. Finally, the assault guns provided accompanying artillery support for both infantry and tanks. To accomplish this direct-fire role, the assault guns began the battle in camouflaged positions from which they could overwatch the advancing tanks and infantry. The assault guns engaged centers of resistance that had survived the Soviet artillery preparation. This freed the assaulting forces to advance without halting to engage the enemy unless a counterattack appeared. At intervals, the assault guns bounded forward to new positions, always keeping within 500 meters of the heavy tanks and infantry.[10] By staying behind in this manner, assault guns avoided meeting enemy armor in a maneuver battle at close range. In such a battle, tank turrets could traverse and fire much faster than the turretless assault guns could turn their entire vehicles to aim their guns. On many occasions, of course, the attacking Soviet unit did not have all three different types of armor, but the assault guns preferred to operate from an overwatch position in any case.

115

Tank Design and Production

These technological trends in antitank weapons and tank surrogates form a necessary background to the actual design and production of tanks during World War II. In general, both the armor and armament of tanks increased along with antitank technology, but different nations followed different design and production strategies. These factors exerted considerable influence on the battlefield.

During the war, German tank design went through at least three generations, plus constant minor variations.[11] The first generation, as already mentioned, included such unbattleworthy prewar vehicles as the Mark (or Panzerkampfwagen) I and II, which were similar to the Russian T-26 and BT series and to the British cruiser tanks. The Germans converted their tank battalions to a majority of Mark III and IV medium tanks after the 1940 French campaign, thereby stealing a march on the Soviets and British, who still possessed the obsolete equipment described earlier. However, the appearance of a few of the new generation T-34 and KV-1 tanks in Russia during 1941 compelled the Germans to begin a race for superior armor and gunpower. Simultaneously, their successes of 1939-41 encouraged them to rely increasingly on armor, rather than infantry, when conducting a rapid breakthrough attack. The German solution was to design third generation tanks that combined greater armor protection with the 88-mm antiaircraft gun that had proved so successful in the antitank role. The third generation included many different variants, but the most important designs were the Mark V (Panther) and Mark VI (Tiger) tanks. Unfortunately for the Germans, their emphasis on protection and gunpower compromised the mobility and reliability of their tanks. The automotive design of Mark V and VI tanks was notoriously underpowered and unreliable.

Moreover, Hitler and his assistants were fascinated with technological improvements and frequently stopped production to apply the latest design changes to the existing tanks. The fighting characteristics of German tanks remained current at the cost of interference with mass production. This interference, plus shortages of raw materials, meant that Germany could not compete in sheer numbers of tanks produced. In 1943, for example, Germany manufactured only 5,966 tanks, as compared to 29,497 for the U.S., 7,476 for Britain, and an estimated 20,000 for the Soviet Union.[12] A disparity in numbers of this magnitude would eventually overcome the highest quality in individual tank design. Similarly, the presence of so many different versions of the same tank, often within the same company or battalion, made it extremely difficult for the Germans to obtain spare parts and repair damaged equipment.

The alternative to constant changes in tank design was to standardize a few basic designs and mass produce them even though technology had advanced to new improvements. This was the solution of Germany's principal opponents. The Soviet T-34, for example, was an excellent basic design that survived the war with only one major change in armament (76.2-mm to 85-mm main gun) and various minor modifications. When the Soviets did introduce new designs, such as the heavier tanks and self-propelled guns of 1944, they did so without halting production of the older types.

The United States had even more reason to standardize and mass produce than did the Soviet Union. By concentrating on mechanical reliability, the U.S. was able to produce vehicles that operated longer with fewer repair parts. This helped alleviate the chronic shortage of shipping space when the army moved to Europe and the Pacific. To further ease the shipping problems and to ensure that American tanks were compatible with American bridging equipment, the War Department restricted tank width to 103 inches and maximum weight to thirty tons. The army relaxed these requirements only in late 1944.[13]

There was also a tactical reason for these restrictions. General McNair wanted to ensure that American tanks were designed in accordance with the U.S. doctrine for employing armored divisions. As already indicated, this doctrine foresaw tank destroyers, not tanks, defeating enemy armor. Chance encounters between tanks might occur, but the primary role of the armored division was to exploit and pursue, not fight enemy armor.

For all these reasons, the U.S. Army standardized on the M4 Sherman medium tank, an excellent compromise between reliability, mobility, armor protection, and gunpower. When the British first employed the Sherman in North Africa during late 1942, it proved to be at least equal, if not superior, to the German second-generation tanks, Mark III and IV. Once the Tiger tank appeared in Tunisia in early 1943, however, the Sherman tank and most of the U.S. antitank force seemed inadequate.

The width limitation further hampered the Sherman by forcing designers to give the tank narrow tracks. These tracks had much less mobility in muddy terrain than the wider tracks used by the Soviets and Germans. The M4's only advantages over later German tanks were superior reliability and a power-driven turret. During meeting engagements at close ranges this latter feature allowed the Sherman's crew to traverse their gun and engage the enemy more rapidly than could German crews using hand-cranked turrets. Sherman tank crews often carried a white phosphorus round in their guns to blind enemy tanks during such maneuvers.

Despite its drawbacks, the Sherman remained the main battle tank of the U.S. Army. In early 1945, apparently as a result of the large-scale German armored attacks during the Battle of the Bulge, the U.S. Army finally allowed a few heavy tanks of the T20 series to be sent to Europe for combat testing. The army's Ordnance Department had developed the T20 series in 1943, but considerations of doctrine, shipping, and mass production had prevented its use in battle until the closing days of the war.[14]

Great Britain also used the Sherman during the latter half of World War II, but was concerned by the limited penetrating power of the M4's 75-mm, medium-velocity main gun. After considerable discussions with the Americans, the British finally modified some of the Shermans they received. The British version of the Sherman, called the "Firefly," included the third-generation British antitank gun, the seventeen pounder (77-mm). This gun's long bore and higher velocity gave it much greater capability against German armor.[15]

Signals Intelligence and Communications

In addition to the tank and aircraft, another piece of technology came of age during World War II. Signals intelligence, or SIGINT, was yet one more instrument or arm that the commander had to integrate and coordinate with others. Recent histories of the war probably have overstated the strategic importance of SIGINT, while they have understated its tactical role. An army's ability to plan for future operations and concentrate the different arms at the decisive location depended in part on such intelligence.[16]

Ultra, the British codeword for intelligence based on decoding highly classified German radio messages, gave the western Allies only limited access to German military intentions and capabilities. The German Army normally used secure landline communications for high-level messages, except when fluid operations forced them to make radio transmissions. Even then the Allies did not necessarily intercept, let alone decode in a timely manner, every German message. The Germans changed their code every twenty-four hours and periodically made major shifts in codes or equipment. The Allies might go for days or even months without being able to decode transmissions on specific radio networks. On 1 May 1940, for example, Germany changed virtually all its codes, blinding the Allies' SIGINT effort until 22 May, by which time the German offensive through the Ardennes had succeeded.[17] Similar problems recurred during most of the war.

Nor were the deciphered messages of Ultra always illuminating for the tactical and operational situation. Only rarely did the most senior German commanders communicate their specific plans, except where Hitler was personally interfering in operations and required detailed reports. Intelligence analysts pieced together much of the most valuable Ultra information over long periods, or inferred capabilities on the basis of logistical messages. Moreover, few Allied commanders below field army level had access to this information.

The worst drawback of Ultra-level SIGINT was that it discouraged the use of other sources of intelligence collection that might confirm or deny Ultra information and blinded Allied commanders to threats that were not discussed in German radio traffic. In early 1943, for example, the Allied forces in Tunisia relied heavily on Ultra; their other intelligence collection means were improvised and largely ineffective. The German offensive of Sidi-bou-Zid-Kasserine Pass in February 1943 (Map 6) surprised the Allies because available SIGINT indicated that higher German headquarters had disapproved such an operation in favor of an attack elsewhere. Of course, SIGINT could not know that Rommel and other German commanders had met face-to-face on 9 February and had developed a plan that led to the attack on Sidi-bou-Zid. This attack mauled a dispersed U.S. armored division.[18] Lack of SIGINT and misinterpretation of available intercepts also had a considerable effect on Allied failure to predict the scale and intensity of the German counteroffensive in the Ardennes in December 1944.

Although the western Allies held a priceless asset in the strategic intelligence they received from Ultra, for much of the war German SIGINT was more effective at the tactical level. From 1940 to 1942, for example, a single Horch (listening or intercept) company in North Africa skillfully interpreted the unencrypted tactical communications of British units, giving Rommel a complete picture of enemy dispositions and intentions during battle. When the British finally became aware of this unit's activities in July 1942, an Australian battalion raided and captured the company. German replacements could not replace the expertise of the analysts lost in that company and thus had more difficulty detecting later British deception operations.[19]

By contrast, relatively little information is available concerning Allied tactical SIGINT, including the British "Y" Service and American "Radio Intelligence." German tactical communications were often unencrypted, or used easily deciphered code systems. From a miniscule prewar basis, the Allies had to develop their knowledge of German tactical radio networks and

TUNISIA

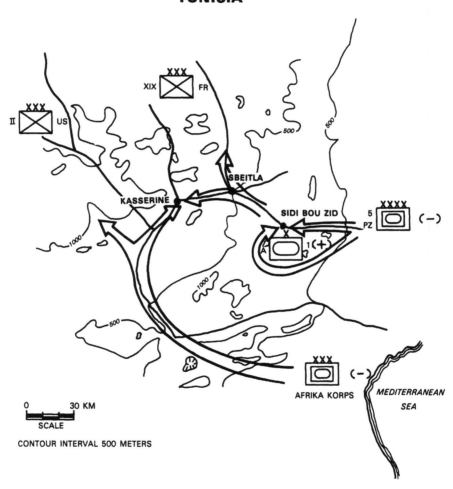

Map 6. SIDI BOU ZID—KASSERINE PASS, February 1943.

84-3330   —120—

procedures. In terms of offensive electronic warfare, the Allies had a number of notable successes. During the evacuation of Dunkirk in 1940, the British effectively jammed German bomber communications, hampering Luftwaffe attacks on the retreating British forces. Two years later, when Montgomery launched the second Battle of Alamein, airborne jammers disrupted German tactical radio communications for hours.[20]

The development of effective tactical radio communications was the basis for controlling fluid, mechanized operations as well as the raw material for tactical SIGINT. The demand for such communications greatly accelerated research and development in this area. In particular, the U.S. Army pioneered the use of frequency modulation (FM) radios for short-range tactical communications, and both very high frequency (VHF) and ultra high frequency (UHF) radios for longer range communications.[21] Unlike the European armies, the U.S. Army used FM extensively, because it provided static-free signals over a wide variety of channels without using a separate crystal for each frequency.

The combination of reliable radio communications with efficient tactical signals intercept services also provided a new opportunity for senior commanders to follow the course of battle without delays in the communications system. Both the British and American armies developed means for senior headquarters to receive battle reports by radio without waiting for the messages to be processed through intermediate layers of command. That is, the senior headquarters could monitor tactical unit radio networks directly, or else assign a radio-equipped liaison detachment to each forward unit to report the situation to the senior headquarters. The British GHQ Liaison (Phantom) units and the American Signal Information and Monitoring (SIAM) companies performed this service admirably during 1944-45, and in the British case as early as 1942. The danger with such a monitoring system, as Gen. Dwight D. Eisenhower noted after the war, was that the senior commander might be tempted to bypass the intermediate headquarters and interfere directly in the battle, using the system for command rather than as a source of timely operational and intelligence information.[22] In the latter role these monitoring services enabled much more effective coordination of the battle, allowing the commander to react through his subordinate commanders to situations as they developed.

Soviet Concepts and Practice, 1943-45

Many of the foregoing technological considerations became evident on the Eastern Front, beginning with the Battle of Kursk in July 1943. The last great German offensive in the east ran directly into an elaborately prepared Soviet defense organized around antitank strongpoints established by all units of company size or larger. The German blitzkrieg stalled because it was unable to achieve the initial penetration of the enemy's defenses--Soviet antitank defenses were simply too strong and, above all, too deep for the Germans to breech without catastrophic losses. If anything, the Germans played into Soviet hands by leading their attack in some areas with massed armor, instead of a more conventional infantry-artillery-engineer-tank attack to create the breech. The Germans apparently led with massed tanks in an effort to increase the tempo of the penetration, but without decisive numerical superiority the result was a disaster.

After Kursk, the Soviet Union held the initiative, although it was not always attacking the Germans and their Axis allies on all fronts. Generally speaking, the Soviets exerted tremendous efforts to penetrate the deep German defenses. In the ensuing exploitation, logistical restrictions usually caused the Soviet offensive to grind to a halt even where there was little German resistance. In the course of the war, improvements in Soviet logistics led to steady increases in the depth of exploitation. Once the Germans gained a respite to reorganize their defenses, the cycle repeated itself. Accordingly, the Red Army developed a variety of techniques for both penetration and exploitation against the German defenders.

One significant development during 1944 was the change in Soviet reconnaissance techniques before a deliberate attack. Prior to that year, the Red Army had been very effective in conducting small, time-consuming long-range reconnaissance patrols. To shorten the time required to prepare for a new offensive, the Soviets in early 1944 sent out experimental company- and battalion-sized units to engage the German outposts or reconnoiter by fire, thereby identifying the main German defensive organization much more rapidly. In the process, the Red Army received an unexpected bonus. Soviet reconnaissance units were often able to seize control of outposts that the Germans were defending only lightly, as part of the long-standing German doctrine of defense-in-depth. By late 1944, the Soviets had transformed their reconnaissance units into the first wave of the deliberate attack. Company and larger units on reconnaissance missions attacked within a few hours of the main offensive, seizing the German outposts and thereby unmasking the main German defenses. Then the main attack focused on those principal defenses.[23]

Although Soviet commanders massed their forces on relatively narrow breakthrough fronts, their successes were due to more than just numerical superiority. Whether in the reconnaissance echelon or the main attack, the Soviets used a variety of procedures to overcome German defenses. First, artillery units fired their preparations under centralized control and according to elaborate plans. The Soviets used a variety of deception measures, such as sending the assault infantry forward during a lull in the firing in order to lure the Germans out of their bunkers so that renewed Soviet artillery fire could destroy them. Heavy tanks to support the infantry and eliminate strongpoints, medium tanks to penetrate rapidly and suppress enemy infantry fires, and assault guns for direct-fire support against antitank guns and strongpoints cooperated as described earlier. Combat engineers or specially trained infantrymen frequently rode on each tank. Their mission was to eliminate obstacles and provide close-in protection for the tank from German short-range antitank weapons.[24] The tank might temporarily assume a hull-down position and provide covering fire while engineers cleared minefields and infantry eliminated enemy short-range antitank weapons.

The Soviets reluctantly accepted the high casualties produced by this technique in an effort to accelerate their rate of penetration. Given the meticulous German defensive preparations and the lack of Soviet armored personnel carriers, the Soviets had to combine engineers, infantry, and tanks in this manner, regardless of losses. Soviet commanders may have used battalions of "expendable" criminals for these tasks. In general, however, by 1944 casualties were a subject of great concern for the Soviets. The best means to reduce casualties were concentration, speed of penetration, and careful task organization of the attacking forces. Instead of advancing on-line and in mass, the Soviet attackers operated in tailored assault groups of platoon to battalion size (Figure 13). Where time allowed, each assault group trained to eliminate a specific German strongpoint, thereby dislocating the German defensive organization. Assault groups normally included four subgroups: a reconnaissance subgroup to clear an approach route to the objective, a blocking subgroup to engage and pin down the defenders, a fire subgroup to isolate the strongpoint from reinforcement, and an attack subgroup, including engineers and heavy tanks or assault guns, to eliminate the objective from the flanks or rear.[25]

Once the Soviets completed their penetration, their commanders sought to sustain the momentum, moving rapidly from encirclement to renewed exploitation and pursuit so that the defenders had no opportunity to reorganize a coherent defense. German exploitations of 1939–42 had normally been centrally controlled, to ensure that all elements moved in the same general direction and were available to support each other in the event of counterattack. Soviet exploitation, particularly after the initial encirclement was completed, tended to be more decentralized and diffuse. Notoriously poor Soviet radio

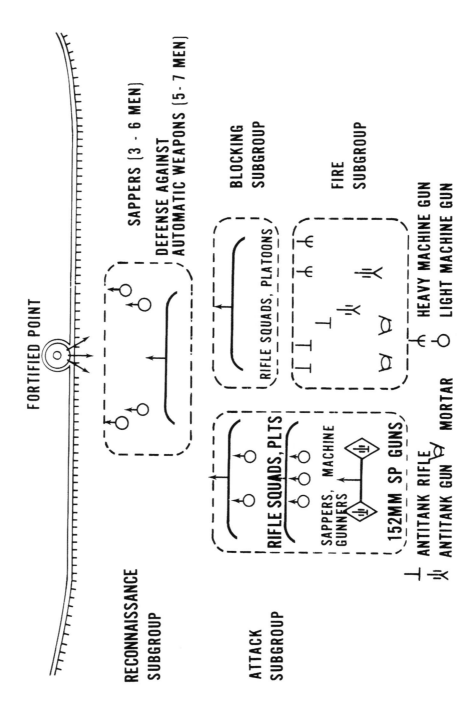

Figure 13. Soviet Assault Group Formation, 1944—45.

FORTIFIED POINT

RECONNAISSANCE SUBGROUP

SAPPERS (3 - 6 MEN)

DEFENSE AGAINST AUTOMATIC WEAPONS (5 - 7 MEN)

BLOCKING SUBGROUP

FIRE SUBGROUP

RIFLE SQUADS, PLATOONS

HEAVY MACHINE GUN
LIGHT MACHINE GUN

ATTACK SUBGROUP

RIFLE SQUADS, PLTS

SAPPERS, MACHINE GUNNERS

152MM SP GUNS

ANTITANK RIFLE
ANTITANK GUN   MORTAR

communications may have been partially responsible for this decentralization, but more to the point the Soviets retained their belief in the interwar theory that rapidly moving forces could fan out and confuse as well as disorganize the defender. Decentralization and small-unit initiative allowed leading Soviet units to seize targets of opportunity, such as bridges and river crossings, that were not immediately obvious to the senior planners. The same decentralization made the Soviets more vulnerable to defeat in detail by massed German counterattacks. Beginning in 1943, a combination of factors, including declining German combat effectiveness, growing Soviet tactical experience, and better close air support of the exploitation forces allowed the Soviets to defeat most German counterattacks and continue their mission.

The most common formation for Soviet exploitation was the "forward detachment," a combined arms organization of great mobility and firepower that was sent ahead of the main unit to seize key objectives and disrupt enemy efforts to reorganize the defense.[26] During the war, both the size of the typical forward detachment and the distance it operated ahead of the main body increased steadily. In the last two years of the war, a forward detachment normally was a tank brigade reinforced by batteries or battalions of field and antiaircraft artillery, heavy tanks, assault guns, and engineers. When available, an air controller accompanied the detachment to direct close air support, and air units were dedicated to support specific detachments. This reinforced brigade operated as much as ninety kilometers ahead of the rest of its parent tank corps, which, in turn, might be acting as a forward detachment for a tank army. A forward detachment did not necessarily follow the same routes as the main body of troops and was not responsible for advance guard security of that main body. Frequently, an efficient forward detachment commander could brush through hasty German defenses along the way, allowing the following troops to continue their exploitation and pursuit without deploying to attack the scattered Germans. When logistics and lack of combat power finally halted a forward detachment, the detachment commander attempted to seize a bridgehead over the next river obstacle as a starting point for a renewed offensive at a later date. In short, the forward detachment led the mobile group envisaged in prewar Soviet doctrine and greatly increased the tempo of exploitation and pursuit.

The German Decline, 1943-45

While the Red Army grew in both equipment and tactical proficiency, the German Army declined not only in numbers but in overall training and tactical ability. When faced with local Soviet superiority achieved by massing on a narrow breakthrough frontage, German defenders naturally ascribed all Soviet successes to overwhelming numerical advantage. In reality, the quality of the German armed forces declined as a result of their declining quantity. As early as the summer of 1942, the German divisions that were not involved in the second German offensive in the east were deliberately filled to only 55 percent of authorized personnel. Even spearhead units received only 85 percent of authorized equipment.[27] In order to maintain their armies in the field, the German leaders progressively reduced the amount of training given to replacements and used training units in combat during Soviet breakthroughs. This became a vicious cycle, in which poorly trained German soldiers survived for only short periods at the front and had to be replaced even more rapidly than before.[28] This decline in infantry quality prompted German commanders to seek ever-increasing amounts of firepower in the form of assault guns, antitank rockets, automatic weapons, and artillery.

Given shortages of personnel, many German infantry divisions operated with only six instead of nine infantry battalions from 1942 onwards. In 1944, the German General Staff formally changed the division structure to reflect this reality. According to the 1944 reorganization, an infantry division consisted of three infantry regiments of two battalions each. This configuration allowed each battalion to have a greater share of the weakened regimental artillery and antitank companies than had been possible with a three-battalion regiment. On the other hand, such a structure retained the large overhead of three regimental staffs and support elements, yet denied the regimental commander a third battalion to act as a local reserve force. In practice some divisions organized themselves into two regiments of three battalions each. In either case, the 1944 German infantry division retained all four artillery battalions of the previous structure, so that, at least on paper, the declining ability of the infantry was offset by a larger proportion of fire support. Recognizing enemy air superiority, the 1944 divisional organization also included a battery of self-propelled antiaircraft guns.[29]

Despite such improved fire support, after 1943 the German defenders found themselves increasingly hard pressed to contain, let alone halt, Soviet offensives. The basis for the German doctrine of defense-in-depth was to absorb enemy attacks and separate armor from its supporting infantry, in order to defeat each element independently. By 1944, improved Soviet cooperation among the arms nullified German efforts to isolate those fighting components from one another. Many German commanders experimented with the idea of a preemptive withdrawal, pulling back their troops just before a Soviet deliberate attack in order to save lives and to force the Soviets to reorganize for another attack a few kilometers farther west. Yet such a withdrawal under pressure required high morale and well-trained troops, the very commodities that were declining most rapidly in the German Army.[30]

While the infantry divisions gradually wore down, the Germans made a belated effort to rebuild their panzer forces. Heinz Guderian dedicated himself to this task as Inspector-General of Panzer Troops (1943-44) and then as Chief of the General Staff (1944-45). However, his continued insistence on the panzer arm as a force separate from the rest of the German Army was no longer appropriate. It was true that panzer divisions were the principal German instrument for counterattacking enemy penetrations and encirclements. Yet these divisions were so few in numbers compared to the great distances on the Russian front that they often counterattacked singly or in pairs, wearing themselves down as fast as Guderian could rebuild them. By removing armor training and doctrine from the appropriate branches of the General Staff, Guderian only increased the estrangement between the panzer and infantry forces and made training between the arms more difficult.[31]

Despite these problems, the balanced panzer division remained an extremely effective force at the tactical level. Only minor changes in organization and tactics occurred after 1941. Production requirements for tanks, assault guns, and other tracked vehicles meant that the panzer grenadiers remained largely motorized, rather than mechanized, throughout the war. Even at its peak in the fall of 1943, the German panzer force had only 26 of 226 panzer grenadier battalions, or 11 percent, mounted in armored half-tracks.[32] Thus, except in certain elite units, no more than one of the four to five infantry battalions in a panzer division was actually mechanized. Generally speaking, one or two companies of such a mechanized battalion accompanied each panzer battalion in advance, with the motorized infantry following later to consolidate and defend the areas seized by the first attacks. Artillery forward observers in tanks or half-tracks accompanied the first wave. Where only motorized infantry was available, these troops went into battle dismounted, following in the lee of the tanks until they were needed to clear obstacles or defend against enemy infantry. To avoid being tied to this dismounted infantry when the attackers met with effective fire, the German tanks sometimes bounded forward, assumed hull-down positions that minimized the target they presented to the enemy, and provided suppressive fires to cover the infantrymen hurrying to rejoin the tanks. To protect the attacking panzer force from enemy armored counterattack, antitank guns leapfrogged into a series of overwatching positions on the flanks of the advance. Assault guns remained with the motorized infantry reserves to consolidate gains or to engage an enemy counterattack that penetrated into the division mass. Because of Allied air superiority on all fronts, German armored forces needed much greater air defense protection in 1944-45 than in 1940. Truck-mounted panzer grenadier battalions therefore included the 20-mm antiaircraft guns that had proven so effective earlier in the war, while tank and half-track mounted infantry received self-propelled antiaircraft guns, in some cases as low as company level.[33] Such, at least, was the theory of panzer organization and tactics; in practice, of course, the declining strength of such units produced a variety of improvised battle groups.

American Concepts and Practice, 1943-45

The initial contact of American forces with Axis troops did not fulfill the promise of previous U.S. developments in doctrine and organization. During the 1942-43 invasion of North Africa a variety of factors, including inexperience, led American commanders to scatter their forces in regimental or smaller units, thereby depriving them of the advantages of the American centralized fire control system. The U.S. armored divisions had stressed decentralized, mobile combat by direct fire so often in training that their self-propelled artillery battalions had neglected the study of indirect-fire techniques. Inadequate logistics forced the Americans to leave their corps artillery far behind the front in Tunisia, further reducing available fire support when the Germans counterattacked in February 1943. In the crisis of Kasserine Pass, however, the artillery of the 1st and 9th Infantry Divisions was finally able to operate on an organized basis, with devastating effect on the Germans (Map 6, above).[34]

Similar problems arose in the Southwest Pacific, where in 1942 General Douglas MacArthur committed the 32d Infantry Division to battle in Papua with no artillery and only a few mortars. Despite the protests of the 32d Division commander, MacArthur's staff mistakenly thought that artillery would be ineffective in the jungles. Moreover, the local air commander, Gen. George C. Kenney, assured the division that "the artillery in this theater flies," and then failed to provide effective air support throughout a long campaign.[35] Weather and terrain prevented such air support on many occasions, and there was so little communication between air and ground that Kenney's pilots attacked Americans by mistake on a weekly basis. Based on the bitter experience of assaulting Japanese bunker complexes without appropriate fire support, the 32d Division learned at great cost the need to coordinate artillery and air support with the infantry.

To some extent the U.S. troops who invaded Normandy in 1944 had to relearn this lesson. Many of the U.S. infantry divisions used in the invasion had not been in combat before and had not had the opportunity for extensive tank-infantry training with the separate tank battalions that supported them. Furthermore, the radios issued to infantry, tank, and fighter aircraft units had incompatible frequencies, making communication among the arms impossible. Even when the infantry commander was riding on the outside of a tank or standing next to it, the noise of the tank engine made it difficult for the infantry and tank commanders to communicate face-to-face.[36]

The U.S. Army gradually corrected these problems and developed more effective combined arms teams during the breakout from Normandy. The need for close tank-infantry cooperation reinforced the habitual association of the same tank battalion and infantry division. Signalmen installed improvised external telephones on tanks, so that the accompanying infantry could enter the tank intercommunications network. In July 1944, the commander of IX Tactical Air Command, Gen. Elwood A. Quesada, provided VHF aircraft radios for installation in the leading tanks of each armored task force. When the U.S. broke out of Normandy beachhead, these tanks could communicate with fighter bombers. The IX Tactical Air Command flew "armored column cover," providing on-call fighter-bombers for close air support. It is true that this tactic was very wasteful of air resources, but the high tempo of exploitation that these tank-aircraft teams could maintain justified the expenditures.

Advancing on parallel routes also facilitated American exploitation and pursuit across France. Where the road network allowed, U.S. armored divisions and combat commands advanced with two or more task forces moving along parallel routes. Frequently, a German strongpoint would halt one column, only to find itself outflanked by another American column a few kilometers away. These tactics and massive air superiority propelled the Allied advance. The Allied forces usually found their progress hindered as much by logistical factors as by enemy defenses. Strategically, logistics hampered the Allies throughout 1944-45. Tactically, some armored units found it more secure to travel with their combat trains in the midst of the column, rather than following behind where they might encounter bypassed enemy resistance. Of course, such a tactic was only appropriate when exploiting against limited enemy defenses. When logistics elements moved on their own, they often required small antiaircraft, tank destroyer, and infantry escorts for local security.[37]

This dispersion of antiaircraft units in small detachments exemplified the fate of specialized American forces when their particular function was not in demand. Although U.S. antiaircraft units conducted a number of air defense operations, most notably the protection of the bridge at Remagen during the conquest of Germany, overwhelming Allied air superiority made an integrated air defense system increasingly unimportant during 1944-45. Instead, senior commanders used antiaircraft weapons in a ground fire-support role and deactivated some antiaircraft units to provide much needed infantry replacements during the fall of 1944. Similarly, chemical smoke generator companies repaired roads when line units did not need smoke support. This misuse developed a set of false attitudes and priorities among combat commanders, but the shortage of manpower was so severe that no unit could stand idle. The excellent performance of such specialized units in an infantry role during the Battle of the Bulge justified the American policy that support troops should be trained and equipped to defend themselves and fight when necessary. Even if, for example, the engineers had been employed to construct barriers in front of the German advance, there were no other forces available to provide firepower in conjunction with those obstacles. At that point, the situation was so desperate that local commanders were fully justified in using all available forces as infantry.

Air-Ground (Non)Cooperation

Air support of ground operations, and especially close air support, was the subject of intense controversy between ground and air services during World War II. No one disputed the importance of air superiority, but ground attack priorities were another matter. That controversy was perhaps most acute in the United States, but the questions involved found echoes in other nations as well.

Throughout the war, the U.S. Army Air Forces (AAF) operated almost independently from the other elements of the Army. Soon after Pearl Harbor President Franklin D. Roosevelt gave the AAF a tremendous mission--precision strategic bombing of Germany and eventually Japan--that strained the limited air resources of the U.S. for most of the war. AAF leaders believed strongly in the value of strategic bombing. This belief only increased their tendency to distance themselves from the ground arms. The result was near disaster on the battlefield, retrieved only by the common sense of tactical commanders on the spot.

Army Air Force doctrine defined three priorities for tactical aviation: first, air superiority; second, "isolation of the battlefield," which in effect meant air interdiction; and third, attacks on ground targets "in the zone of contact" between opposing armies.[38] Throughout the war, the AAF phrase for close air support was "third phase" or "priority three" missions, reflecting a basic belief that such targets were an uneconomical, inefficient, and unimportant use for air power, and rightfully belonged to the field artillery. Some basis for this belief existed, of course--close air support required extremely careful training and coordination and suffered from the difficulty of differentiating friend from foe while flying at high speed. Moreover, the air leaders were probably correct in their belief that the air weapons of World War II had only limited destructive effect against small, point targets of the type found near the line of contact. Centrally directed interdiction of the enemy by tactical air assets, the AAF argued, was the most efficient use of this weapon. Yet the ground commanders valued the psychological effects of close air support on both friend and foe, while the unseen interdiction attacks had no such effects. In addition, close air support was an excellent means of rapidly massing combat power at the decisive point. The more that air leaders opposed the decentralized use of their aircraft for close air support, the more ground commanders felt the need to control some air assets to ensure their availability when needed.

As commander of the Army Ground Forces, General McNair led a vain effort to change Army Air Force priorities. He argued that, even if close air support missions were the exception rather than the rule, that exception should be stressed in training because it was the most difficult form of ground attack mission. Yet the AAF was unwilling to provide aircraft even for major ground maneuvers, let alone small-unit training. Six months before the Normandy invasion, thirty-three U.S. divisions in England had experienced no joint air-ground training, and twenty-one had not even seen displays of friendly aircraft for purposes of recognition in battle. As noted above, in 1943 the AAF arbitrarily changed the radios in fighter-bombers to a type that was incompatible with ground radios. Air and ground units had little understanding of the tactics and capabilities of their counterparts.[39]

The results were predictably poor. During the North African invasion, ground forces received little air support, and ground commanders with no experience in the employment of tactical air support misused the little that was available. U.S. ground troops saw so few friendly aircraft that they fired on anything that flew. One American observation squadron lost ten aircraft in North Africa--two to enemy air attack, three to enemy ground fire, and five to American ground fire. Gradually, both sides learned to recognize and cooperate with each other, but the process was painful.[40]

131

The United States did not develop a formal doctrine and training procedure for air-ground cooperation until late in the war. In the interim, effective air support depended upon personalities and initiative in the field. The XII Air Support Command collocated its headquarters with the fifth U.S. Army in Italy, meeting each evening to plan strikes for the next day and improvising a common network of liaison officers and radios. Within the air resources allocated by higher headquarters, the ground operations officer established priorities that the air operations officer rejected only when the proposed use was a technical impossibility. A similar relationship gradually developed between the 9th U.S. Tactical Air Force and some of the U.S. field armies in France and Germany. Yet, even in 1946, AAF officers assigned to study the lessons learned from tactical air operations in Europe continued to describe close air support as a "priority three" mission and recommended the continued use of AAF doctrine on this subject. Meanwhile, in the absence of effective aerial observation support, the ground forces had developed their own aviation, using light aircraft for artillery adjustment, command and control, and movement of critical supplies.[41]

Not even the German armed forces were immune to this type of interservice misunderstanding and rivalry. As late as November 1941, for example, the Luftwaffe refused Erwin Rommel's request for a single air liaison officer to arrange on-call aircraft for the Afrika Korps, because such an arrangement "would be against the best use of the air force as a whole." With such attitudes, it is not surprising that German Stukas dive-bombed their own armored divisions on at least one occasion.[42] On the Eastern Front, of course, German air-ground cooperation reached its peak during the period 1941-43. Thereafter, the growing strength of the Red Air Force and the demands of air defense for Germany against American and British strategic bombardment caused a steady decline in the number and quality of German tactical aircraft. In addition, from 1942 onward the improved quality of Soviet tanks caused the Luftwaffe to experiment with better air-ground antitank weapons, including 30-mm automatic cannon and shaped-charge armor-piercing bombs.[43] Thus, although the Luftwaffe developed adequate procedures for air-ground cooperation in most respects, the lack of sufficient aircraft to conduct such support and the technological decline of the Luftwaffe in comparison to its opponents made this support rare after 1943.

The Royal Air Force continued its policy of independence from the British Army well into World War II. As in the U.S., RAF leaders considered strategic bombing and air superiority much more important than air-ground cooperation. From 1942 onward, however, a working compromise developed in three different theaters almost simultaneously. First, the battles of North Africa demonstrated the importance of air-ground cooperation there. Bernard Montgomery developed an entire network of liaison officers and collocated ground and air headquarters to provide such support while still leaving much independence to the RAF. Second, the British and Commonwealth forces that reconquered Burma eventually developed an even closer relationship with their airmen, a relationship based on their mutual sense of having to depend on themselves because of poor support from Britain. Meanwhile, in Great Britain, RAF Fighter Command sought a more active mission once it had won the Battle of Britain. This institutional need for a new mission coincided with the rise in Fighter Command of one of the few British fliers with extensive experience in close air support--Air Vice-Marshal Sir Trafford Leigh-Mallory. The irritating but effective Leigh-Mallory built the British 2d Tactical Air Force as an instrument to support the Normandy invasion; he then directed both this force and the American 9th Air Force during the 1944 campaign. Even then, the proportion of ground-attack sorties expended on close air support was often much lower than that on interdiction missions that searched for targets almost at random.[44]

By 1945, most armed forces had developed unofficial techniques for effective air-ground cooperation in the field. Such techniques did not resolve the basic doctrinal differences between air and ground components. These disputes persisted in peacetime long after the procedures for close air support were forgotten.

Air Transportation and Air-Landing Forces

One of the neglected aspects of air-ground operations during World War II was the use of air transportation to move supplies and even nonparachute troops within a theater of operations. Just as railroads and trucks had changed the logistical and operational mobility of earlier armies, so air transportation promised to eliminate the historical vulnerability of all ground forces--their land-based lines of communication. Leaving aside for the moment the use of true airborne troops, the techniques of air transportation and supply bear closer examination.

The most significant use of these techniques was in Asia, where vast distances, poor road networks, and few railroads made aerial supply almost a necessity. In order to understand the British use of air transport in Burma, however, we must digress briefly to consider the tactics of Britain's opponent, Japan.

As previously noted, Japanese industry could not hope to compete with the mass production of weapons by its enemies. Much as the Japanese Army would have liked to have had such weapons, it often had to rely on unorthodox tactics to make up for lack of equipment and firepower. In particular, surprise attacks by night or from unexpected directions seemed to allow the Japanese to close rapidly with the enemy. In hand-to-hand fighting, Japanese leaders believed that their superior morale and training would compensate for shortages of equipment and manpower.[45]

During the conquest of Malaya and Burma in 1942, the Japanese tactics made a virtue out of the lack of heavy weapons. Generally speaking, British and Commonwealth defenders were tied to the few available roads for supply purposes and considered the surrounding hills and jungles almost impassible. Upon contacting the enemy, the Japanese therefore used a small demonstration attack along the road to fix the attention of the enemy and sent a lightly armed infantry force in a long flank march through difficult terrain into the enemy rear. Once in position, the outflanking Japanese force would attack British logistical installations and set up roadblocks behind the bypassed British defenders. The British response was predictable--they turned their combat forces around to fight through the roadblocks behind them and rejoin their logistical support, allowing the Japanese to defeat them in detail. As the war continued and Japanese supplies became even thinner, many Japanese commanders acquired a habit of planning to live off captured enemy supplies. Having achieved their objectives, the Japanese would then establish elaborate bunker defenses that were difficult to identify, let alone destroy, when the British counterattacked.

Some of the British responses to these tactics were simple and effective. Divisions reduced their establishment of wheeled vehicles and trained to secure their flanks and move through "impassable" terrain. To destroy Japanese bunkers, the British 14th Army developed two tactics, which incidentally represented partial solutions to the continuing problems of how to keep the defender pinned down by fire while the attacker covered the final few meters in the assault. First, British tanks accompanying the attack fired a careful sequence of ammunition at the bunkers--simple explosive to clear the jungle, then high explosive with delayed action fuzes to break into the bunkers, and finally solid armor-piercing shot as the infantry made the final assault. So long as the infantrymen stayed out of the tank's direct line-of-fire, they could safely close with the Japanese because this solid shot had no explosive effect. Later in the war, the extremely high degree of cooperation and mutual confidence between air and ground elements in Burma allowed the British close air support aircraft to fly a final, "dummy" bombing pass against the enemy, causing the Japanese to stay under cover until the Allied infantry and tanks were on top of them.[46]

The key to defeating Japanese infiltration tactics was air transportation. In March 1944, Gen. William Slim, the 14th Army commander, correctly predicted a major Japanese offensive against his logistical base area around the town of Imphal (see Map 7). Using large numbers of RAF and U.S. transport aircraft, Slim was able to parachute or air-land supplies to all his bypassed elements, thus allowing them to fight without being tied to their threatened lines of communication. Furthermore, Slim air-landed most of the 5th Indian Division on the airfields around Imphal, and these fresh troops went straight into battle against the infiltrating Japanese.

By 1945, the victorious advance of the 14th Army in the more open country of central Burma was made possible only by a combination of air and surface transportation. Two of Slim's divisions reorganized into an unusual configuration for this advance. Two out of three infantry brigades in each division reequipped with their wheeled transportation, so that they could accompany attached army tank brigades in a mechanized advance down major arteries. As each objective fell, one of these two brigades paused long enough to construct an air strip for resupply. The third brigade in each division was specially equipped with very light trucks and narrow artillery gun carriages that would fit onto transport airplanes. Thus the entire brigade could be air-landed onto airstrips or captured airfields to reinforce the ground elements when they encountered significant resistance. Until that time, the brigade was in essence a divisional reserve that did not burden the logistical system in the combat zone. This combination of armor, wheeled infantry, and air-landed infantry established a tempo of advance that the poorly equipped and foot-mobile Japanese could not hope to match. The only drawback to this form of aerial resupply and redeployment was the need for air superiority or at least air parity to allow hundreds of transport flights into forward areas each day.[47]

Other nations also used air transport for resupply and limited movement of troops. In the German case, air transport--like close air support--was a promising concept that the Luftwaffe was too weak to sustain in many cases. Thus, the surrounded German forces in encirclements like Stalingrad rarely received adequate air resupply.

Airborne Operations

All the considerations and difficulties of close air support and of air transportation loomed even larger when ground troops used parachutes and gliders to land behind enemy lines. In fact, the Americans and British finally decided that the only solution

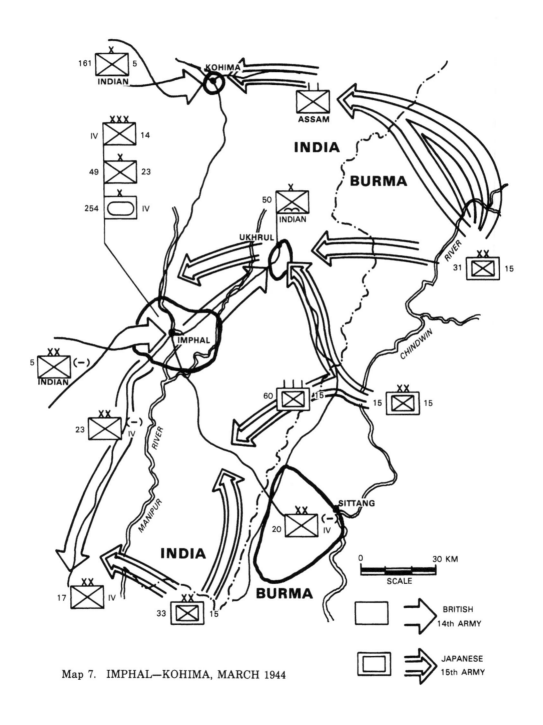

Map 7. IMPHAL—KOHIMA, MARCH 1944

to such coordination problems was to establish a joint and combined organization--the 1st Allied Airborne Army, which controlled both the troops and the troop carrier aircraft. Even with close integration of air and ground assets, the potential for error in planning and executing airborne operations was great.

In theory, airborne operations appeared as an answer to the difficulties of penetrating prepared defenses--the attacker simply flew over those defenses and assaulted the enemy rear areas. Sudden assault from above had the same psychological effects as early armored penetrations, confusing and disorganizing the structure of the defending army. In practice, of course, planning and communications between the air and ground elements of such an operation were complicated in the extreme. The effects of German air defense, the inaccuracies of air navigation, and the difficulty of controlling early parachutes and gliders during landings meant that most airborne drops were widely scattered. Paratroops had to land prepared to fight as individuals or in ad hoc small groups and without the advantages of organization that make any military unit so much more effective than the sum of its individual members.

In a few operations, such as the German capture of the island of Crete in 1941, airborne troops took and held an objective almost unsupported, but only at great cost in men and equipment. Generally, airborne operations were best conducted in conjunction with a conventional ground offensive, so that the paratroops could link up with the attacking ground forces within a few hours or days of the initial airdrop. Finding such an ideal situation was difficult. Commanders had to abort many planned airborne operations because, by the time the decision was made and planning completed, the advancing ground troops had overrun the proposed drop zones.

Because of the difficulties of transporting heavy weapons and vehicles even in gliders, airborne units could not be equipped like conventional infantry forces. Furthermore, the parachuting personnel often found themselves separated from the gliders and cargo parachutes carrying their heavy weapons. Thus, an airborne unit lacked much of the firepower, protection, and ground mobility of ordinary infantry divisions. Once on the ground, an airborne division was extremely vulnerable to enemy mechanized attack and had to seize and hold its objectives before the enemy could react. Gen. James Gavin and other U.S. airborne commanders concluded that it was better to accept heavy casualties and parachute injuries by landing on or close to the objective than to descend on a safer drop zone that was several miles from the objective.[48]

The poor firepower and mobility of an airborne division was especially significant for the British and Americans, because the shortage of combat troops of all kinds meant that airborne divisions frequently remained in ground combat alongside conventional divisions even after the two forces had linked up. Ultimately, U.S. airborne commanders urged that their divisions be organized and equipped like conventional infantry divisions, with the heavy weapons and vehicles rejoining the airborne division overland after the drop zone had been secured.[49]

Many of the same problems plagued the Soviet efforts in airborne warfare. Despite an initial lead in airborne concepts and training during the 1930s, by 1941 the Red Army's higher level paratroop commanders suffered from the same problems of their more conventional peers--poor leadership and staffwork, inadequate intelligence, and lack of key equipment, including transport aircraft. Of the two division-sized Soviet airborne operations of World War II, the Vyazma landing in early 1942 was at best a partial success, because attacking ground elements never established firm contact between the airborne pockets and the main Soviet lines. The Dnepr landing of September 1943, on the other hand, was a disaster because the troops landed on an unsuspected concentration of German troops. As a result of these experiences, Joseph Stalin virtually ignored airborne tactics and development after the war.[50]

Amphibious Operations

If airborne operations required meticulous cooperation and coordination between two services, air and ground, amphibious operations were far more complex. The opposed amphibious landings of World War II foreshadowed the nature of future wars, when sea, air, and land forces would have to be integrated and coordinated with each other and often with the forces of other nations.

Tactically, the U.S. Marine Corps had developed the doctrine of amphibious landing during the interwar period, at a time when most armies considered such operations impossible. When war broke out, the marines were still struggling to resolve the problems of fire support. An amphibious assault against prepared enemy defenses has all the problems of a deliberate attack, plus the inability of the attacker to bring his own artillery onto the beach immediately and the difficulties of wind and tide as the attacker comes ashore. The solution to these problems, besides careful organization and command and control, was fire support from naval and air units. Yet as late as 1940, the USMC's own aviators followed the familiar argument that air strikes should be used only when conventional artillery was unavailable. Even during the invasion of Saipan in June 1944, there was only one frequency available for forty-one air liaison teams to control marine close air support, causing considerable delays in air strikes. Still, by the end of the war the USMC had extremely effective and responsive air support, and even naval gunfire was so refined that it could provide a rolling barrage in front of the marine attackers on the beach. Only the flat trajectory of naval guns limited their ability to provide fire support inland.[51]

In addition to coordinating the elements of fire support, there was the question of moving the assault infantry and support forces across the beaches and through enemy shoreline defenses. The amphibious tractor gave the attacker that ability even where the water was too shallow for ordinary landing craft. The British Army developed an entire armored division, the 79th, which was equipped with specialized weapons such as amphibious Sherman tanks and mine-roller or flail tanks. This equipment proved invaluable, not only during the invasion of Normandy in June 1944, but also in the assault river crossing of the Rhine in 1945. Both of these operations, with the combination of ground, air, amphibious, and parachute forces of several nations, were models of the steps required to combine many different weapons and units into an effective whole.

Unconventional Warfare

One final specialized weapon was prominent in World War II--unconventional warfare or guerrilla forces. Dozens of German divisions were involved in rear-area protection against partisan forces in the Soviet Union and the Balkans. In France and again in the American reconquest of the Philippines, these guerrilla armies were much more than an additional irritant to the occupying army. On a number of occasions, U.S. and British forces used the guerrillas as an economy-of-force tool, bypassing enemy positions and leaving the guerrillas to protect friendly flanks and rear. This, plus the great intelligence and sabotage potential of guerrillas, made them a significant weapon.

The principal drawback to the Allied use of guerrillas was largely one of perception. Because most military planners regarded the guerrillas as an auxiliary force, dependent upon the conventional armies for weapons and training, they tended to underestimate the capability of guerrillas for independent actions of the type that dominated the 1950s and 1960s.

To some extent, the experience of the German Army reflects the experience of all armies in World War II. Initially, Germany had advantages in training and experience, advantages that allowed its soldiers to integrate the different weapons on the battlefield and to move so rapidly that their opponents became disoriented and incapable of rapid response. As the war lengthened, the Germans tended to rely increasingly on their air support and high-quality armored formations to perform missions that were inappropriate for such formations, such as penetration of a prepared defense. Heavy tanks took precedence over half-tracks for the accompanying infantry, and thus German production was never able to support a fully mechanized force. Simultaneously, Germany's opponents were learning how better to integrate their forces at a tactical level and how to organize an effective antitank defense-in-depth. Moreover, from 1943 onward inprovements in both the quantity and quality of Allied air and ground forces dissipated the early German advantages of training and weaponry. The twin issues of quality and quantity became even more acute for the Japanese, who were never able to compete in manpower and production with their enemies, especially because hundreds of thousands of Japanese troops were tied down in China.

Sheer mass was not sufficient to defeat the Axis forces on the battlefield, however. The Soviet, British, and American armed forces also gained greater skill in combined arms and adjusted their organizations to improve this combination. By 1945, these armies had developed true combat effectiveness at the small unit level, even though that effectiveness was sometimes a product of field improvisation rather than of careful institutional development. At that point, the problem of combined arms integration shifted, at least temporarily, to a higher level of organization. The lingering problems of combining the arms in 1945 were not so much at battalion or division levels as they were between the army and the other services. Air support in particular was a critical link in the success of most offensives in World War II, yet the U.S. Army had only achieved a temporary truce on this issue with the Army Air Forces. Once the war was over, the practical lessons of small unit integration and of air-ground cooperation were frequently forgotten.

CHAPTER SIX
COMBINED ARMS AFTER 1945

By 1945, the victorious armies of the United Nations had developed a very sophisticated, equipment-intensive form of combined arms mechanized war. Even in the Pacific theater, the Americans and British used generous amounts of air power, specialized landing craft, and armored vehicles to support their infantry operations. Yet during the immediate postwar years, the same armies faced two trends that argued against the mechanized, armored solution to the problems of combined arms combat. First, the destructive power of the atomic bomb convinced many strategists that traditional land combat was obsolete and caused others to expect radical modifications to any future land combat. The atomic weapon made dense concentrations of ground forces on narrow frontages extremely dangerous and caused the air power advocates of the world to regard air-ground cooperation as even less important than they had previously viewed it, because the super weapon seemingly made close air support unnecessary. Especially during the late 1940s, when the United States had a nuclear monopoly, the future role of armies appeared to be to secure the bases for strategic bombers before a war and to mop up and occupy enemy territory after a nuclear bombing. Until the early 1950s, technological limitations restricted the design and production of truely small-yield, tactical nuclear weapons. Thus by definition nuclear warfare meant using large-scale, strategic nuclear weapons; consequently, ground combat fell into neglect.

The second, and opposing, challenge to the mechanized armies of 1945 was the so-called "war of national liberation" that employed unconventional warfare tactics. During the later 1940s, insurgencies in China, Indo-China, Greece, and Malaya made conventional armies appear too expensive and too musclebound to compete efficiently against the politicized peasant outfitted with a rifle and a bag of rice. To meet this challenge, western armies had to neglect the development of new generations of expensive armored weapons in favor of renewed interest in increased mobility for light infantry forces. The French in Indo-China and Algeria, and the British in Malaya, Kenya, and Aden, were clearly distracted from the mechanized trends of 1945. In the 1960s, the Europeans were again able to focus on home defense in an intensive, mechanized war, but almost simultaneously the U.S. became involved in Vietnam. Not until the mid-1970s were all the NATO Allies actively studying and developing doctrine for their own defense in Europe. In the interim the Soviet Union had gone far to make up its previous technical disadvantages in conventional combat. Of course, some developments in counterinsurgency wars may have application in a more intense, mechanized environment. For example, despite the potentially high air defense threat posed by Soviet-equipped forces, airmobility is clearly one of the major new tactical trends of the later 20th century.

Most major armies, including that of the Soviet Union, have been forced to adjust to the challenge of nuclear warfare or guerrilla insurgency, or both. The only major exception has been Israel, and even there persistent terrorism has posed a difficult problem for the mechanized Israeli forces. Thus, major themes in combined arms since World War II are difficult to identify. Different armies have faced the same problems, but rarely at the same time. This chapter will examine the postwar period from three different perspectives: the development of organization and doctrine in the Soviet Army, the experience of the United States and to a lesser extent its European allies, and finally the rapid development of the Israeli Defense Forces from guerrillas to armor-heavy conventional soldiers.

The Soviet Army, 1945-66: The Decline of Conventional Forces

The Soviet Army, as it was renamed after World War II, has experienced at least three distinct periods of doctrine and organization since 1945. First, from the end of the war to the death of Stalin in 1953, the Soviets demobilized a portion of their forces but continued with the same tactical and operational doctrines and organizations developed during the war. Second, from 1953 to approximately 1967, the ground forces took a back seat to the nuclear-equipped arms of the Soviet state. During this period, the Soviet Army shrank in size and neglected its historical experience in combined arms in favor of an armor-heavy force designed to survive and exploit nuclear strikes. Finally, since the late 1960s the Soviet Union has reversed this decline of land forces, restudied the experience of the "Great Patriotic War," and prepared for the possibility of an extensive, combined arms mechanized conflict with or without the use of nuclear weapons.[1]

Immediately after World War II, the Soviet Union had no nuclear weapons and therefore sought to refine its increasingly mechanized conventional forces for any European eventuality. At the time, this was the only possible Soviet counterweight to the U.S. nuclear monopoly. Although the Soviet Union demobilized from a total of over 500 division-sized units to approximately 175 divisions during the period 1945-48, the number of armored and mechanized units actually increased from thirty-nine to sixty-five. In the process, "tank corps" became tank divisions, and "mechanized corps" became mechanized divisions (see Figure 14).[2] Each of these divisions reflected the experience of World War II, including integration of tanks, self-propelled guns, infantry, artillery, and air defense at regimental level.

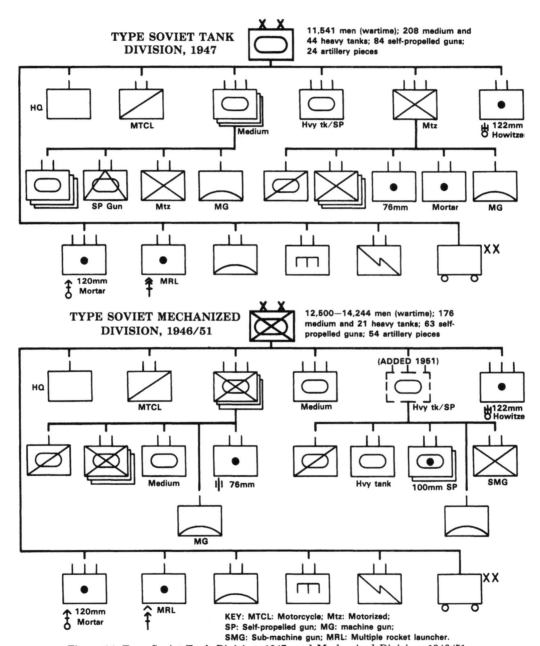

TYPE SOVIET TANK
DIVISION, 1947

11,541 men (wartime); 208 medium and
44 heavy tanks; 84 self-propelled guns;
24 artillery pieces

HQ
MTCL
Medium
Hvy tk/SP
Mtz
122mm Howitzer

SP Gun
Mtz
MG
76mm
Mortar
MG

120mm Mortar
MRL

TYPE SOVIET MECHANIZED
DIVISION, 1946/51

12,500—14,244 men (wartime); 176
medium and 21 heavy tanks; 63 self-
propelled guns; 54 artillery pieces

HQ
MTCL
Medium
(ADDED 1951)
Hvy tk/SP
122mm Howitzer

Medium
76mm
Hvy tank
100mm SP
SMG

MG

120mm Mortar
MRL

KEY: MTCL: Motorcycle; Mtz: Motorized;
SP: Self-propelled gun; MG: machine gun;
SMG: Sub-machine gun; MRL: Multiple rocket launcher.

Figure 14. Type Soviet Tank Division, 1947, and Mechanized Division, 1946/51.

Indeed, the addition of a heavy tank/self-propelled gun regiment to the mechanized division in 1951 made this division almost too unwieldy for a small Soviet staff to control.

Simultaneously, the Soviets motorized their rifle divisions. The demobilization of 1945-48 allowed them to equip the remaining divisions completely with motor transportation, as evidenced by a three-fold increase in the number of trucks in a rifle division between 1944 and 1946. The first Soviet armored personnel carriers, the BTR-152 series, came into production in late 1945, but even the motorized rifle regiment of a tank division was truck-mounted until well into the 1950s. At that point, the tracked BTR-50 series came into production for the mechanized units, and apparently other motorized rifle units inherited the BTR-152.[3]

Soviet doctrine remained essentially unchanged until 1953. During this period the Soviets produced their first nuclear weapons, so that their conventional ground forces became less vital to national strategy. Then Stalin's death in 1953 allowed Marshal Georgi Zhukov to return to power within the armed forces.* By 1955, Zhukov had won government approval for a major reorganization of the ground forces. His primary goal was to adjust the ground forces to the realities of nuclear warfare. All units had to become smaller for better command and control, and better armored for protection against the effects of nuclear weapons. The tubed artillery preparations of the Great Patriotic War declined in significance, giving way to a doctrine that viewed mechanized, armor-heavy forces as the exploitation element after nuclear strikes had shattered the enemy defenses.

In the realm of organization, Zhukov abolished the rifle corps, the unwieldy mechanized division, the rifle division, and the remaining horse cavalry divisions. The motorized rifle division replaced both the mechanized and the rifle division. By 1958, only three types of division remained: tank, motorized rifle, and airborne rifle. Armies consisted only of three to four tank divisions in a tank army, or two to three motorized rifle divisions and one tank division in a combined arms army. Missile-equipped artillery and air defense replaced much of the conventional artillery of the Soviet Army.[4]

———————————

*Because of his great prestige, Zhukov posed a potential political threat to Stalin. As a result, Stalin banished Zhukov to minor posts for a number of years after World War II.

At the same time, the influx of new equipment and the
reduction in the overall size of the army meant that all units,
with the exception of airborne divisions, were at least motorized
and in many cases mechanized. The term "mobile group," which for
three decades had designated cavalry and mechanized forces that
were more mobile than conventional infantry, lost its meaning and
fell out of use. The function of exploiting penetrations
remained, however, becoming a role for the tank and motorized
rifle divisions.

Perhaps most significantly, the entire concept of combined
arms seemed less important once the Soviet Army decided that any
future war would be a nuclear war. In particular, infantry as
well as conventional artillery shrank within existing
organizations. In 1947, for example, a typical "mechanized army"
consisted of two tank and two mechanized divisions. Because all
the maneuver regiments in these divisions had integrated infantry
units, there was a total of thirty-four motorized or mechanized
infantry battalions in this mechanized army. By contrast, the
1958 "tank army" consisted of only four tank divisions, and these
four divisions had lost the motorized rifle battalions from their
tank regiments. Consequently, the tank army had only twelve
infantry battalions, all of them mounted in armored personnel
carriers in part to shield them from the blast and radiation
effects of nuclear weapons.[5]

Beginning in 1960, Nikita Khrushchev further slighted the
conventional ground forces in favor of the "Strategic Rocket
Forces." Individual army organizations, as well as the total
strength of the army, declined to a postwar low of 140 small
divisions. The Soviet Union appeared totally committed to the
concept of the "single option," the expectation that any major
war must be a nuclear war.

Rebirth of Soviet Combined Arms After 1967

Following Khrushchev's ouster in 1964, a debate began within
the Soviet military about the general direction of military
affairs. The exact causes of this debate remain unclear,
although to some extent it may have been a response to the
American doctrine of flexible response. This U.S. doctrine,
which will be discussed below, called for military forces that
would be capable of fighting along the entire range of possible
conflicts, from terrorism and guerrilla warfare up to full
conventional and even nuclear war. Regardless of the causes of
the Soviet reappraisal, by 1966-67 the Kremlin had apparently
determined that the "single option" was too simplistic. In
January 1968, for example, Maj. Gen. S. Shtrik publicly announced
that:

a situation may arise in which combat operations begin
and are carried out for some time (most probably for a
relatively short duration) without the use of nuclear
weapons, and only subsequently will a shift to
operations with these weapons take place.[6]

To meet this possibility, the Soviet military renewed its
study of conventional combined arms warfare. The government
allowed many senior commanders of World War II to publish their
memoirs, openly identifying the operational and tactical errors
that the Soviets had made while fighting the Germans. More
importantly, these memoirs focused on the continuing relevance of
certain techniques of the Great Patriotic War. In particular,
Soviet military scholars paid attention to the concepts of the
mobile group and the forward detachment, both of which were key
to Soviet methods of mechanized exploitation and pursuit.
Although the term "mobile group" no longer applied in a fully
mechanized Soviet Army, the functions involved remained relevant
to conventional Soviet tactics.[7]

Soviet organization reflected these doctrinal and historical
concerns. During the 1970s, Soviet tank regiments gradually
regained the mechanized infantry and conventional artillery
battalions that they had lost under Zhukov's regime. Perhaps
most important, some Soviet divisions received a "new" formation,
the separate tank battalion. Viewed as a pure tank unit, this
battalion might seem to be an additional reserve for the division
commander. Within the context of renewed Soviet interest in the
Great Patriotic War, however, the separate tank battalion might
well be the nucleus for a forward detachment in any future
exploitation and pursuit.

Thus, by the mid-1970s the Soviet Union had come full circle
in the doctrine and organization of combined arms combat. While
the United States lost a decade of mechanized development because
of its involvement in Vietnam, the Soviet Union had developed new
generations of armored fighting vehicles to implement fully its
long-standing doctrine of deep battle and mechanized combined
arms.

The U.S. Army: Demobilization to Korea

In contrast to Soviet commanders in 1945, American field
commanders were only partially satisfied with their organization
and equipment. In 1945-46, the General Board of the U.S.
European Theater of Operations conducted an exhaustive review of
past and future organization. This review recognized the actual
practices of the army in 1944-45, thereby departing from McNair's
concepts to a considerable extent.

For example, in reviewing the performance of the triangular infantry division, both the General Board and the War Department concluded that armor should be organic to that division in order to provide support for infantry attacks and to act as the primary antitank weapon of the army. The infantry's 57-mm antitank gun seemed ineffective, and the tank destroyer was too specialized to justify in a peacetime force structure. In a reversal of previous doctrine, the U.S. Army concluded that "the medium tank is the best antitank weapon."[8] Although such a statement may have been true, it ignored the difficulties of designing a tank that could outshoot and defeat all other tanks. Moreover, even if the tank was the best antitank weapon, using it to defeat enemy armor might not be the best employment of available tanks, which found themselves tied to their own infantry instead of attacking and exploiting enemy vulnerabilities. In any event, each infantry regiment in the postwar U.S. Army received authorization for an organic tank company, with the division as a whole acquiring an additional tank battalion.

By the time the War Department finally approved a new infantry division structure in November 1946, a variety of changes had occurred based on wartime experience (Figure 15). The self-propelled antiaircraft machine guns and 4.2-inch mortars that had frequently provided fire support to the World War II division became organic to that division. Regimental cannon companies and antitank companies disappeared, but each infantry battalion received recoilless rifles. Even the infantry squad and platoon changed. After a conference at Fort Benning, Georgia, in 1946, the army reduced the rifle squad from twelve to nine men. This change not only facilitated the squad leader's control of his squad, but also released personnel to man a light machine gun and an antitank rocket launcher in the weapons squad of each reorganized platoon. These new platoons had a greater capacity for independent fire and maneuver than their wartime predecessors. On the other hand, the nine-man squad had little staying power once it suffered casualties.[9]

In the armored division, similar modifications occurred. The limiting factor in most armored operations during 1944-45 was the shortage of armored infantry, even in the smaller 1943 divisions. At the end of the war, Gen. George S. Patton estimated that the armored infantry suffered 65 percent of all casualties in these divisions while inflicting only 29 percent of the German casualties.[10] Conventional infantry and armored engineers found themselves pressed into service to perform the infantry's close security and urban combat functions for armored task forces. In 1946, the War Department therefore increased the armored infantry in each armored division from three battalions of three companies each to four battalions of four companies each.

147

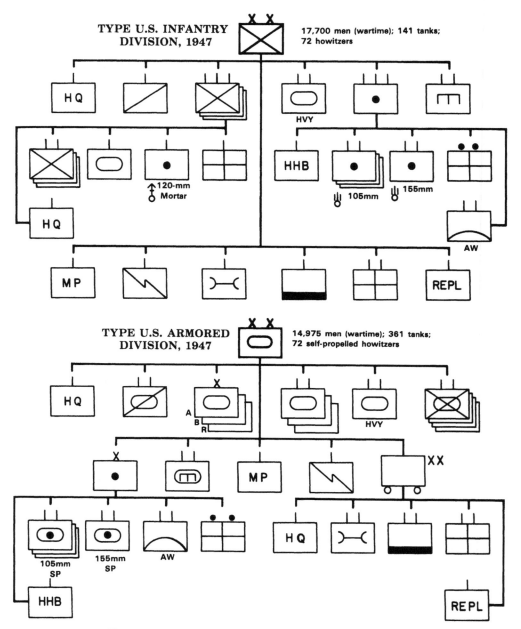

Figure 15. Type U.S. Infantry and Armored Divisions, 1947.

Just as in the infantry division, the postwar armored division acquired a number of units that had previously been attached to it. A "heavy" tank battalion, actually equipped with M26 medium tanks because of their 90-mm high-velocity guns, replaced the departed tank destroyers as the antitank element of an armored division. Battalions of 155-mm self-propelled artillery and self-propelled antiaircraft machine guns also became organic. The three armored engineer companies of the World War II division had proved inadequate for mobility missions, let alone for doubling as armored infantry, and so the postwar engineer battalion received a fourth line company and a bridge company. The two truck companies normally attached to any armored division were not added as separate units, but the division's available wheeled transportation certainly grew during the postwar reorganization. To cite but one example, the number of two and one-half ton cargo trucks increased from 422 in 1943 to 804 in 1947.[11]

Most of these notable improvements in the combination of arms were stillborn because of postwar demobilization. The U.S. Army shrank to a garrison force occupying Germany and Japan, with only skeleton units at home. Given America's nuclear monopoly, few people outside the army saw any requirement for combat ready forces. Except for one division in Germany, the U.S. Army had no formations that even approched the 1946-47 tables of organization and equipment. All four divisions occupying Japan in 1950 had only two-thirds of their wartime authorization in men and equipment. Each of these divisions had only one tank company and one antiaircraft battery and was missing one out of every three infantry battalions and artillery batteries.[12]

The Korean Conflict

When the Soviet-equipped North Korean People's Army invaded South Korea in June 1950, the understrength American divisions in Japan entered combat in a matter of days. This sudden commitment to battle revealed more than a simple lack of combat power; it also demonstrated that the U.S. Army had a force structure that did not fit its doctrine. Regimental commanders were deprived of their primary antitank weapon, the tank, and had only the obsolete 2.36-inch rocket launcher for short-range antitank defense. With only two infantry battalions instead of three, a regiment had no reserve if it tried to defend on a normal frontage of two battalions. The shortage of manpower and the hilly terrain of the Korean peninsula increased the dispersion and isolation of defending units. Such dispersion allowed the North Koreans to practice tactics that were a combination of Japanese offensive operations in 1942 and the Soviet forward detachment. A small unit of Soviet-supplied T-34 medium tanks led each column as the North Koreans moved south. If this tank force encountered a strongpoint that it could not overrun, light infantry forces bypassed that strongpoint through the surrounding hills, cut the defender's line of communications behind him, and forced the defender to withdraw or be cut off.[13]

Later in the war, the Americans, like the British a decade before them, learned to accept being cut off and under attack from flank and rear. Throughout the war, the most common American defensive position was a company entrenched for all-round defense of a ridge or hilltop, separated by hundreds or even thousands of meters from the units to its flanks. This type of dispersed, strongpoint deployment has become increasingly common in most armies since 1945, but it requires excellent fire support and, if possible, active patrolling to provide an effective defense. In the case of Korea, U.S. infantry frequently had to forego patrols and outposts, relying on superior firepower to defeat sudden enemy attacks delivered at close range. When such attacks occurred, a combination of artillery, heavy infantry weapons, and the organic weapons of the infantry proved effective in halting them.[14]

The initial contacts with the Chinese Communist Force (CCF) in October and November 1950 were not deliberate attacks or small-unit defenses, but rather a series of meeting engagements in which both sides were trying to use the same roads and streambeds as avenues of movement. By late 1950, the U.S. divisions had built up to their full tables of organization and were oriented on the few roads in an effort to occupy North Korea rapidly. Although much more lightly equipped, the CCF also used the low ground, moving southward in solid columns with security screens out and hiding in woods or villages when aerial reconnaissance searched the area. Once the initial surprise encounter was over, the CCF, many of whom were veterans of the guerrilla wars of China in the 1940s, shifted their attention to the high ground, moving around the U.S. and allied forces tied to the roads. American firepower soon made any daytime movement dangerous for the communists, and the establishment of company and battalion perimeter defenses on high ground further hampered the CCF movements. Thus, during the later years of the Korea conflict, the preferred CCF maneuver once again became the advance along the low ground at night, seeking to bypass enemy strongpoints in order to attack from unexpected directions.[15]

When the front began to stabilize in 1951, the Korean War became a war of attrition, with each side launching limited attacks to destroy enemy personnel. The U.S. used its World War II doctrine for combining the different arms in such attacks, modifying that doctrine slightly to maximize the available firepower and to minimize casualties. One small example of this operational technique was the second phase of Operation Punch, a

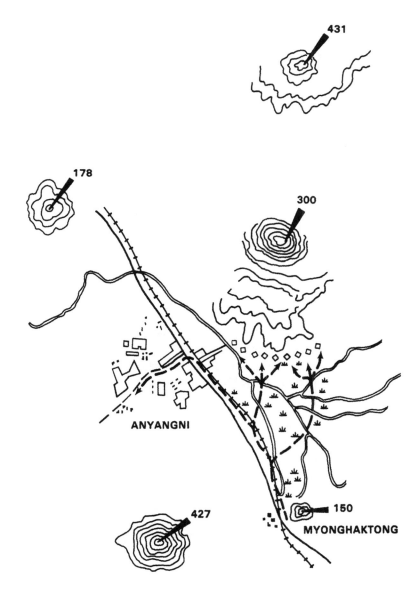

431

178

300

427

ANYANGNI

150

MYONGHAKTONG

Map 8. Task Force Dolvin, Anyang-ni, Korea, 5 February 1951.

multi-battalion limited attack conducted by the 25th U.S. Infantry Division during early 1951 (Map 8). Two task forces advanced along parallel roads to reduce CCF resistance, withdrew at night to avoid infiltrations, and then returned to inflict additional casualties after the enemy had reoccupied his defenses. One of these two U.S elements was Task Force Dolvin, which consisted of a battalion headquarters and two companies of medium tanks, a battalion of infantry, a 4.2-inch mortar platoon from a regimental mortar company, a self-propelled antiaircraft machine gun platoon, a combat engineer platoon, and elements for communications, medical aid, and tactical air control. Because the intent was to clear enemy bunkers in the area of Hill 300, the infantry commander controlled the entire force. Communication between tank crews and the infantry riding on those tanks was difficult, because the newer M46 tanks, like the M4 tanks of 1944, had no external telephones mounted on them.

On 5 February 1951, the entire task force moved up the highway and deployed around the base of Hill 300. The self-propelled antiaircraft guns, with the enormous firepower of multiple heavy machine guns, deployed behind the tanks, with the two lines of vehicles staggered so that all could aim at the hill to engage the enemy defenses. For thirty minutes, the 4.2-inch and 81-mm mortars, the infantry recoilless rifles, the antiaircraft machine guns, and the tank weapons methodically blasted Hill 300, trying to suppress and if possible destroy enemy resistance. Then the infantry, which was sheltered behind the tanks during this preparatory fire, advanced up the hill. One man in each platoon deliberately exposed himself by wrapping a colored panel, originally intended for signalling aircraft, around his body. Whenever these leading men took cover because of enemy fire, all supporting weapons knew exactly where the friendly troops were, together with the approximate area of enemy resistance.[16]

In November 1951, the United Nations and its communist opponents tentatively agreed to a demarcation line for the armistice they were negotiating. Thereafter, the United States and its U.N. allies had little opportunity for maneuver attacks even as small as that of Operation Punch, because there was no object in clearing ground that would be lost at the armistice. Except for patrols, raids, and counterattacks in response to communist advances, the war became largely a matter of holding defensive positions.[17] Many observers compared this phase of the Korean War to the artillery and trench struggles of World War I, but in fact there were notable differences. Instead of a defense-in-depth along relatively narrow unit frontages, U.N. units in Korea formed a very thin line of strongpoints on high ground. Centralized fire control and artillery proximity fuzes

152

gave the U.N. defenders unprecedented firepower in the defense, while the attacking communists often had only limited fire support. In 1951, the U.S. Army further improved its fire direction capability by introducing rotating plotting boards, allowing an F.D.C. to adjust fire on a target without knowing the observer's location. Upon report of a communist attack, a horseshoe-shaped concentration of artillery and mortar fire, called a "flash fire," would descend around a U.N. outpost. This firepower isolated the area from further enemy reinforcement for hours and provided illumination to assist the defenders. Within the horseshoe of artillery shells, the defending infantry had to deal with the attackers who had closed on the strongpoint. A defending infantry company often had up to a dozen machine guns above its normal authorization and, in some cases, could call on self-propelled antiaircraft machine guns for ground fire support. On occasion, the artillery of an entire corps would fire in support of one such outpost. During a 24-hour period in April 1953, nine artillery battalions fired a total of 39,694 rounds to protect one infantry company.[18]

Artillery fire, even on such a lavish scale, could stop a determined enemy only while the shells were actually falling. By contrast, air support had a tremendous psychological effect on both sides in a ground action. Recognizing this, the U.S. Marine Corps in the Korean War maintained the tradition of intimate air-ground cooperation. This was especially important for the Marines, who had less nondivisional artillery and other fire support than the army. The U.S. Air Force preferred to concentrate on interdiction missions and established a cumbersome procedure for requesting close air support. In December 1951, the commander of the Eighth U.S. Army, Lt. Gen. James Van Fleet, expressed the dissatisfaction of his subordinate commanders on this issue. In a formal proposal to the U.N. commander, Gen. Mark Clark, Van Fleet requested that each of his four army corps receive an air force fighter-bomber squadron as a permanent attachment. This would ensure that the pilots were familiar with the units and terrain in a particular area and would respond rapidly when needed. General Clark studied the matter and finally rejected the proposal because it would divert scarce aircraft from other missions such as interdiction. He did, however, get both the Navy and Air Force to provide a much larger proportion of available aircraft for close air support, culminating in 4,500 sorties in October 1952. Gradually, the air and ground leaders became more familiar with each other's operations and capabilities. For example, the army learned that firing high explosive rounds with proximity fuzes just before an air strike would help protect the aircraft by suppressing enemy antiaircraft fire in the target area.[19]

One new area of air-ground operations in Korea was the use of helicopters. At the end of World War II, both the U.S. Marine Corps and the U.S. Army had purchased a few primitive helicopters and studied their employment. The Marines organized an experimental helicopter squadron in 1947 and used those helicopters in small assault landings during amphibious exercises. Interservice agreements meant that the U.S. Air Force controlled design and procurement of helicopters for the army, significantly impeding development of this capability. Moreover, the U.S. Army stressed parachute and glider mobility at the expense of newer concepts. Still, by 1953 both the army and the marines had used helicopters not only for medical evacuation and liaison but also for limited movement of troops and supplies.[20]

In Search of a Mission: U.S. Army Organization From Triangle to ROAD

The genuine success of the U.S. Army in the Korean War caused a temporary increase in its size and budget. Armored forces especially profited from the example of North Korean tanks in 1950, and the army increased its armored strength from one combat command to four armored divisions between 1948 and 1956.[21]

At the same time, the Eisenhower administration chose to base its national strategy on "massive retaliation" with nuclear weapons. In order to justify its existence and mission, the U.S. Army had to develop a doctrine and organization that would allow ground forces to function effectively on a nuclear battlefield. Concentrated, fixed defenses of the type used in both world wars appeared to be vulnerable to nuclear attack, and so the army had to find a means of greater dispersion and flexibility, yet still retain efficient command and control. Unlike the Soviet Army, which had to fight only in the terrain of Europe and Asia--terrain favorable to mechanization--the U.S. Army had to remain relatively light in equipment, so that it would deploy rapidly to any trouble spot in the world.

These strategic considerations greatly influenced the tactical structure and concepts of the army. Tactical units had to be sufficiently small so that they would not present a lucrative nuclear target, sufficiently balanced between the arms so that they could defend themselves when isolated, and sufficiently self-supporting that they could fight without vulnerable logistical tails. Army commanders also wanted to streamline the command structure in order to speed the passage of information and decisions. The need for dispersion and for fewer command echelons prompted some theorists to consider increasing the span of control from three subordinate units to five. Five units, spread over a greater area, could report to one higher headquarters, thereby reducing the number of such headquarters needed at any level.

The result of all these concerns was the "Pentomic Division," a public relations term designed to combine the concept of five subordinate units ("penta") with the idea of a division that could function on an atomic or nonatomic battlefield. Five "battle groups" were at the core of the pentomic infantry division (Figure 16). Each battle group was an infantry formation that was smaller than a regiment but larger than the established triangular battalion. The authors of this design believed that they were eliminating the battalion level of the chain of command while retaining the reconnaissance, heavy weapons, and command and control elements of the triangular infantry regiment. In retrospect, however, a battle group appeared to be an oversized battalion, consisting of a headquarters and service company, four infantry companies of four rifle platoons and a heavy weapons platoon each, as well as a 4.2-inch mortar battery. Within the headquarters and service company, a variety of specialized units were available. The reconnaissance platoon, for example, integrated light tanks, an 81-mm mortar, and an armored infantry squad. The assault gun platoon, equipped with the unarmored, self-propelled M56 gun, provided both antitank and limited offensive gun support for the infantry. The infantry companies, which included the 81-mm mortars and 106-mm recoilless rifles previously located at battalion level, proved to be too large for effective control. In 1959 the battle group therefore acquired a fifth rifle company, but each company was reduced to only three rifle and one weapons platoon. Even the squad changed, increasing from nine to eleven men and officially acquiring a second automatic rifle. As a result, the pentomic infantry squad was able to practice the fireteam, fire and movement tactics used by all Marine Corps and some army squads during and after World War II.[22]

The pentomic division structure allowed the division commander to attach to each battle group, if necessary, one tank company, one engineer company, and one 105-mm howitzer battery. This fire support proved inadequate, and in 1959, the division's five direct-support batteries gave way to five composite direct-support battalions, each consisting of a 105-mm battery and a 155-mm battery. Such a composite battalion posed notable problems in training, ammunition supply, maintenance, and fire control of two dissimilar weapons. Because mortars had again proved unsuitable as an artillery weapon, the 1959 modifications also reduced the number of 4.2-inch mortars in a battle group and returned control of those mortars to the infantry.

Fire support was not the only difficulty with this organization. The division commander had only one brigade headquarters, commanded by the assistant division commander, to help control the five battle groups, the tank battalion, and the armored cavalry squadron. Even with a new division trains

155

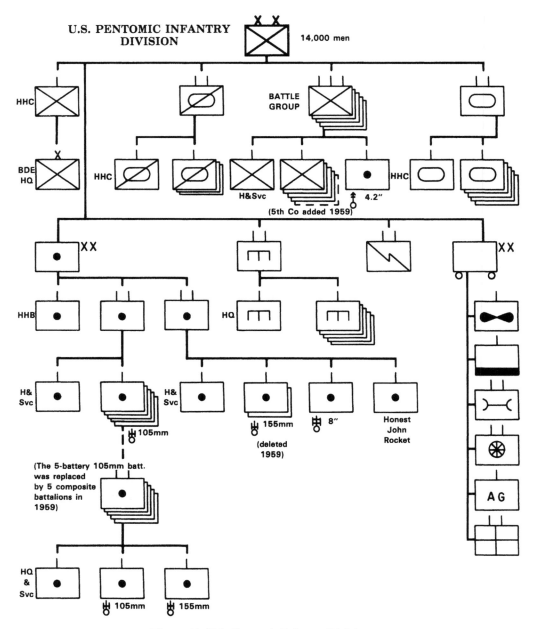

Figure 16. U.S. Pentomic Infantry Division.

headquarters to control logistical support, the division commander and headquarters risked being overwhelmed by the number of subordinate units involved. The growth of the signals element of the infantry division from a company to a battalion illustrated these command and control difficulties. Similar problems existed at the battle group level, where a colonel and his small staff had to control four or five rifle companies, a mortar battery, reconnaissance and assault gun platoons, a tank company, and direct-support artillery. By eliminating one level of headquarters, the pentomic infantry structure left all other headquarters with an excessive span of control. The loss of any one of those headquarters could be disastrous in battle.

Mobility was another problem. The pentomic structure included both a helicopter company and, for the first time, a large number of armored personnel carriers. These carriers, grouped in a transportation battalion, were able to move one battle group at a time. Because the carrier drivers belonged to one unit and the infantry to another, close cooperation between the two was difficult. Any battle group without these armored carriers had only limited protection and mobility. In addition, many senior commanders anticipated that their divisions would be deployed for nonatomic struggles in various areas of the world. Such a deployment could well mean leaving the tank battalion and other heavy equipment behind.

The effects of the Pentomic concept on the rest of the U.S. Army were much less drastic. The armored division retained its three combat commands, four tank battalions, and four armored infantry battalions. It acquired an aviation company to centralize existing aviation assets and received the same general support artillery battalion (155-mm/8-inch/Honest John rocket) as the infantry division, instead of the previous 155-mm battalion. As in the infantry division, the armored signal company grew to a battalion.

The pentomic changes also brought the nondivisional armored cavalry regiment, the descendent of the World War II cavalry reconnaissance group, to the structure it retained into the 1970s. Each of three reconnaissance squadrons in this regiment received enough logistical support elements to enable it to operate semi-independently. Such a squadron consisted of a headquarters and headquarters troop, three armored reconnaissance troops, a tank company, and a self-propelled howitzer battery. A reconnaissance troop represented an ideal of combined arms organization, because each of its three platoons integrated tanks, infantry, scouts, and a mortar.[23]

This organization of cavalry reconnaissance organizations served two purposes. First, the variety of main battle vehicles in such units made it difficult for an opposing force to distinguish between U.S. cavalry and other combined arms forces and, therefore, to determine whether the U.S. force in question was simply a cavalry screen or a major force. Second, this combination of weapons and vehicles allowed U.S. reconnaissance forces to fight, if necessary, to develop intelligence about the enemy. As the Soviets had discovered in 1944, a reconnaissance force that is not able to fight in this way will be much less effective even in its primary role of intelligence collection and screening.

By 1959, the U.S. Army had a radically new structure and operational concept to meet the changing demands of nuclear warfare. This structure and concept differed markedly from the armor-heavy solution of the post-Stalin Soviet Army, but the American commanders were no happier with the results than were their Soviet counterparts.

During the same time period, the possibility of nonnuclear conflict increased. The Kennedy administration came into office in 1961 committed to the concept of flexible response. Despite the army's original purpose, the pentomic division was heavily oriented for nuclear warfare. Thus, the army needed new structures to fight across the entire spectrum of possible conflicts from "low intensity" terrorism and guerrilla wars up to fully mechanized and even nuclear warfare. The new administration quickly approved ongoing army studies for a different division organization, the Reorganization Objectives Army Division (ROAD) (Figure 17). The different types of ROAD division shared a common division base, including a cavalry reconnaissance squadron of some type, three brigade headquarters, division artillery, division support command, engineer battalion, and eventually an air defense battalion. The brigade headquarters, like the combat commands of the World War II armored division, could control a varying number of combat and combat support elements. The combat arms battalion replaced the battle group as the largest fixed-maneuver organization, but retained many of the battle group's elements, including reconnaissance, mortar, and service support units.

The unique aspect of the ROAD division was the ability to "task organize" and tailor structures at any level. Strategically, the army could choose to form and deploy armored, mechanized, conventional infantry, airborne, and later airmobile divisions, depending upon the expected threat. Although there were recommended configurations of each division type, in practice planners could further tailor these different division types by assigning various numbers and mixes of armored,

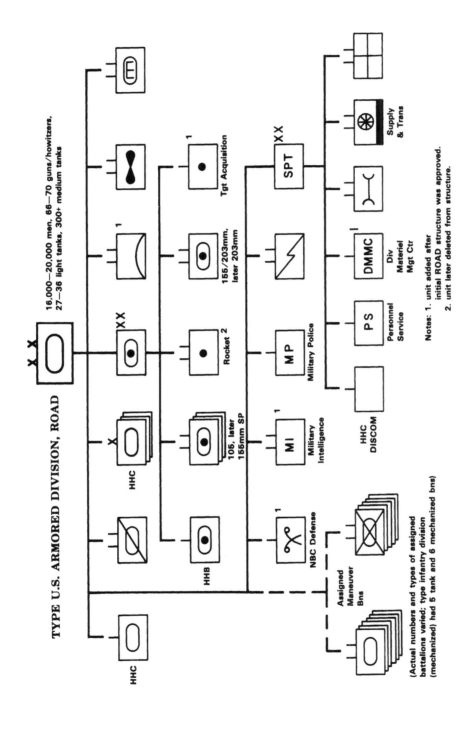

TYPE U.S. ARMORED DIVISION, ROAD

16,000—20,000 men, 66—70 guns/howitzers, 27—36 light tanks, 300+ medium tanks

HHC

HHC

X

HHC

XX

Tgt Acquisition

155/203mm, later 203mm

Rocket 2

105, later 155mm SP

HHB

Military Intelligence

MI

Military Police

MP

NBC Defense

(Actual numbers and types of assigned battalions varied; type infantry division (mechanized) had 5 tank and 6 mechanized bns)

Assigned Maneuver Bns

SPT

XX

Supply & Trans

Div Material Mgt Ctr

DMMC

Personnel Service

PS

HHC DISCOM

Notes: 1. unit added after initial ROAD structure was approved.

2. unit later deleted from structure.

Figure 17. Type U.S. Armored Division, ROAD, 1965—1983.

84-3330

mechanized infantry, infantry, airborne infantry, and airmobile infantry battalions, for a total of anywhere from seven to fifteen maneuver battalions. The division commander and staff had considerable flexibility in attaching these battalions to the three brigade headquarters. Finally, within the brigades and battalions, commanders could task organize combined arms forces by temporarily cross-attaching infantry, mechanized, and armored companies and platoons, as well as attaching engineers, air defense artillery, and other elements. Thus a battalion task force or company team might receive a variety of subordinate units of different arms, allowing integration of the arms as the mission required. In practice, of course, such tailoring and task organizing were prey to the same problems that the World War II system of pooling and attachment had suffered. Constantly shifting units resulted in inefficiency and poor coordination between subordinate elements that were unfamiliar with each other. As a result, battalion and brigade commanders tried to keep the same elements "habitually associated" with each other unless a radical change of mission or terrain occurred. Nevertheless, the ROAD structure gave the U.S. Army the span of control and flexibility of organization it had lacked under the pentomic structure.[24]

Air Assault

The Kennedy administration's dedication to flexible response also brought the long-standing question of helicopter mobility to resolution. The result was a noteworthy new capability in air-ground interaction and in tactical operations in general.

During the later 1950s, the USMC continued to lead the other services in the application of helicopters for battalion and larger unit assaults. While the army struggled with the pentomic structure, the marines reconfigured their divisions and regiments to eliminate much heavy equipment, relying on mortars, naval gunfire, and aircraft rather than on howitzers for direct-support artillery. The assault elements of a marine division became completely air transportable as a result.[25] The more limited army experiments focused on helicopters in a cavalry role, with small aviation units for screening, raids, and reconnaissance. Brig. Gen. Carl I. Hutton, commandant of the U.S. Army Aviation School during the period 1954-57, conducted extensive experiments to improvise gun and rocket armament for helicopters and then to use armed helicopters tactically. The U.S. Army Infantry School made similar efforts, and the Director of Army Aviation, Maj. Gen. Hamilton H. Howze, attempted to popularize the concept of completely heliborne units. The U.S. Air Force adamantly opposed any expanded role for army aviation as a challenge to air force missions, and thus only limited progress was possible during the 1950s.[26]

Then in 1962, following the suggestions of several army aviation advocates, Secretary of Defense Robert McNamara asked the U.S. Army to study the bold use of aviation to improve tactical mobility for ground forces. The result was the Howze Board of 1962. General Howze and his staff conducted tests on everything from dispersed fuel stockpiles for helicopters to close air support bombing by army fixed-wing aircraft. Howze recommended the formation of a number of air assault divisions depending almost entirely on army aircraft, as well as separate air cavalry brigades for screening and delay roles and air transport brigades to improve the mobility of conventional divisions. He noted that an air assault division could maneuver freely to attack a conventional foe from multiple directions and could use both artificial and natural obstacles to delay or immobilize an enemy while itself remaining free to fly over those obstacles.[27]

After a considerable internal struggle, the Defense Department authorized the creation of a division for further testing. From 1963 to 1965, the 11th Air Assault Division (Test) at Fort Benning acted as the vehicle for extensive tactical training and experimentation. The 11th itself was so small that it often had to borrow elements of another division to conduct exercises. When the division first formed, army regulations still forbade army aircraft to fly in formation, and thus many techniques had to be developed with little or no background experience. In order to make the division's supply system as mobile as its maneuver elements, the division commander, Maj. Gen. Harry Kinnard, developed refueling and rearming points camouflaged and dispersed near the battle area. Artillery, aviation, and infantry had to cooperate closely to suppress enemy resistance during an assault landing. Artillery and available air force aircraft fired on the proposed landing zone (LZ) until assault aircraft began their final approach, one or two minutes prior to landing. The last artillery rounds were smoke, to signal helicopter gunships to take up direct-fire suppression around the LZ while troop helicopters landed and discharged their infantry. Early helicopter weapons were rather inaccurate, but their fire had a considerable psychological effect on both friend and foe. Artillery and infantry changed location frequently by helicopter and often conducted false, temporary landings in multiple locations to confuse the enemy as to their actual dispositions and intentions.

The division's air cavalry squadron combined elements for aerial observation, insertion and recovery of ground reconnaissance teams, and armed helicopter "gunships" within each air cavalry troop. The air cavalry conducted the traditional cavalry missions of reconnaissance, screening, and raids almost entirely from the air. After a number of tests, the air assault division had clearly demonstrated its potential. The two most obvious vulnerabilities of such a unit were the loss of mobility and resupply capability in darkness or extremely poor weather, and the debatable effects of enemy air defense on helicopter tactics.[28]

During the same period, U.S. Army helicopter units, both armed and unarmed, supported the Army of the Republic of Vietnam (ARVN). This provided a combat test for the concepts developed by Howze, Kinnard, and others, and personnel and ideas passed frequently between Vietnam and the 11th Air Assault Division at Fort Benning. Initially, American helicopters in Vietnam did little more than transport troops from one place to another. By 1964 American helicopter gunships and transports formed small air assault units with Vietnamese infantry on a semi-permanent basis.[29]

Inevitably, the U.S. Air Force protested the U.S. Army's use of armed helicopters and even armed fixed-wing aircraft in a close air support role in Vietnam. The government of South Vietnam was so concerned about possible disloyalty in its own forces that it further complicated the already cumbersome process of requesting air support from Vietnamese Air Force elements. Despite USAF protests, American and Vietnamese ground commanders felt compelled to use any air support that was available, including army aviation when air force channels proved unresponsive. By 1967, the U.S. involvement had reversed the situation, providing large amounts of air force close support for ground forces in most circumstances. Because there was no enemy air threat over South Vietnam, the USAF supported the ground forces to such an extent that Congress held hearings about the neglect of the air superiority mission. This artificially high level of air-ground cooperation temporarily buried much of the rivalry between the U.S. Army and U.S. Air Force.[30] However, no air force would have been able to provide such sustained support to ground forces while simultaneously struggling for air superiority against a comparably equipped enemy air force.

In the interim, the U.S. Army fully integrated the helicopter and its tactics. In the summer of 1965, the 11th Air Assault Division became the 1st Cavalry Division (Airmobile) and deployed to Vietnam (see Figure 17). General Howze's plan to use fixed-wing army aircraft in a ground-attack role had failed, but many of his other recommendations were reflected in the new airmobile division. An aerial artillery battalion armed with rocket-firing helicopters replaced the general support artillery battalion found in other ROAD division structures. A division aviation group, including two light and three medium helicopter battalions and a general support aviation company, could redeploy several infantry battalions simultaneously.

162

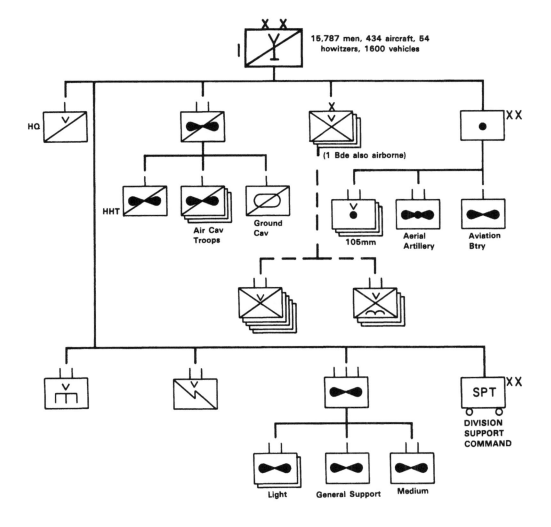

Figure 18. 1st Cavalry Division (Airmobile), 1965.

Entering combat in the fall of 1965, the 1st Cavalry much more often found itself fighting North Vietnamese conventional light infantry regiments than small guerrilla bands. On 14 November 1965, for example, a battalion landed by helicopter in the base camp of the North Vietnamese 66th Regiment, forcing the enemy to turn and fight in his own rear area. Superior mobility and firepower of this type temporarily halted a North Vietnamese invasion of the south.[31]

One key to the airmobile or air assault concept was the close integration, within the same unit, of helicopter and ground forces. By contrast, using helicopter gunships and transports from one major unit to airlift infantry or artillery elements of another unit was much less efficient, requiring more time and effort to ensure coordination and mutual understanding between the parties involved. In practice, the U.S. Army lacked sufficient helicopter assets to make all the American, Korean, and Vietnamese units fully airmobile with their own organic aviation. Instead, the 1st Aviation Brigade controlled up to 100 company-sized aviation units of various types. Battalions from this brigade were habitually associated with different divisions. Even the two airmobile divisions, the 1st Cavalry and 101st Airborne, frequently had to lend their assets to support neighboring units.[32]

Airmobility did more than put the enemy off balance and neutralize conventional obstacles. It also forced the U.S. Army to change many procedures to accomodate operations over a large territory without a defined "front line." For example, both field artillery and signal units ordinarily oriented their support towards a particular front line or axis of advance. By contrast, in Vietnam these branches had to operate on an area concept, providing fires and communications in any direction from a pattern of small bases. Even this system did not always give sufficient artillery support for a large-area operation, and thus the 1st Cavalry Division controlled a nondivisional 155-mm artillery battalion that could be lifted by heavy transport helicopters.[33]

Lam Son 719

When the 1st Cavalry Division deployed to Viet Nam in 1965, it used the tactic of terrain flying--hugging the ground with helicopters--to present a fleeting target for ground air defense. This procedure worked well in jungle and rough terrain, but in more open areas the enemy on the ground had more time to react and to fire on helicopters. Because the principal air-defense threat was small arms and automatic weapons fire at low altitudes, at least some aviation units began to fly above the effective range of such weapons. Many observers argued that such high altitude, level flight would be suicidal against an enemy with larger and more sophisticated air defense weapons. One battle in 1971, known as Lam Son 719, became the center of the debate on the vulnerability of helicopters in combat.[34]

The purpose of Lam Son 719 (Map 9) was to destroy the North Vietnamese base area in Laos, specifically the large logistical installations around Tchepone. This would forestall a major North Vietnamese offensive to take control of the northern provinces of the Republic of Vietnam. I ARVN Corps planned to make the main effort with the 1st ARVN Airborne Division conducting airmobile operations north of the Ye Pon River, while the 1st Armored Brigade, which was attached to the airborne division, advanced westward along Route 9 into Laos. The 1st ARVN Infantry Division would conduct a secondary attack south of the Ye Pon River, providing fire support and flank protection for the main attack. Finally, a three-battalion force of Vietnamese rangers was responsible for the northern (right) flank of the 1st Airborne Division.

This plan had problems even before the offensive began. First, the U.S. government would not permit U.S. forces to operate on the ground inside Laos, and thus the ARVN units had to fight for the first time without their American advisors. Although most ARVN units were capable of such operations, the absence of advisors made coordination of air support and airmobile transport much more difficult. On the other hand, the ARVN units depended upon American helicopters and air support for their mobility and firepower. U.S. Army aviation and ARVN ground unit commanders had to plan each operation as equals, which inevitably slowed down the planning process even though both sides tried to cooperate.

Terrain was another major handicap. The Ye Pon River valley, including Route 9 that paralleled the river, was the natural avenue of approach between Viet Nam and Tchepone. This valley was so narrow that the 1st ARVN Armored Brigade lacked maneuver space for its three armored cavalry squadrons. The valley was also a natural air corridor, especially when clouds reduced visibility over the high ground on either side of the valley. The Ye Pon River was the most prominent terrain feature for helicopter navigation. As a result, much air traffic was channeled down the valley, and once the ARVN forces began their advance, their future axis of attack was immediately obvious to the defending North Vietnamese. Huge ARVN convoys near the border gave the North Vietnamese ample warning of the projected attack.

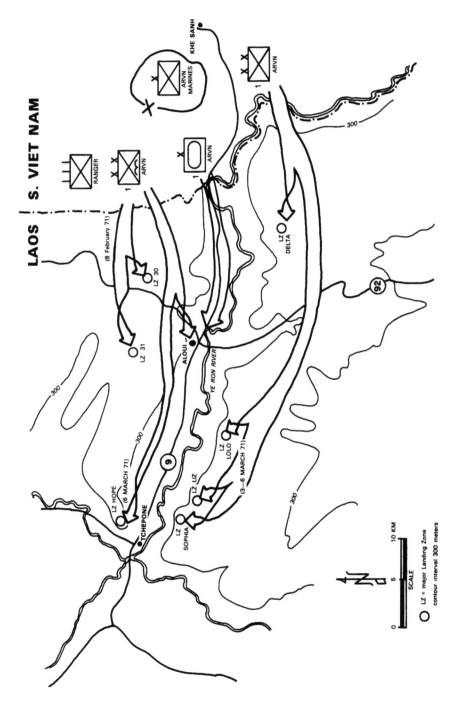

Map 9. Lam Son 719, February—March 1971.

For several years prior to Lam Son 719, the communists had established an integrated air defense oriented on the valley and on the few natural helicopter LZs. Nineteen antiaircraft artillery battalions were in the area, including 23-mm, 37-mm, 57-mm, and 100-mm antiaircraft guns, and 12.7-mm machine guns. The antiaircraft coverage was thickest around the Tchepone supply dumps. In addition, the North Vietnamese had preplanned artillery fires on all likely LZs. The North Vietnamese reinforced their defenses during the battle, reaching a total of twelve infantry regiments, two tank battalions, and considerable artillery support.[35]

The result was a "mid-intensity war" rather than a counterinsurgency operation. The ARVN began its attack on 8 February 1971, but had to delay operations the next day because of poor weather. Throughout the offensive, air force air support was often unavailable because of low cloud cover. Even single helicopters on medical evacuation or supply flights needed armed helicopter support to suppress enemy air defense. This in turn strained the available resources of AH-1 attack helicopters and forced the U.S. Army to use the slower, more vulnerable, and generally obsolete UH-1C gunships.

The helicopters engaged North Vietnamese light tanks, destroying six and immobilizing eight. At the same time, T-34 medium tanks overran the ARVN firebase at LZ 31 after repeated attacks. Because the U.S. and ARVN forces had rarely needed large-caliber antitank weapons before this battle, they had few effective defenses available. The U.S. Army aviation commander for Lam Son 719 urged the army to renew its study of antitank helicopters.[36]

After several weeks of limited success, the ARVN commander abandoned plans for a ground advance west of Aloui. Instead, during the first week of March 1971, the 1st ARVN Infantry Division established a series of temporary firebases on the escarpment along the southern side of the river. On 6 March, two battalions of the 1st ARVN Airborne Division air assaulted into LZ Hope. This LZ was in the center of the enemy air defense umbrella, but the two battalions lost only one helicopter out of 120 in the attack. These later air assaults were carefully planned and supported operations. Strategic and tactical bombers suppressed local enemy defenses and often created clearings to be used as new, unexpected LZs. Gunships and air-delivered smoke screens protected the infantry during their landings.

The ARVN accomplished its mission, destroying the support facilities around Tchepone before withdrawing with considerable losses. This operation delayed a major North Vietnamese offensive for a year, but the cost seemed excessive. In addition to several infantry battalions virtually destroyed, the U.S.-ARVN attackers lost a total of 107 helicopters shot down in six weeks. Many observers cited Lam Son 719 as proof that airmobile operations were too vulnerable to enemy air defense and could not be conducted in complex, mechanized wars.

Yet these helicopter losses must be evaluated carefully. One hundred and seven helicopters represented perhaps ten percent of the number of U.S. Army aircraft involved at any one time, but only a small loss in an offensive during which the U.S. Army flew more than 100,000 sorties. This was true even though many of these sorties were only short "hops." The terrain neutralized most of the advantages of an air assault force, allowing the defender to focus his attention on a few critical areas through which the advance and withdrawal had to pass. This concentration of antiaircraft fires, in combination with poor weather, forced the helicopters to avoid terrain flying by increasing their altitude to about 4,000 feet above ground level. Finally, since 1971, helicopters have acquired improved navigation devices and more survivable mechanical designs. Similar circumstances of weather and terrain might still hamper air assault operations, but Lam Son 719 by itself did not definitely prove such operations to be impossible.[37] Certainly the other NATO powers and the Soviet Union used the airmobile experience of Vietnam to help in the development of their own army aviation doctrine.

The Nato Powers

For fifteen years after 1945, the military policies and posture of Western European powers resembled those during the same period after 1918. The war had exhausted the Europeans, who were reluctant to finance major new weapons systems for their armed forces. The Allies allowed West Germany to rearm only after a decade of occupation, and even then only because of the conflict between East and West. The new Bundeswehr could not afford to mechanize all its formations in accordance with the experience of World War II, and so the first-line units had different equipment and tactics from the other German ground forces. France and Britain had even greater problems, developing three elements within their armies: a fully mechanized force committed to defense of central Europe, a less-equipped conscript and reserve force at home, and a lightly equipped but well-trained and strategically mobile element for conflicts outside of Europe. Such conflicts and the demands of strategic mobility encouraged British and French interest in light tanks and armored cars that might be used both at home and abroad.

In the 1960s, the end of conscription in Britain and the gradual termination of counterinsurgency wars abroad caused both the British and French armies to reorient on defense in Europe.

Even then, democracies were naturally suspicious of "offensive" weapons such as tanks, preferring to develop "defensive" weapons such as the antitank guided missile (ATGM). The French SS-11 was the first effective ATGM in NATO, and many nations including the United States adopted it during the early 1960s.

Britain, France, and West Germany all accepted the concept of combined arms or "all-arms cooperation" as a principle of tactics. This similarity of concept was reflected by some similarity in large-unit organization. All three armies converged on fixed combined arms forces that in U.S. terms are of brigade rather than divisional size. By contrast, within the U.S. ROAD division, brigades might change their configuration to adjust to different situations and missions. The evolution of the fixed European brigade may be a result of orientation on the single mission of mechanized operations in Europe. In any event, this evolution deserves a brief review.

At the end of World War II, the British Army retained its two-brigade armored division and three-brigade infantry division with only minor changes. The mixture of three tank and one motor battalion in an armored brigade, and three infantry and one tank battalion in an infantry brigade, allowed for cross-attachment at battalion and company level. The resulting combinations would be in the proportion of three companies or platoons of one arm with one of another. During the 1950s, the British Army of the Rhine (BAOR) developed a "square brigade" structure that was more suitable for a variety of tactical situations. Each brigade then consisted of two tank and two mechanized infantry battalions. These brigades came to have a fixed organization of other arms, generally including a 105-mm artillery battalion, two engineer companies, and more service support than any other NATO brigade. Although these units might nominally belong to the division as a whole, they were habitually assigned to specific brigades. Thus, the two levels of command, division and brigade, became redundant. Many brigade headquarters disappeared or became "field forces" in 1977-78. This, plus the needs of economy, prompted the BAOR to reduce the division to only six maneuver battalions--three tank and three mechanized infantry--in 1982. Pairs of tank and mechanized infantry battalions still carried the designation of "brigade," and might control a semi-permanent combination of artillery, engineers, and other arms. This structure bore a considerable resemblance to the 1943 U.S. armored division. Outside of the BAOR, the brigade level of command was more important. Although designated divisions existed in the United Kingdom, the deployable unit was usually the infantry brigade, consisting of approximately five infantry battalions plus other arms.[38]

As late as 1954, the French Army, whose Free French divisions had been equipped by the U.S. during World War II, retained the equipment and organization of the U.S. armored division. After the Algerian War ended in 1961, the French Army renewed its study of mechanized operations and organizations, culminating in the Type-67 (1967) mechanized division consisting of three mechanized brigades. Each of these brigades, like their German and British counterparts, had a permanent structure. The brigade included one main battle tank battalion, two mixed mechanized battalions, a self-propelled artillery battalion, and an engineer company. As in the case of Britain, this structure for European operations was so fixed that the brigade and division levels of command were somewhat redundant. As a result, in the mid-1970s, the French Army began to convert all of its units to a new structure, labeled a division, that was in fact an oversized brigade. The armored division, for example, consisted of only 8,200 men, organized into two tank, two mechanized, one artillery, one engineer, and one headquarters and service battalion. The infantry division within France became even smaller, totaling 6,500 men in three motorized infantry and one armored car battalion, plus other arms as in the armored division. The French hoped that this smaller division structure would be more responsive and fast-moving on the nuclear battlefield. For the French Army, the function of armored divisions in such a battle was to cause the enemy forces to mass and present a vulnerable target for French tactical nuclear weapons.[39]

One of the unique aspects of French Army structure during the 1960s and 1970s was the organic combination of different arms within one battalion. The French began experiments with combined arms battalions in the early 1960s, culminating in the mixed or "tank-infantry" battalion of 1967. Within this battalion, two light tank companies each consisted of four tank platoons plus an antitank guided missile platoon, while two mechanized infantry companies had three mechanized platoons each. The two types of companies cross-attached platoons for tactical operations. The battalion headquarters controlled other arms, including communications, reconnaissance, and mortar platoons. Use of the same basic vehicle chassis simplified the maintenance problems of each battalion and ensured that all elements had uniform mobility. First the AMX-13 and later the AMX-10 family of armored vehicles included compatible vehicles for light armor, ATGM launchers, and infantry. The French had to extend greatly the amount of training given to junior leaders to enable them to control three types of platoons. This problem helped force the French Army to reduce the size of both tank and mechanized infantry platoons to three vehicles each, a unit easier to supervise and control. Finally, because these tank-infantry battalions could no longer provide infantry support for pure tank units, the medium or main battle tank battalion in each

170

mechanized brigade acquired an organic mechanized infantry company. In practice, this tank battalion often had to support the tank-infantry battalions because of their limited armor protection against massed enemy attack.[40]

While France led the western powers in the integration of different arms within the infantry battalion, West Germany led in the development of mounted infantry integrated with armor. Based on the experience of World War II panzer-grenadiers, the postwar German commanders were determined to provide effective armored fighting vehicles for their infantry. The resulting Marder was the first mechanized infantry combat vehicle (MICV) in NATO. The Marder had a turret-mounted automatic cannon, NBC protective system, and gunports for infantry weapons. German commanders intended the mechanized infantry to fight from their MICVs, dismounting only when necessary for special operations such as patrols or urban combat. The German panzer-grenadiers had the smallest dismounted squad size--seven men--of any western army. The Marder itself became the base of fire around which the dismounted squad maneuvered as the assault team.

The German concept and design for a MICV drew considerable attention and imitation both in the Soviet Union and in the other members of NATO. Yet, if tanks and mounted infantry operated as a team under all circumstances, the MICV required the same mobility and protection as a tank, becoming in essence another tank. The British Army had recognized this at the end of World War II, when it had used a limited number of Sherman tank chassis without turrets as "Kangaroo" heavy personnel carriers. The Marder itself went a long way in the same direction, but its weight of 27.5 tons made crossing obstacles difficult, and its production cost prevented the Bundeswehr from equipping all German infantry with this vehicle.[41]

The Germans were also the only power to field new armored tank destroyers during the 1960s, although a decade later the Bundeswehr replaced those tank destroyers with tanks. The Jagdpanzer was organic to German brigades and sometimes carried ATGMs as well as a 90-mm high-velocity gun. A gun-equipped antitank vehicle of this type seemed too specialized to maintain in peacetime, especially when ATGMs were so much more effective and flexible. In the later 1970s, however, new forms of ceramic and other specialized armor protection greatly reduced the effectiveness of the shaped-charge chemical energy warheads used on most ATGMs and low-velocity guns. The shaped-charge round was not totally useless, because no nation could afford to use ceramic armor on all its combat vehicles, or even on all surfaces of main battle tanks. Still, the tank or a high-velocity gun on a tank surrogate was again the most effective weapon against enemy tanks, and infantry units were potentially more vulnerable

171

to armored attack than they had been since 1943. Both high-and low-velocity antitank weapons can neutralize the armor of existing MICVs, but nothing the mechanized infantryman has can effectively neutralize ceramic-armored tanks. Further weapons development must occur before the low-velocity, man-portable antitank weapons that were so popular in the 1970s can again compete on an equal basis with tank or tank destroyer high-velocity guns.

From Home Defense to Blitzkrieg: The Israeli Army to 1967

In four wars and numerous undeclared conflicts since 1948, Israel has become famous as an expert practitioner of highly mechanized combined arms warfare. Yet to understand the strengths and weaknesses of the Israeli Defense Forces we must remember the origins of those forces.

In 1948, the Israeli portions of Palestine declared independence from Great Britain while under attack by their Arab neighbors. At the time, the Israeli armed forces were a loose confederation of self-defense militia, anti-British terrorists, and recent immigrants. A number of Israelis had training as small-unit leaders, both in the local defense forces and in the British Army of World War II. What Israel lacked were commanders and staff officers with experience or formal training in battalion or larger unit operations. Even after independence, Great Britain would allow only a few Israelis to attend British military schools. Moreover, until the 1960s Israel could find neither the funds nor the foreign suppliers to purchase large quantities of modern weapons.

As a result, the Israeli Army of 1948-56 was an amateur army, poorly trained and equipped. It relied on its strengths in small-unit leadership and individual initiative, strengths that were sufficient for self-defense until the Soviet Union began to supply Egypt with large quantities of modern heavy weapons. The honored elite of this light infantry army were the paratroopers of 202d Brigade, who conducted raids into Arab territory. Indeed, throughout its history Israel has always assigned the cream of its army recruits to the airborne brigades.

Moshe Dayan became Chief of Staff of this unusual army in 1953. In 1939, Dayan had been one of a number of Jewish self-defense soldiers who received unauthorized small-unit training from Capt. Orde Wingate, the erratic British genius who later founded long-range British attacks in the jungles of Burma. During the 1948 War of Independence, Dayan commanded the 89th Mechanized Commando Battalion, a ragged collection of half-tracks and light vehicles that conducted daring raids into Arab rear areas. While visiting the United States, Dayan by chance met Abraham Baum, the famous World War II tank company commander who had led a small raiding party behind German lines to release American prisoners of war at Hammelburg, Germany. Baum's account of American armored tactics in World War II reinforced Dayan in his belief in speed, mobility, and commanders going forward to make decisions on the spot. Thus, Dayan discovered that his own ideas were in part a reinvention of the principles used by both Americans and Germans in World War II.[42]

Dayan's genius in the 1956 war lay in his recognition of Arab vulnerability to rapid attacks:

> The Egyptians are what I would call schematic in their operations, and their headquarters are in the rear, far from the front. Any change in the disposition of their units, such as forming a new defense line, switching targets of attack, moving forces not in accordance with the original plan, takes them time--time to think, time to receive reports through all the channels of command, time to secure a decision after due consideration from supreme headquarters, time for the orders then to filter down from the rear to the fighting fronts.
>
> We on the other hand are used to acting with greater flexibility and less military routine . . .[43]

The Egyptian defenders of the Sinai desert in 1956 occupied a string of positions at key terrain points lacking both depth and flank security. These defenses were vulnerable to outflanking Israeli movements and lacked a large counterattack force to support them. Dayan planned to disorganize and ultimately collapse the defense by rapid thrusts at Egyptian lines of communication.

Still, the instrument that Dayan planned to use for the 1956 campaign was not a mechanized force. On the contrary, he depended on the Israeli strengths in small-unit leadership and light infantry operations. An airborne drop at the critical Mitla Pass would assist the ground infantry columns, which moved across the desert in commandeered commercial vehicles, plus a few light tanks and artillery pieces. Initially, Israel's only armored brigade, the 7th, remained in reserve, with no mission except to use its tank guns as additional indirect-fire weapons.

The 7th was a fairly typical armored brigade of the immediate post-World War II period.[44] It consisted of a battalion of Sherman medium tanks, a battalion of AMX-13 light tanks, a battalion of half-track mounted infantry, a reconnaissance company, and an artillery battery. The brigade commander, Col. Uri Ben-Ari, was dissatisfied with his symbolic role, and almost derailed the entire Israeli plan by crossing the border too early. His reconnaissance company penetrated the poorly guarded Dyka Pass on the southern flank of the key Egyptian position of Abu Agheila-Um Katef (Map 10). Although this reconnaissance indicated that the road through the pass would support only a few vehicles, Ben-Ari took a calculated risk and committed his three cross-attached task forces on three different axes to fracture the Egyptian defense. Task Force A attacked in vain against the southern side of the Um Katef defenses, where two other Israeli brigades were already making expensive frontal assaults. Task Force C exploited to the southwest, towards the Suez Canal. Ben Ari sent Task Force B, consisting of one company of Sherman tanks and one company of mechanized infantry, through the Dyka Pass and into the middle of the Egyptian position. The task force commander, Lt. Col. Avraham Adan, held this position against limited Egyptian attacks from two directions and strafing by his own aircraft. Only the 7th Brigade's artillery battery gave Adan effective support. This small task force greatly discouraged and confused the Egyptian defenders in the area, who felt that their line of communications had been cut. The frontal infantry attacks were therefore able to overrun the Egyptians.

The 7th Armored Brigade did not win the 1956 war by itself, yet its actions at Abu Agheila and elsewhere convinced Dayan that armored forces were a superior instrument for future wars of maneuver. During the decade after 1956, the Israeli Defense Forces gave the armored corps almost as high a priority for men and material as the air force and paratroopers received. As deputy commander of the Armor Corps from 1956 to 1961, and commander after 1964, Israel Tal shaped Israeli armor into an effective force. Tal soon discovered that complicated armored tactics and equipment required the same discipline and methodical maintenance that had long been common in western armies, but which were rare in Israeli forces.

The main problem was that Israel lacked the resources to maintain a superior air force and elite paratroop element while still developing a balanced mechanized army. Tal got the government to purchase modern American and British tanks and to improve the older Shermans, but the rest of the armored force suffered. Most of the Israeli infantry still rode in the 1941-vintage M3 American half-track, a vehicle with no overhead protection, limited side armor, and increasing maintenance and mobility problems as it aged. Tal insisted that the tank-mechanized infantry team was a European tactic that was less important in the Middle East. In the open spaces of Sinai, Israeli tanks needed less infantry security against short-range enemy antitank weapons. To Tal, infantry was useful for reducing bypassed centers of resistance and mopping up after the battle. Otherwise, he agreed with the British in North Africa, who had considered ordinary infantry more a burden than a help.[45]

174

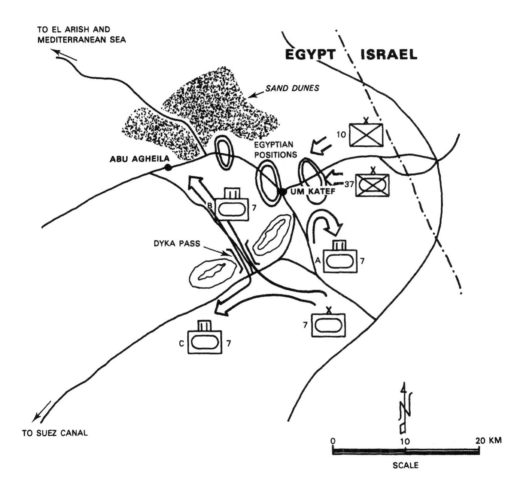

TO EL ARISH AND
MEDITERRANEAN SEA

EGYPT ISRAEL

SAND DUNES

EGYPTIAN
POSITIONS

ABU AGHEILA

UM KATEF

10

37

B
7

DYKA PASS

A
7

7

C
7

TO SUEZ CANAL

N

0   10   20 KM

SCALE

Map 10. 7th Armored Brigade at ABU AGHEILA, 1956.

The Six Day War of 1967 seemed to confirm these arguments. The set-piece attacks conducted by teams of Israeli infantry, paratroops, artillery, and tanks to break open the Egyptian border defenses were forgotten in the euphoria of another armored exploitation to the Suez Canal. The technology of 1941 half-tracks could not keep pace with the technology of 1961 tanks, either under fire or across difficult terrain. The close and constant assistance of the Israeli Air Force made army air defense and field artillery seem unimportant, especially in fluid operations when the Air Force could arrive more quickly than the artillery could deploy. Consciously or otherwise, Israel came to rely largely on the tank-fighter-bomber team for its victories.

Israel: The Failure of Combined Arms, 1967 to 1973

Many of these trends continued and intensified after the 1967 success. The Israeli armored force grew from nine armored and two mechanized brigades in 1967 to an estimated sixteen armored and four to eight mechanized brigades by 1973. The rest of the army remained relatively stable in size. Because Israeli doctrine regarded the tank as the best means of defeating other tanks, the Israeli Defense Forces refused an American offer to supply new TOW ATGMs.[47]

Armor became the main avenue for promotion in the Israeli Army. Aside from the small number of paratroop units, no mechanized infantry officer could expect to command above company level without first qualifying as an armor officer. Israel distinguished between paratroop, conventional, and mechanized infantry, with the latter being part of armor branch, but having the lowest priority for quality recruits. Most conventional and mechanized infantry units were in the reserve, where they received less training and priority than tanks. For example, the three armored brigades located in the Sinai when the 1973 war began had all their tanks and crews at a high level of availability, but their mechanized infantry components were still in the unmobilized reserve. These brigades went into battle as almost pure tank forces.[47]

As commander of the armor corps from 1969 to 1973, Maj. Gen. "Bren" Adan, the task force commander at Abu Agheila in 1956, tried to reverse these developments. He assigned higher quality recruits to the mechanized infantry forces of the Israeli Army, only to have those recruits seek reassignment away from such an unprestigious branch. Adan also tried to obtain large numbers of M113 armored personnel carriers to replace the dilapidated M3s. Upon becoming chief of staff in 1972, Gen. Israel Tal opposed this purchase. Tal argued that the true role of mechanized infantry, if it had a role, was to fight mounted, as in the West German doctrine. Although the M113 was a considerable improvement over the M3, neither vehicle had enough armor protection and firepower to act as the MICV Tal sought. The Chief of Staff therefore opposed spending scarce funds on a good but not perfect vehicle.[48] Israel continued to emphasize the tank and the fighter-bomber to the neglect of other arms.

This neglect was also apparent in Israeli unit structures. Despite the great increase in the Israeli Army, all echelons above brigade remained ad hoc task forces, rather than deliberate designs to integrate an appropriate balance of arms.

By contrast, the Egyptian Army carefully analyzed its weaknesses and strengths between 1967 and 1973. Indeed, one reason for its initial success in the 1973 war was that for the first time the Arabs initiated a war with Israel according to a detailed plan, rather than having Israel conduct a preemptive attack. Moreover, President Anwar Sadat recognized that a holy war to destroy Israel completely was impossible. In 1972 he appointed a new staff and commanders to plan a rational, limited war.[49]

This staff recognized the same problems that Dayan had exploited since 1948. Egyptian leadership and control procedures could not react quickly to sudden changes in mission, and the Egyptian troops became demoralized rapidly in a maneuver battle where Israeli troops could bypass them and attack from unexpected directions.

The classic World War II solution to this problem would be to prepare the troops psychologically to continue fighting when cut off and surrounded, and then develop a defense-in-depth to absorb Israeli armored attacks before they could penetrate. Yet the Egyptians recognized the lack of cohesion and mutual trust in their units and, therefore, sought a different answer to their problem. They planned to force the Israelis to attack Egyptian positions at a time and place of the Egyptians' choosing. This would allow the Egyptian soldier to fight at his best, stubbornly defending his own position from frontal attack without worrying about his flanks or his fellow soldiers. To do this, the Egyptians planned a surprise attack across the Suez Canal, the line of contact between Egypt and Israel since the 1967 war. This attack would isolate the small Israeli outposts known as the "Bar Lev Line" along the eastern bank of the canal. Egyptian units that were not involved in this attack surrendered their ATGMs and surface-to-air (SAM) missiles to the assault echelons, who therefore had three times the normal complement of such weapons. The first waves of these well-armed troops rushed about four kilometers east of the canal and then set up defensive positions. When the local Israeli armored reserves counterattacked to relieve the Bar Lev outposts, the missile-armed Egyptian infantry faced perfect targets of pure tank units without infantry or fire support.

The decision to defend only a few kilometers east of the canal also enabled the Egyptians to seek shelter under the integrated air defense system that they had constructed with Soviet materials on the western bank. Israeli aircraft suffered heavily when they tried to support their armor inside the range of the Egyptian SAMs.

The Egyptians also profited from the famous Israeli method of command, which depended on leaders operating well forward and communicating with each other in a mixture of slang and codewords on the radio. The Egyptian Army jammed many of the Israeli command nets and captured codebooks that enabled them to interpret messages they could not jam. Moreover, Israeli commanders committed the classic mistake of becoming personally involved in local battles instead of directing their troops. On the night of 8 October 1973, the third day of the war, an Israeli brigade commander, battalion commander, and artillery commander all risked themselves to rescue personally the garrison of one of the outposts that had escaped to the east. Their involvement showed an admirable concern for the safety of their troops, but left them unable to coordinate and control the battle.[50]

The Arab armies also made mistakes in 1973. In contrast to the carefully prepared Egyptian plan, Syria attacked on the Golan Heights in a rigid carricature of Soviet doctrine, with all units moving on a fixed schedule and no one assigned to mop up bypassed centers of resistance. Soviet advisors may have taught these tactics because they considered Arabs incapable of more sophisticated operations. Israeli armor fought these dense masses from prepared tank positions that minimized the target presented to the Syrians. The defenders moved between engagements, rather than leaving their positions to maneuver during a battle. Although hard pressed, the Israelis were able to halt and counterattack the Syrians, despite the tremendous initial advantage the Syrians had in numbers and surprise. Syria then appealed to Sadat for help, and thus on 14 October 1973 the Egyptians gave up most of their advantages by attacking eastward into Sinai, away from their prepared infantry positions and air defense umbrella. By this time, nine days into the war, all surprise was lost, and the Israeli forces in Sinai were fully mobilized and ready to fight.[51]

In the ensuing days, the Israelis arrived at improvised solutions to their immediate problems. Airborne units functioned as conventional and even armored infantry, because of the low regard armored commanders had for their own mechanized infantry.

After counterattacking and crossing to the west side of the canal, the Israeli forces concentrated on eliminating Egyptian SAM sites, destroying the integrated air defense system, and thereby allowing the Israeli Air Force to provide more support.

Still, the 1973 war completed the cycle in which the Israeli Defense Forces almost exactly repeated the experience of the German Wehrmacht in the use and misuse of mechanized forces. Like the Germans in World War I, the Israelis before 1956 had regarded tanks as specialized weapons that they could not afford to maintain. In 1956 a few armored experts like Col. Ben Ari showed the Israeli commanders the value of mechanized units for penetrating and disorganizing thin enemy defenses, just as Guderian had taught his seniors in 1939-40. Nineteen sixty-seven was the heyday of the Israeli blitzkrieg, but then, like the Germans before them, they came to rely on the main battle tank and the fighter-bomber to the neglect of the other arms. Once their Arab opponents developed more effective means of antitank and antiaircraft defense and adjusted their defensive systems to the threat of armor penetration, the Israeli commanders found mechanized operations almost as difficult as the Germans had found them in 1942-45. Blitzkrieg was still possible, but it required much greater combat power and much less reliance on psychological confusion than had been the case in earlier campaigns.

The Aftermath of 1973

As the most significant mechanized war since 1945, the 4th Arab-Israeli War of 1973 attracted immense concern and study by all professional soldiers. The Israelis themselves were understandably reluctant to talk about the detailed problems they had encountered. The renewed Israeli interest in organic mortars for maneuver battalions and increased procurement of armored personnel carriers certainly indicated that they placed greater stress on the need for fire support and mechanized infantry to support their armor.

At the time of the 1973 war, the U.S Army was just reorienting its doctrine and force structure to deal with the Soviet threat in Europe. It was therefore natural that the U.S. would seize upon the Israeli example as an indicator of future tactical problems. For much of the 1970s, the influence of Israeli experiences on the U.S. was evident in such areas as the great emphasis placed on ATGMs and on fighting from hull-down positions to wear down a numerically superior mechanized opponent.

Yet the lessons of 1973 and indeed of the entire Israeli experience are sometimes obscure. First, the Israeli Army is organized and trained to fight only one type of war in a relatively narrow variety of terrain; conclusions about the way that the Israeli Army fights may not apply to some of the many possible situations for which the U.S. Army must prepare. Second, as noted above, the Egyptian defensive system along the Suez Canal in 1973 was an artificial one, carefully crafted to use concentrations of antitank and air defense weapons that were far above what any army in the world issues to its field units. Moreover, since 1973 the development of ceramic armor has made the shaped-charge warhead ATGM significantly less effective. Third, the Israelis played into Egyptian hands by neglecting combined arms organization and practice, producing artificially high tank losses that gave a mistaken impression about the future role of armor.

What is clear from the 1973 war is that all weapons and arms, and especially high performance aircraft, are quite vulnerable on modern battlefields. This realization simply reinforces the need for mutual support by different weapons to negate the threats posed to other arms. To cite one obvious example, since 1973 suppression of enemy air defense has become a much higher priority for ground units if they wish to have friendly rotary and fixed-wing aircraft support the ground battle.

Thus in some ways, the experience of the Israeli wars revalidates the experience of World War II. Successful operations in mechanized warfare require not only combined arms organization, but also compatible equipment, so that all arms and services can move over the same terrain with the same degree of protection. Combined arms training must ensure that the different arms and the aviation assets can actually cooperate with each other on a complicated battlefield. ATGMs and air assault or army aviation units must be integrated into existing organizations and practices, instead of treated as special cases.

CONCLUSION

Summary

Prior to World War I, the various combat arms existed independently of each other, with very little doctrine or training in cooperation. Thoughtful professional soldiers frequently discussed the concept of combining the different arms for mutual support, but in practice such combination was the exception rather than the rule, at least below the level of a division or corps. In particular, there was profound disagreement over the organization and role of field artillery on the battlefield and the degree of cooperation needed between artillery and maneuver forces. Some armies, notably those of Germany and Japan, became aware of the importance of indirect fire to aid the infantry while protecting their own artillery from enemy fire. Other armies, especially the French, maintained the tradition of massed artillery in a direct-fire role to suppress enemy defenses at close range.

More generally, professional soldiers were acutely conscious of the effects of the new firepower developed during the previous century. However, even where official doctrine allowed for dispersion and maneuver to minimize the attacker's exposure to firepower, professionals felt compelled to accept the risks of a relatively dense attack. They believed that the need for a quick victory and the inadequate training of their conscript and reservist troops left few alternatives to such attacks.

After an initial period of maneuver warfare in which prewar doctrine seemed to justify itself at least inpart, European nations gradually developed the elaborate trench systems of 1915-18. Restoring mobility on the battlefield required a number of developments. First, all armies had to apply and refine procedures for indirect-fire support. Between 1915 and 1917, the British, French, and German field artillery learned how to place massed fire on any preplanned target, although targets of opportunity remained difficult to engage. Mapping and survey techniques, aerial and ground forward observer procedures, and concern for such variables as weather, ammunition production quality, and the wear of the gun tubes all became common. However, this preplanned fire was possible only because of a series of rigid phase lines and schedules of targets, with no means to change the firing once it began and little opportunity for the infantry to communicate with its supporting artillery.

During the same period, infantry regained some of its firepower and mobility by developing the weapons and organization which have dominated that branch ever since. Led by the French, European armies produced and issued mortars and rifle grenade launchers for indirect fire, automatic rifles and light machine guns for mobile direct fire, and small caliber accompanying guns to reduce enemy strongpoints. With these weapons came the familiar infantry structures of today: a section or squad integrating rifles, grenade launchers, and an automatic weapon, and companies and battalions combining such maneuver elements with heavier support weapons. The German Army then mastered these new weapons and organization, giving infantry the tactics to advance or defend in a decentralized, flexible manner. The linear deployment of infantry that had been used to maximize firepower for three centuries was no longer necessary; the target that infantry presented to enemy fire was thus reduced.

Developments in Allied artillery and infantry could not accomplish much without changes in command, control, and communications. Even if the artillery succeeded in suppressing the power of enemy defensive fires, the infantry had to struggle forward across No Man's Land with no means of communicating either with the guns or with higher headquarters. Long delays ensued while the advancing infantry sent runners and telephone messages up the chain of command and waited for decisions to come back down that same chain. General officers had to command from the rear, because the inflexible nature of telephone communications and the poor visibility inside the trenches made control from the front almost impossible. Even when the commander was able to receive information and communicate in a timely manner, supplies, artillery, and reinforcements all had to cross zones of destruction produced by the attacker's own artillery preparations. By contrast, the German defenders accepted the risk of allowing junior commanders on the spot to make independent decisions and even to commit the reserves of their parent units, thereby increasing the difference in decision-cycle times between French and British attackers and German defenders. Hence the trenches largely immobilized opposing armies, even when German infiltration tactics or the Allied artillery-infantry-tank-aircraft team achieved tactical successes.

By 1918 most armies had come to imitate the German doctrine of defense-in-depth, leaving only lightly held outposts in the forward area and thereby absorbing enemy artillery preparations and infantry attacks forward of the intended main line of resistance.

Nevertheless, the seeds of future combined arms attacks were present in 1918. German infiltration tactics in the west and the British cavalry exploitation in Palestine both acted as forerunners for the mechanized doctrine of their respective countries.

Between the world wars a number of factors common to all nations hampered the development of such doctrine and practice. Anti-war sentiment, tight defense budgets, and the huge stockpiles of 1918 equipment all discouraged innovation. Confusing terminology, the extreme and contradictory claims of various abrasive but visionary theorists, and constant changes in technology also made it difficult for professional soldiers to develop a rational basis for changes in equipment, organization, and doctrine. Despite such problems, few armies stood still, although they varied in the exact compromise they reached along the long continuum between military conservatism and total mechanization.

Great Britain could not afford to become so mechanized that its battalions were unable to function in the low intensity operations required to police the British Empire. This need for one army to fight in various types of war foreshadowed the even greater problems of the U.S. Army since 1945. For Britain between the wars, this restriction, plus the problems described above and a number of unfortunate experiments with mechanization, caused the nation that developed the tank to lose its lead in armored warfare during the 1930s. Instead, British armor developed in two divergent directions, a pattern repeated to some extent in the French and American armies of the same period. British armor and cavalry officers sought tanks that were lightly armed and armored, providing the mobility to function as armored cavalry both in Europe and the empire. On the other hand, slow, heavily armored tanks were still necessary to support the deliberate infantry attack. As a consequence, no British vehicles or armored organizations emphasized firepower. Even the British infantry, which improved its mobility somewhat by developing lighter and more effective weapons, lacked effective antitank capability in 1939. Only the Royal Artillery had such a capability, and it had neglected the indirect-fire experience of World War I.

In Germany, the determination of Heinz Guderian and other visionaries, plus the limited support of Adolf Hitler, produced the panzer division. Guderian built a fully mechanized force in which all arms were integrated, although the service and maintenance elements were never as mobile as the units they supported. As in other armies, the traditional combat arms controlled some of Germany's mechanized equipment, but two-thirds of the available armored vehicles remained concentrated in the panzer divisions by 1939. Germany's first tanks were in some ways inferior to those of France and Britain, but the Germans produced such equipment several years before the hasty rearmament of their opponents. Thus, the panzer units had enough equipment in their hands before the war to train and experiment extensively.

Prior to 1937, the lead in mechanized warfare belonged to the Red Army. From the Russian Civil War of 1918-21 to the present, the Soviets have been remarkably consistent in their doctrine. This doctrine envisioned a "deep battle" fought by combined arms mechanized formations that could rupture conventional enemy defenses and then simultaneously attack all echelons of that defense with artillery, paratroops, air strikes, and the maneuver of mechanized "mobile groups." However, the Red Army purge of 1937-41 was a major factor which caused the Soviets to fall behind Germany, producing the incredible unpreparedness that contributed to the initial German victories of 1941-42.

If the Soviet Union was the most advanced in military doctrine between the world wars, France was the most conservative. The French reserve system was inferior in quantity and quality to that of 1914, reinforcing French commanders in their belief that only methodical, set-piece operations of the World War I variety were possible. The same reserve system prompted the French government to construct the Maginot Line. The purpose of this line was not to hold the Germans indefinitely, but to act as a shield for French mobilization and as an anchor for French maneuvers in the low countries. The cost of the Maginot Line, the limitations of French industry, and the French distrust of elite standing armies all delayed the formation of armored divisions until the war began, denying French soldiers the experience and training that their German counterparts had gained in the last years of peace. When Germany invaded France in 1940, French armor was largely dispersed in an infantry support role, or functioning as mechanized cavalry in Belgium, too far from the main German thrust to redeploy under the rigid French command structure. In any event, France lacked sufficient troops to establish an effective defense-in-depth and maintain counterattack forces to repel German penetrations.

The United States was heavily under French influence during the 1920s, but did develop new structures and doctrine in the following decade. The triangular infantry division gave the United States Army, at least on paper, a more mobile, responsive, and strategically deployable force than it had had in World War I. Unfortunately, the organizational concepts of that division required significant modification under the test of combat. Also during the interwar years, the U.S. Field Artillery School far outstripped its European competitors by inventing the fire direction center procedures that allowed massed artillery to concentrate rapidly on targets of opportunity. Such centralized and flexible fire direction has been a major advantage of all subsequent American field units.

Germany's initial victories in 1939-41 defined blitzkrieg as the standard for mechanized combined arms. Although all armies eventually developed the psychological and technical capability to react to the blitzkrieg, the principles involved had considerable merit. The German panzer division was a combined arms mechanized formation in which the balance between the arms improved as the war progressed, and in which all elements had trained to regroup and reorganize to meet different conditions. The principal role of this force was exploitation, encirclement, and pursuit after a more conventional attack penetrated the enemy defenses on a narrow, concentrated frontage. This exploitation was not a random scattering of forces; German commanders strove to focus the actions of their subordinate mechanized units throughout the battle, seeking to disorganize and encircle the enemy forces. After the success of 1940, the limited German capability for close air support expanded to assist the ground units in such operations.

In German hands, these tactics produced difficulties that were not immediately apparent to observers. In their heyday, German tankers concentrated on exploitation, leaving antitank guns, not tanks, to defeat enemy armor. From 1942 onward, by contrast, the Germans redesigned their equipment to put increasing responsibility on the tank-aircraft team for both penetration and antitank defense. When Germany's opponents developed effective antitank defenses and challenged German air superiority, this system fell apart. Germany denied the infantry, artillery, and other elements of the panzer force the production priorities that they needed to remain equal partners with the increasingly sophisticated German tanks. Moreover, limited transportation and maintenance assets had restricted the German force from the start, making sustained operations such as those in the Soviet Union a tremendous strain.

Poor deployments, training, and command and control were largely responsible for the British and French defeat in 1940. The British response was to readjust both organization and training. Gradually infantry, armor, artillery, and antitank forces became equal partners in the British armored division at home, although the forces in North Africa were too pressed by combat to adjust until 1942. At the same time, Gen. Bernard Montgomery led a group of officers who used large-scale exercises to develop a common set of concepts and procedures for mobile warfare. Realizing that the British Army still had slow command procedures and considerable branch prejudices, Montgomery "stage-managed" large unit operations to ensure integration of all elements of the combined arms teams. The result, while much less responsive and fluid than the German battlegroups, at least enabled the British to use their forces to best advantage.

The Soviet Union also had to change its organization and training in response to the German menace. German accounts of the war in the east usually describe the Red Army during 1941-42, the period when Soviet leadership and staff procedures were poorest, and when the necessities of the moment forced the Soviets to abandon temporarily their prewar organization and doctrine. Beginning in 1942, however, the Red Army rebuilt its tank and mechanized forces and retrained its leaders to solve the problems of penetration and exploitation against the Germans. Popular German accounts rarely speak of these techniques, which became standard by 1944-45. In the deliberate attack, the Soviets used deception operations and selective massing on narrow frontages to achieve an overwhelming superiority at a few points even when they could not claim such superiority across the entire front. A wave of task-organized company- and battalion- sized units then initiated the offensive by fighting to develop information about the enemy and to occupy German outposts. Combined arms assault groups reduced specific strongpoints, while heavy tanks, medium tanks, assault guns, engineers, infantry, and artillery cooperated to push rapidly through the main German defenses. Once this penetration developed, combined arms forward detachments led the larger mechanized formations in rapid exploitation, seeking to preempt German efforts to organize a new defensive line.

As remarked before, the U.S. Army entered the war with a triangular infantry division that was designed to adjust its combat power by frequent attachment and detachment of specialized units. Unfortunately, most commanders concluded that the infantry division was incapable of sustained attack or defense without such attachments under all circumstances. Moreover, frequent changes in these attachments caused much inefficiency and misunderstanding between those attachments and the gaining divisions. Thus, the U.S. infantry and armored divisions, although nominally small and strategically mobile, actually fought as larger formations because of the habitual attachment and association of nondivisional armor, antitank, antiaircraft, field artillery, and transportation assets. At least some of these attachments became organic to the division structures when the U.S. Army recognized the reality of its practice after the war.

The other developments of World War II were obvious to everyone. The shaped-charge antitank warhead allowed all arms to acquire limited capacity to kill tanks with low-velocity guns and rockets. The demands of infantry units for long-range antitank defense and for armor support in the attack produced a number of tank surrogates, primarily armored assault guns. Most nations, including Germany, had considerable difficulties in achieving effective air-ground cooperation, because air commanders saw only the inefficiency and limited destructive capacity of close air support, while ground commanders appreciated the rapid response and psychological effect of such support. Although this issue did not prevent temporary cooperation between air and ground forces on the battlefield, air-ground problems were symptomatic of the larger difficulties of coordination and combination when all operations became joint service, and most combined the forces of more than one nation.

Since 1945, the atomic bomb has called into question the entire role of land combat and has certainly made massing on the World War II model quite dangerous. In the 1950s and 1960s, the Soviet response to this new development was to organize and equip their ground forces for an armor-heavy exploitation, with penetration left to nuclear fires. Since the late 1960s, however, the Soviets have recognized the possibility of renewed conventional warfare and have restudied the lessons of World War II while restoring the balance of arms within their divisions and regiments.

The U.S. Army, by contrast, faced challenges not only from nuclear warfare, but also from insurgencies and a variety of other conflicts around the world. The necessity to fight any war any place at any time with only a handful of divisions places a tremendous burden on American doctrine and organization, a burden rarely understood by America's allies or even the general public. The skeleton configuration of garrison forces in the later 1940s was inadequate to fight a limited conventional war, while the pentomic division structure of the 1950s lacked the flexibility of command and control required to fight in nonnuclear environments. The requirements of flexible response to a variety of possible threats go far to explain not only the ROAD structure, with its variety of strategic and tactical task organizations, but also the American emphasis on firepower to make up for inadequate forces and mobility in different environments. Airmobility is another major new development that promises to give the U.S. Army both firepower and mobility on the battlefield, but only if the U.S. has the strategic transportation assets to move bulky helicopters and large amounts of supplies to an overseas battlefield.

Today Israel and many of America's NATO Allies are not confronted with the prospect of conducting extended contingency operations outside of their own regions; they need only limited forces for such contingencies. Thus, the British, French, and German armies have tended to standardize on integration of mechanized assets at smaller unit levels, producing fixed organizations equivalent in size to an American brigade or armored cavalry regiment. Israel was also able to focus on a limited number of possible conflicts. The tremendous armored successes of 1967 and the lack of resources in a small nation led the Israelis to repeat the error of Germany in World War II, relying on the tank and fighter-bomber to the neglect of the other combined arms. This error, plus the limited variety of terrain and threat that Israel faces, make generalizing lessons from the Arab-Israeli wars to other future conflicts rather hazardous.

Trends and Principles

Certain trends or principles recur in all these developments. Some of these trends are so self-evident that the military rarely discusses them, yet because they have survived the test of different technologies and armies over different periods, they merit some attention.

First, major armies have tended to integrate more and more arms and services at progressively lower levels of organization, in order to combine different capabilities of mobility, protection, and firepower while posing more complicated threats to enemy units. Integration does not necessarily mean combining individual weapons or even companies of different arms together in a permanent organization in garrison; indeed, such a fixed structure would be almost as dangerous tactically as the current organization, because battalions and companies could not adjust the balance of weapons in response to varying terrain, enemy, or mission. To be effective the different arms and services must train together at all times, changing task organization frequently. When making such changes in task organization, however, it is more effective to begin with a large combined-arms unit, such as a division or fixed brigade, and select elements of that unit to form a specific task force, rather than to start with a smaller brigade or division and attach nondivisional elements to that formation. In the former case, all elements of the resulting task force are accustomed to working together and have a sense of unit identity that can overcome many misunderstandings. In the latter case, confusion and delay may occur until the nondivisional attachments adjust to their new command relationships and the gaining headquarters learns the capabilities and limitations of these attachments. Frequent changes in the partnership of units, especially changes that are not practiced in peacetime, will produce inefficiency, misunderstanding, and confusion. Only the need to adjust the proportion of arms to different tactical situations limits the degree to which those arms can be grouped together permanently.

One corollary is that all arms and services need the same mobility and almost the same degree of armor protection as the units they support. Not only infantry, engineers, field artillery, and air defense, but also logistics units need to be able to go where the tank units go in order to conduct sustained operations.

Another corollary is that the arms must be balanced within an organization, grouped together to perform according to a particular doctrine. Units above battalion level in which one arm dominates the others numerically may be useful in certain circumstances, but lack flexibility. Similarly, specialized arms and elites of all kinds, like the tanks and tank destroyers of World War II, have special capabilities that must be balanced against their vulnerability when not supported by other arms.

A fourth trend is the continuing problem of air-ground cooperation. Artillery and infantry learned to function together in World War I, and with much difficulty tanks, antitank weapons, engineers, and antiaircraft artillery joined that team during and after World War II. Yet the aircraft is still not integrated into the combined arms team. In three wars since 1941, the U.S. Army and U.S. Air Force have had to develop ad hoc compromises and procedures for air-ground cooperation because their peacetime training and doctrine were always inadequate. To some extent, the development of the helicopter has been an army effort to acquire a capability that receives low priority in the air force. As General Howze argued at the time that the air assault team developed,

> We drew a parallel to the indirect fire support available to the infantry company commander. That gentleman had call on battalion 4.2-inch mortars, brigade 105-mm howitzers, division 155-mm and eight-inch howitzers, and 240-mm howitzers. Even so, he would not give up that crummy little platoon of three 81-mm mortars that was part of his own company. For he had to ask no one's permission to use them—they were totally responsive, always available, a precious asset even though a small part of the total firepower backing up the infantry company.[1]

The United States is not unique in suffering this problem; even the German Luftwaffe and army had similar disagreements during World War II. Until the legitimate concerns of both services are adjusted, air support of ground forces will remain a broken reed at the start of each new conflict.

A final problem of combining the different arms and services is the difficulty of defense against enemy penetration. The Germans in 1915-17, the Allies in 1939-42, and the Egyptians in 1956 and 1967 have all suffered in this regard. Few armies have the time and troops in peacetime to train in the establishment of a true defense-in-depth, to prepare their troops psychologically as well as technically to continue to fight when penetrated and bypassed by enemy forces. In the mid-1970s, the U.S. Army conducted such preparation as part of the "Active Defense" doctrine in Europe, only to be maligned by critics who considered that doctrine too oriented on defense and on firepower. If anything, however, the true test of an army's skill in combined arms is its ability to reorient and orchestrate the different arms under the pressure of a fast-moving enemy attack.

Abbreviation used in the notes:
CARL-U.S. Command and General Staff College Combined Arms
Research Library, followed by the document call number.

INTRODUCTION ENDNOTES

1. Gerald Gilbert, The Evolution of Tactics (London, 1907),
   183-84.
2. John F. C. Fuller, The Foundations of the Science of War
   (London, 1925), 148.
3. U.S. Department of the Army, Field Manual 100-5: Operations
   (Washington, 1982), 7-4.

CHAPTER ONE ENDNOTES

1. Bernard Brodie and Fawn M. Brodie, From Crossbow to H-Bomb,
   rev. and enl. ed. (Bloomington, IN, 1973), 82.
2. Ibid., 132.
3. Dennis E. Showalter, Railroads and Rifles: Soldiers,
   Technology and the Unification of Germany (Hamden, CT,
   1976), 75-139.
4. David Woodward, Armies of the World, 1845-1914 (New York,
   1978), 30, 46, 74. Actual forces in maneuver units were
   about half the size of these totals.
5. David G. Chandler, The Campaigns of Napoleon (New York,
   1966), 351-63.
6. The division structures discussed here are derived
   primarily from James E. Edmonds and Archibald F. Becke,
   History of the Great War: Military Operations France and
   Belgium, 1914, vol. I, 3d ed. (London, 1933), 6-7, 490-97.
   For Russian division organization, see A.A. Strokov,
   Vooruzhennye Sily i Voennoe Iskusstvo v Pervoi Mirovoi
   Voine [The Armed Forces and Military Art in the First World
   War] (Moscow, n.d.), 142, 144-47, 588-89. On machine gun
   organization, see Wilhelm von Balck, Development of
   Tactics-World War, trans. Harry Bell (Fort Leavenworth, KS,
   1922), 176.
7. Pascal Lucas, L'Évolution des Idées Tactiques en France et
   en Allemagne Pendant la Guerre de 1914-1918, 3d ed. rev.
   (Paris, 1932), 29.
8. Michael Howard, The Franco-Prussian War: The German
   Invasion of France, 1870-1871 (New York, 1969), 156-57.
9. Lucas, Idées Tactiques, 6; H. Burgess, Duties of Engineer
   Troops in a General Engagement of a Mixed Force, Occasional
   Papers No. 32, U.S. Army Engineer School (Washington, DC,
   1908), 20, 28-32.
10. Howard, Franco-Prussian War, 85-117.
11. Jonathan M. House, "The Decisive Attack: A New Look at
    French Infantry Tactics on the Eve of World War I,"
    Military Affairs 40 (December 1976): 164-65.
12. Balck, Tactics, 31.
13. See, for example, S.L.A. Marshall, World War I (New York,
    1975), 76-88, 100-5.

191

14. Henri Bonnal, _La premiere bataille; le service de deux ans; Du caractère chez les chefs; Discipline-Armée nationale; Cavalerie._ (Paris, 1908), 59-60.
15. House, "Decisive Attack," 165-67.
16. Woodward, _Armies_, 30-33; Lucas, _Idées Tactiques_, 31-34.
17. Wilhelm von Leeb, _Defense_, trans. Stefan T. Possony and Daniel Vilfroy (Harrisburg, PA, 1943), 62; Lucas, _Idées Tactiques_, 6.
18. Shelford Bidwell and Dominick Graham, _Fire-Power: British Army Weapons and Theories of War, 1904-1945_ (Boston, 1982), 14.
19. Robert H. Scales, Jr., "Artillery in Small Wars: The Evolution of British Artillery Doctrine, 1960-1914" (Ph.D. dissertation, Duke University 1976), 308-17.
20. Bidwell and Graham, _Fire-Power_, 10-11.
21. Ibid., 17; Lucas, _Idées Tactiques_, 37.
22. Marshall, _World War I_, 44.
23. Brodie and Brodie, _Crossbow_, 126.

CHAPTER TWO ENDNOTES

1. Ferdinand Foch, _The Memoirs of Marshal Foch_, trans. T. Bentley Mott (London, 1931), 16-17.
2. Ibid., 80, 83.
3. Lucas, _Idées Tactiques_, 115.
4. Ibid., 55-58.
5. Ibid., 57-58, 103n; Bidwell and Graham, _Fire-Power_, 101-7.
6. Balck, _Tactics_, 244.
7. Graeme C. Wynne, _If Germany Attacks: The Battle in Depth in the West_ (London, 1940), 26, 30.
8. John Monash, _The Australian Victories in France in 1918_ (New York, n.d.), 124-25, 171-72.
9. Ian V. Hogg, _Barrage: The Guns in Action_ (New York, 1970), 28.
10. Wynne, _If Germany Attacks_, 19; Lucas, _Idées Tactiques_, 75.
11. The best account of this German defensive system remains Wynne, _If Germany Attacks_, 126-29, 202-12. See also Wynne's "The Development of the German Defensive Battle in 1917, and its Influence on British Defence Tactics," _The Army Quarterly_ 24 (1937): 15-32, 248-66; Balck, _Tactics_, 151-68.
12. Wynne, "The Development of the German Defensive Battle," 22-27.
13. Lucas, _Idées Tactiques_, 75-76; George C. Marshall, _Memoirs of My Services in the World War_ (Boston, 1976), 61-63.
14. Alan Clark, _The Donkeys_ (New York, 1962), 77-82, 84-85, 145-49.
15. Brereton Greenhous, "Evolution of a Close Ground-Support Role for Aircraft in World War I," _Military Affairs_ 39 (February 1975): 22-28.

16. Bryan Cooper, <u>The Battle of Cambrai</u> (New York, 1968), 107-20; Greenhous, "Evolution," 25.

17. George H. Raney, "Tank and Anti-Tank Activities of the German Army," <u>Infantry Journal</u> 31 (1927): 151-58.

18. John Wheldon, <u>Machine Age Armies</u> (London, 1968), 24-26. See also Samuel D. Rockenbach, "Tanks" (Fort Meade, MD, 1922), 17; Balck, <u>Tactics</u>, 130-31.

19. Ian V. Hogg, <u>The Guns, 1914-1918</u> (New York, 1971), 72-76.

20. Balck, <u>Tactics</u>, 39-40, 181.

21. Wynne, <u>If Germany Attacks</u>, 53-58; Lucas, <u>Idées Tactiques</u>, 109.

22. John A. English, <u>A Perspective on Infantry</u> (New York, 1981), 24-26; Lucas, <u>Idées Tactiques</u>, 230-31. See also Lazlo M. Alfoldi, "The Hutier Legend," <u>Parameters</u> 5 (1976): 69-74.

23. Georg Bruckmüller, <u>The German Artillery in the Break-Through Battles of the World War</u>, 2d ed. trans. by J.H. Wallace and H.D. Kehm (n.d.), 41, 44-46.

24. Ibid., 49-50, 65-70, 73; S. L. A. Marshall, <u>World War I</u>, 346-47.

25. Balck, <u>Tactics</u>, 186.

26. U.S. War Department, General Staff, Historical Branch War Plans Division, <u>A Survey of German Tactics, 1918</u> (Washington, DC, 1918), 12. See also Bruckmüller, 54, 73-74; Robert R. McCormick, <u>The Army of 1918</u> (New York, 1920), 171.

27. Erwin Rommel, <u>Infantry Attacks</u>, trans. by G.E. Kidde (Washington, DC, 1944), 177-204.

28. John F.C. Fuller, <u>Memoirs of an Unconventional Soldier</u> (London, 1936), 253.

29. John Terraine, <u>To Win A War - 1918, The Year of Victory</u> (Garden City, NY, 1981), 45, 55-57.

30. This account of second Armageddon is based primarily on Cyril Falls, <u>Armageddon, 1918</u> (Philadelphia, 1964) and on Archibald W. Wavell, <u>The Palestine Campaigns</u>, 2d ed. (London, 1929).

31. Balck, <u>Tactics</u>, 188.

32. Ibid., 259.

33. Ibid., 37; Lucas, <u>Idées Tactiques</u>, 299-300; René Altmayer, <u>Études de Tactique Générale</u>, 2d ed. (Paris, 1937), 20.

34. U.S. War Department, General Staff, War College Division, <u>Order of Battle of the United States Land Forces in the World War: American Expeditionary Forces, Divisions</u> (Washington, DC, 1931), 446-47; George C. Marshall, <u>Memoirs</u>, 25, 61-63; John J. Pershing, <u>My Experiences in the World War</u>, Vol. I (New York, 1931), 101n.

CHAPTER THREE ENDNOTES

1. Constance M. Green, Harry C. Thomson, and Peter C. Roots, The Ordnance Department: Planning Munitions for War, The United States Army in World War II (Washington, 1955), 205.
2. Edward J. Drea, Nomonhan: Japanese-Soviet Tactical Combat, 1939, Leavenworth Paper No. 2 (Fort Leavenworth, KS, 1981), 17-20; John J. T. Sweet, Iron Arm: The Mechanization of Mussolini's Army, 1920-1940 (Westport, CT, 1980), 49, 73, 184.
3. C. Serré, Rapport Fait Au Nom de la Commission Chargée d'Enquêter sur les Événements survenus en France de 1933 à 1945, Vol. 2, (Paris, 1947-51), 298-99, 313.
4. Sweet, Iron Arm, 17; Harold Winton, "General Sir John Burnett-Stuart and British Military Reform 1927-1938" (Ph.D. Dissertation, Stanford University, 1977), 2-3.
5. Comment by General Sir George Milne, Chief of the Imperial General Staff, on a 1926 proposal for mechanized formations. Quoted in Kenneth Macksey, The Tank Pioneers (London, 1981), 69.
6. Fuller, Memoirs, 318-41.
7. Winton, "Burnett-Stuart," 95, 198.
8. Great Britain, War Office, Field Service Regulations, Volume II: Operations (1924) (London, 1924), 25; Great Britain, War Office, Field Service Regulations, Volume II: Operations-General (1935) (London, 1935), 16; Bidwell and Graham, Fire-Power, 261-74.
9. Giffard LeQ. Martel, In the Wake of the Tank (London, 1935), 243, 251-55; Winton, Burnett-Stuart, 4.
10. War Office, Field Service Regulations Volume II: Operations (1924), 122-23; Great Britain, War Office, Field Service Regulations, Volume II: Operations (1929), 117.
11. Martel, In the Wake, 147-48; Winton, "Burnett-Stuart," 198; Macksey, Tank Pioneers, 81.
12. Martel, In the Wake, 227-28.
13. Ibid., 120-22; Macksey, Tank Pioneers, 99.
14. Macksey, Tank Pioneers, 132-4; Winton, "Burnett-Stuart," 341-64.
15. Winton, 509 and passim; Macksey, Tank Pioneers, 139, 180-81.
16. Macksey, Tank Pioneers, 86-87.
17. G. MacLeod Ross, The Business of Tanks, 1933 to 1945 (Infracombe, UK, 1976), 81-137.
18. Helmut Klotz, Les Leçons Militaires de la Guerre Civile en Espagne, 2d ed. (Paris, 1937), 61-62, 85-93; Ross, Business of Tanks, 130-39; Macksey, Tank Pioneers, 142, 160-62.
19. English, Perspective, 74-78; Bidwell and Graham, Fire-Power, 194-95.
20. Bidwell and Graham, Fire-Power, 164-65, 198.

21. Heinz Guderian, 1940, quoted in Guderian, Panzer Leader (NY, 1952), 105.
22. Germany, Ministry of National Defense, Command and Combat of the Combined Arms, (1921-23). Translated by U.S. Army General Service Schools (Ft. Leavenworth, KS, 1925), 107.
23. Ibid., 23-24, 91, 116, 118.
24. Kenneth Macksey, Guderian: Creator of the Blitzkrieg (NY, 1975), 6-10.
25. Guderian, Panzer Leader, 24.
26. Charles Messenger, The Blitzkrieg Story (NY, 1976), 77-79.
27. Macksey, Guderian, 65.
28. Robert M. Kennedy, The German Campaign in Poland (1939), Dept. of the Army Pamphlet 20-255 (Washington, DC, 1956), 28-30; Matthew Cooper and James Lucas, Panzer: The Armoured Force of the Third Reich (NY, 1976), 22-23.
29. Kennedy, Poland, 28.
30. Paul Deichmann, German Air Force Operations in Support of the Army, U.S.A.F. Historical Studies No. 13 (Maxwell Air Force Base, AL, 1962), 33-36, 131-33.
31. Cooper and Lucas, Panzer, 23.
32. France, Ministère de la Guerre, Instruction Sur l'Emploi Tactique des Grandes Unités (Paris, 1936), 16.
33. France, Ministère de la Guerre, Instruction Provisoire sur l'Emploi Tactique des Grandes Unités (Paris, 1922), 23.
34. Ibid., 24.
35. Jeffrey J. Clarke, "Military Technology in Republican France: The Evolution of the French Armored Force, 1917-1940" (Ph.D. Dissertation, Duke University, 1969), 94-97.
36. Jean Baptiste Estienne, "Etude sur les missions des Chars blindés en Campagne," 25 May 1919, quoted in Georges Ferré, Le Défaut de l'Armure (Paris, 1948), 34-47.
37. Estienne, Conférence Faite le 15 Février 1920 sur les Chars d'Assaut (Paris, 1920), 37-38, 42.
38. Messenger, Blitzkrieg Story, 89; Robert A. Doughty, "The Enigma of French Armored Doctrine, 1940," Armor 83 (Sep-Oct 1974): 41.
39. Charles de Gaulle, Vers l'Armée de Metier (Paris, [1934] 1963), 97.
40. Serré, Rapport, Vol. 2, 377; Clarke, "Military Technology," 152; Robert Jacomet, L'Armement de la France, 1936-1939 (Paris, 1945), 123-26.
41. Ferré, Le Défaut, 74-75.
42. Ministère de la Guerre, Instructions (1936), 16, 18, 21, 23, 44, 46, 111, 154; Clarke, "Military Technology," 82.
43. The Soviet concept of "Deep Battle" is summarized in David M. Glantz, "Soviet Operational Formation for Battle: A Perspective," Military Review 63 (February 1983): 4.
44. Albert Seaton, Stalin as Military Commander (NY, 1976), 62-63.

195

45. USSR, Commissariat of Defense, General Staff, Field Service Regulation, 1936 (Tentative) translated by U.S. Army War College (typescript 1937), 4-6, 83-84.

46. A. Ryazanskiy, "The Creation and Development of Tank Troop Tactics in the Pre-War Period," Voyennyy vestnik, 1966, no. 11: 25, 32.

47. A. Yekimovskiy and N. Makarov, "The Tactics of the Red Army in the 1920's and 1930's," Voyennyy vestnik, 1967, no. 3: 11.

48. John Erickson, The Road to Stalingrad: Stalin's War With Germany, Volume I (New York, 1975), 6, 19-20.

49. Messenger, Blitzkrieg Story, 100.

50. Erickson, Road to Stalingrad, 18, 32.

51. This account of Khalkin-Gol is based primarily on Drea, Nomonhan, 23-86.

52. U.S. War Department, General Staff, War College, Provisional Manual of Tactics for Large Units (Washington, 1922-23).

53. U.S. War Department, General Staff, Field Service Regulations, U.S. Army, 1923 (Washington, 1923), 11.

54. John J. Pershing, Wrapper Indorsement (Forwarding Report of A.E.F. Superior Board on Organization and Tactics) to Secretary of War, General Headquarters, A.E.F., 16 June 1920; Fox Conner, letter to Major Malin Craig (concerning division organization), 24 April 1920, copy in U.S. Army Military History Institute.

55. The primary sources for this discussion of the triangular division development are Kent R. Greenfield, Robert R. Palmer, and Bell I. Wiley, The Army Ground Forces: The Organization of Ground Combat Forces. United States Army in World War II (Washington, 1947), 271-78; Harry C. Ingles, "The New Division," Infantry Journal 46 (1939): 521-29; Janice E. McKenney, Field Artillery Army Lineage Series (Washington, 1980), 255-61; U.S. Army, Headquarters 2d Division, "Special Report Based on Field Service Test of the Provisional 2d Division, conducted by the 2d Division, U.S. Army, 1939," National Archives File 52-83.

56. Ernest F. Fisher, Jr., Weapons and Equipment Evolution and its Influence Upon Organization and Tactics in the American Army From 1775-1963 (Washington, 1963), 61-67, 77.

57. Blanche D. Coll, Jean E. Keith, and Herbert H. Rosenthal, The Technical Services: The Corps of Engineers: Troops and Equipment. United States Army in World War II (Washington, 1958), 10-20; Paul W. Thompson, Engineers in Battle (Harrisburg, PA, 1942).

58. On the development of fire direction centers, see McKenney, Field Artillery, 266-73; Riley Sunderland, "Massed Fires and the F.D.C.," Army 8 (1958): 56-59.

59. The primary sources for this discussion of U.S. armor between the wars are Timothy K. Nenninger, "The Development of American Armor, 1917-1940" (M.A. Thesis, University of Wisconsin, 1968), 55-188; James M. Snyder (ed.), History of the Armored Force, Command, and Center, Army Ground Forces Study No. 27 (Washington, 1946), 1-17; Mildred H. Gillie, Forging the Thunderbolt: A History of the Development of the Armored Force (Harrisburg, PA, 1947), 37-178.
60. Coll et al., Engineers, 17.
61. Frank D. Lackland, "Attack Aviation," student paper written at the Command and General Staff School (Ft. Leavenworth, KS, 1931); U.S. War Department, General Staff, FM 100-5: Tentative Field Service Regulations-Operations (Washington, 1939), 22. See also Brereton Greenhous, "Aircraft Versus Armor: Cambrai to Yom Kippur," in Timothy Travers and Christon Archer (eds.) Men at War: Politics, Technology and Innovation in the Twentieth Century (Chicago, 1982), 96.

CHAPTER FOUR ENDNOTES

1. This critique of the Polish campaign is based on Guderian, Panzer Leader, 65-82; Kennedy, Poland, 130-35; and Cooper and Lucas, Panzer, 25-28.
2. Kennedy, Poland, 61-62.
3. Cooper and Lucas, Panzer, 24, 27, 29.
4. Kennedy, Poland, 28-30 and 133; Guderian, Panzer Leader, 89.
5. Cooper and Lucas, Panzer, 27.
6. J. L. Moulton, A Study of Warfare in Warfare in Three Dimensions: The Norwegian Campaign of 1940 (Athens, OH, 1967), especially 61-63.
7. James E. Mrazek, The Fall of Eben Emael (Washington, DC, 1971).
8. R. H. S. Stolfi, "Equipment for Victory in France in 1940," History: The Journal of the Historical Association, 55 (February 1970): 1-20.
9. Ibid.; Ferré, Le Défaut, 185-95.
10. Macksey, Tank Pioneers, 160-62.
11. Guderian, Panzer Leader, 98, 101-2.
12. I. S. O. Playfair, F. C. Flynn, C. J. C. Molony, and S. E. Toomer, The Mediterranean and Middle East: Vol. II: The Germans Come to the Help of Their Ally (1941). History of the Second World War (London, 1956), 175.
13. Ibid.; Ross, The Business of Tanks, 151.
14. This discussion of British developments after Dunkirk is derived largely from the following sources: Nigel Hamilton, Monty: The Making of a General, 1887-1942 (New York, 1981), 394-545; Martel, Our Armoured Forces (London, 1945), 75-181; English, Perspective, 155-63, 199-201; and on artillery, Bidwell and Graham, Fire-power, 230-34.
15. Hamilton, Monty, 459-60, 533-55.

16. Martel, Our Armoured Forces, 159-61.
17. Ibid., 379-80. The detailed organization is included in Great Britain, War Office letter number 20/GEN/6059 (S.D. 1), dated 1 October 1942, CARL N-6136.
18. Playfair et al., The Mediterranean and Middle East, Vol. I: The Early Successes Against Italy (to May 1941) (London, 1954), 261-68.
19. On equipment in North Africa, see Playfair et al., The Mediterranean and Middle East, Vol. II, 13-14, 173, 175, 341-45; Vol. III, 27-28; U.S. War Department, General Staff, Military Intelligence Service, Artillery in the Desert, Special Series No. 6 (25 November 1942), 2-30; Macksey, Afrika Korps (New York, 1968), 36, 39-41; J. A. I. Agar Hamilton and L. C. F. Turner, The Sidi Rezeg Battles, 1941 (Cape Town, S.A., 1957), 33-55.
20. U.S. War Department, General Staff, Military Intelligence Service, Special Bulletin No. 36: The Battle of Salum, June 15-17, 1941 (Washington, DC, 1941), 26.
21. Great Britain, Middle East Command, "Notes on Main Lessons of Recent Operations in the Western Desert," dated 10 August 1942. Typescript copy by U.S. War Department, General Staff, Military Intelligence Service, in CARL, N-3915; Playfair et al., The Mediterranean and Middle East, Vol. III, 213-14, 223-24, 254, 287.
22. Hamilton, Monty, 653-54, 680-81.
23. Ibid., 732-844.
24. A. Eremenko, The Arduous Beginning (Moscow, n.d.), 12-22; U.S. War Department, General Staff, Military Intelligence Division, Special Bulletin No. 2: "Soviet-Finnish War: Operations From November 30, 1939, to January 7, 1940" dated 10 January 1940, G2 document 2657-D-1054.
25. On Soviet reforms in 1940-41, see Erickson, Road to Stalingrad, 13-49; A. Yekimovskiy, "Tactics of the Soviet Army During the Great Patriotic War," Voyennyy vestnik, 1967, no. 4: 12.
26. Erickson, Road to Stalingrad, 32-34.
27. Guderian, Panzer Leader, 138; Cooper and Lucas, Panzer, 40-42.
28. Martin Van Creveld, Supplying War: Logistics from Wallenstein to Patton (New York, 1977), 160-80; Daniel R. Beaver, "Politics and Policy: The War Department Motorization and Standardization Program for Wheeled Transport Vehicles, 1920-1940," Military Affairs 47 (October 1983): 101; Guderian, Panzer Leader, 190.
29. The Soviet theory is summarized in N. Kobrin, "Encirclement Operations," Soviet Military Review, 1981, no. 8: 36-39.
30. Erickson, Road to Stalingrad, 173; V.D. Sokolovskiy (ed.), Soviet Military Strategy, 3d ed., translated by Harriet Fast Scott (New York, 1975), 163.

31. Erickson, 341, 358; A. Ryazanskiy, "Tactics of Tank Forces During the Great Patriotic War," Voyennyy vestnik, 1967, no. 5: 13-20; Sokolovskiy, Soviet Military Strategy, 165.

32. Stalin's Order No. 306, 8 October 1942, captured and translated by the German Army, retranslated by U.S. Army. Copy in CARL N-16582.256. E. Bolton, "Talks on the Soviet Art of War: 2, Strategic Defence, The Struggle to Capture the Initiative," Soviet Military Review, 1967, no. 6: 45.

33. Erickson, Road to Stalingrad, 442.

CHAPTER FIVE ENDNOTES

1. This discussion of McNair's concepts is based on Greenfield, Palmer, and Wiley, Organization of Ground Combat Forces, 271, 273, 185.

2. Ibid., 356-59.

3. Ibid., 307.

4. Ibid., 322-35; Snyder, History of the Armored Force, 29-43.

5. U.S. Army, European Theater of Operations, General Board, "Organization, Equipment, and Tactical Employment of the Armored Division," Study No. 48 (Washington, DC, n.d.), Appendix 1.

6. For an excellent nontechnical explanation of antitank design factors, see John Weeks, Men Against Tanks: A History of Anti-Tank Warfare (New York, 1975), 12-16.

7. Ibid., 100-2, 67-69; Green, Thomson, and Roots, Planning Munitions, 355-61.

8. Green, Thomson, and Roots, Planning Munitions, 388-90, 402-4; Baily, Faint Praise, 12-38.

9. U.S. Army, European Theater of Operations, General Board, "Organization, Equipment, and Tactical Employment of Tank Destroyer Units," Study No. 60. (Washington, DC, n.d.), 1-2, 10.

10. Pavel Rotmistrov, "Cooperation of Self-Propelled Artillery With Tanks and Infantry," Zhurnal brontetankovykh i mekhanizirovamykh voisk, 1945, no. 7: 8-13, translated by U.S. Department of the Army, G2, n.d.; K. Novitskiy, "Coordination Between Medium and Heavy Tanks in Offensive Combat," Tankist 1947, no. 9: 40-43, translated by U.S. Department of the Army, G2, n.d. Copies of both translations in Military History Institute.

11. Green, Thomson, and Roots, Planning Munitions, 246-56, 283-86; Cooper and Lucas, Panzer, 54 ff.

12. Richard M. Ogorkiewicz, Design and Development of Fighting Vehicles (Garden City, NY, 1968), 36.

13. Army Regulation 850-15, cited in Green, Thomson, and Roots, Planning Munitions, 278.

14. On the M4 Sherman, see ibid., 282-87 and 302-4; Baily, Faint Praise, iii, 7, 41-48.

15. Ross, Business of Tanks, 213, 263-300.

16. On Ultra and its limitations, see Ralph Bennett, _Ultra in the West: The Normandy Campaign, 1944-45_ (New York, 1979), 13-20; Patrick Beesly, _Very Special Intelligence: The Story of the Admiralty's Operational Intelligence Centre, 1939-1945_ (London, 1977), 63-65, 110-11.

17. F.H. Hinsley, E.E. Thomas, C.F.G. Ransom, and R.C. Knight, _British Intelligence In the Second World War: Its Influence on Strategy and Operations_, Vol. I (London, 1979), 144.

18. Ibid., Vol. II (London, 1981), 582-87, 739-46; 757-63.

19. Anthony Cave Brown, _Bodyguard of Lies_ (New York, 1975), 102-4.

20. Hinsley et al., _British Intelligence_, Vol. I, 148; Hamilton, _Monty_, Vol I, 777; see also Aileen Clayton, _The Enemy Is Listening_ (London, 1980); H.W. Everett, "The Secret War In the Desert," _British Army Review_ 60 (December 1978): 66-68.

21. Dulany Terrett, _The Signal Corps: The Emergency (To December 1941)_, United States Army in World War II (Washington, DC, 1956), 118-20, 141-47, 178-85.

22. Eisenhower letter to the General Board, 4 October 1945, reproduced in U.S. Army, European Theater of Operations, The General Board, "Army Tactical Information Service," Study No. 18 (Washington, DC, n.d.), appendix.

23. Vasili I. Chuikov, _The Fall of Berlin_, translated by Ruth Kisch (New York, 1968), 30-33.

24. See, for example, S. Alferov, "Wartime Experience: Breakthrough of Enemy Defenses by a Rifle Corps," _Voyenno-istoricheskiy zhurnal_, 1983, No. 3: 53-56.

25. David M. Glantz, _Autumn Storm_, Leavenworth Paper No. 7 (Ft. Leavenworth, KS, 1984).

26. On the development of forward detachments, see ibid., and N. Kireyev and N. Dovbenko, "From the Experience of the Employment of Forward Detachments of Tank (Mechanized) Corps," _Voyenno-istoricheskiy zhurnal_ 1982, no. 9: 20-27.

27. Earl F. Ziemke, _Stalingrad to Berlin: The German Defeat in the East_ (Washington, DC, 1968), 17.

28. Timothy A. Wray, _Standing Fast: German Defensive Doctrine on the Russian Front During the Second World War_ (MMAS Thesis, Ft. Leavenworth, KS, 1983), 162, 221-35.

29. Ibid., 227, 273; U.S. War Department, Technical Manual E 30-451, _Handbook On German Military Forces_, 15 Mar 1945 (Washington, DC, 1945), II-8, II-14.

30. Wray, _Standing Fast_, 275, 298-303.

31. Ibid.; Guderian, _Panzer Leader_, 290-91; 249-51.

32. Richard E. Simpkin, _Mechanized Infantry_ (Oxford, UK, 1980), 22.

33. TM E 30-451, II-46 to II-51, IV-9 to IV-13.

34. David M. Hazen, <u>Role of the Field Artillery in the Battle of Kasserine Pass</u> (MMAS thesis, Ft. Leavenworth, KS, 1973), 38-42, 77-79, 147, 174-75, 187; Snyder, <u>History of the Armored Force</u>, 17.
35. Samuel Milner, <u>Victory in Papua</u>, United States Army in World War II (Washington, DC, 1957), 92-95, 135, 375-76.
36. This account of combined arms problems in Normandy is based on Martin Blumenson, <u>Breakout and Pursuit</u>, United States Army in World War II (Washington, DC, 1961), 41-43, 208.
37. U.S. Army Armor School, "Armor in the Exploitation," Student Project (unpublished, 1949), 60-61; CARL N-2146.74.
38. Kent R. Greenfield, <u>Army Ground Forces and the Air-Ground Battle Team, Including Organic Light Aviation</u>, AGF Study No. 35 (Washington, DC, 1948), 47. Much of this discussion of U.S. close air support is derived from this brilliant analysis.
39. Ibid., 30, 43, 74.
40. Ibid., 49, 53.
41. Ibid., 58-67, 178-83, 87-92; U.S. Army, European Theater of Operations, General Board, "The Tactical Air Force in the European Theater of Operations," Study No. 54 (Washington, DC, 1946), 10, 15; Frederic C. Bergerson, <u>The Army Gets an Air Force</u> (Baltimore, MD, 1980), 29-37.
42. Playfair et al., <u>The Mediterranean and Middle East</u>, Vol. III, 71, 241.
43. Deichmann, <u>German Air Force</u>, 37-48.
44. On British air-ground cooperation, see Bidwell and Graham, <u>Fire-Power</u>, 185-87, 260-75; W.A. Jacobs, "Air Support for the British Army, 1939-1943," <u>Military Affairs</u> 46 (December 1982): 174-82; William Slim, <u>Defeat Into Victory</u> (New York, 1961), 260, 337-38, 346.
45. Headquarters, U.S. Army Forces, Far East, Japanese Research Division, <u>Japanese Night Combat</u> (Tokyo, 1955), Vol. I, 8-15.
46. Slim, <u>Defeat Into Victory</u>, 199, 337-38.
47. Ibid., 249, 260-2, 321, 376, 409.
48. James M. Gavin, <u>Airborne Warfare</u> (Washington, DC, 1947), 81.
49. U.S. Army, European Theater of Operations, General Board, "Organization, Equipment, and Tactical Employment of the Airborne Division," Study No. 16 (Washington, DC, 1946), 20, 29-30.
50. David M. Glantz, "Soviet Airborne Forces in Perspective" (unpublished, 1983), Chapter 2.
51. Jeter A. Isely and Philip A. Crowl, <u>The U.S. Marines and Amphibious War: Its Theory, and Its Practice in the Pacific</u> (Princton, NJ, 1951), 3-4, 36-39, 59, 233, 334.

201

1. A. Ryazanskiy, "Land Forces Podrazdeleniye Tactics in the Postwar Period," Voyenny vestnik, 1967 No. 8: 15.
2. John Erickson, "The Ground Forces in Soviet Military Policy," Strategic Review 4 (April 1976): 65.
3. Simpkin, Mechanized Infantry, 31; M.V. Zakharov (ed.), 50 Let Vooruzhennykh sil SSSR [50 Years of the Soviet Armed Forces] (Moscow, 1968), 483.
4. Erickson, "The Ground Forces," 66; David M. Glantz, "Soviet Offensive Military Doctrine Since 1945," Air University Review 34 (March-April 1983): 27.
5. U.S., Department of the Army, Assistant Chief of Staff for Intelligence, Intelligence Research Project No. A-1729, "Soviet Tank and Motorized Rifle Division" (Washington, DC, 1958).
6. S. Shtrik, "The Encirclement and Destruction of the Enemy During Combat Operations Not Involving the Use of Nuclear Weapons," Voyennaya mysl', 1968, No. 1: 279.
7. Glantz, "Soviet Offensive Military Doctrine," 29; Kireyev and Dovbenko, "Forward Detachments," 20-27; R.Y. Malinovskiy and O. Losik, "Wartime Operations: Maneuver of Armored and Mechanized Troops," Voyenno istoricheskiy zhurnal, 1980, no. 9: 18-25.
8. Quoted in Robert A. Doughty, The Evolution of U.S. Army Tactical Doctrine, 1946-76, Leavenworth Paper No. 1 (Fort Leavenworth, KS, 1979), 4; see also U.S. Army, European Theater of Operations, General Board, "Organization, Equipment, and Tactical Employment of Tank Destroyer Units," Study No. 60 (Washington, DC, n.d.), 27-29; "Types of Divisions-Postwar Army," Study No. 17 (Washington, DC, n.d.), 8.
9. "The New Infantry, Armored, and A/B Divisions," typed explanation and tables issued by Headquarters, U.S. Army Ground Forces, 24 January 1947, copy in CARL.
10. George S. Patton, 1945, quoted in Ney, Evolution, 114.
11. Comparison between Staff Officers' Field Manual 101-10 (Tentative), U.S. Army Command and General Staff School, with changes to 1943; "Armored Division" table in "The New Infantry, Armored and A/B Divisions;" and Greenfield et al., Organization, 320-21; see also U.S., Department of the Army, The Armored School, "Armored Division Organizational and Manning Charts, TO&E 17N," Instructional Pamphlet No. CS-2 (Fort Knox, KY, 1949), 1-2.
12. James F. Schnabel, Policy and Direction: The First Year, United States Army in the Korean War (Washington, DC, 1972), 54.
13. T.R. Fehrenbach, This Kind of War: Korea: A Study in Unpreparedness (New York, 1964), 126-51.

14. S.L.A. Marshall, <u>Commentary on Infantry Operations and Weapons Usage in Korea, Winter of 1950-51</u>, Operations Research Office Study ORO-R-13 (Chevy Chase, MD, 1951), 6-7.
15. Ibid., 128-31; Marshall, "CCF In the Attack (Part II)" Operations Research Office Study ORO-S-34 (EUSAK) (Tokyo, 1951), 7-18.
16. S.L.A. Marshall, <u>Operation Punch and the Capture of Hill 440, Suwon, Korea, February 1951</u>, Technical Memorandum ORO-T-190 (Baltimore, MD, 1952), 9-10, 43-44, 69.
17. Walter G. Hermes, <u>Truce Tent and Fighting Front</u>, United States Army in the Korean War (Washington, DC, 1966), 119-21.
18. S.L.A. Marshall, <u>Pork Chop Hill: The American Fighting Man in Action; Korea, Spring, 1953</u> (New York, 1956), 47, 196; Hermes, <u>Truce Tent</u>, 370-72.
19. Bergerson, <u>The Army Gets an Air Force</u>, 52; Hermes, <u>Truce Tent</u>, 325-28.
20. John R. Galvin, <u>Air Assault: The Development of Airmobile Warfare</u> (New York, 1969), 254-56.
21. Doughty, <u>Evolution</u>, 23.
22. This discussion of the Pentomic Division is derived from Theodore C. Mataxis and Seymour L. Goldberg, <u>Nuclear Tactics; Weapons, and Firepower in the Pentomic Division, Battle Group, and Company</u> (Harrisburg, PA; 1958), 103-112; John H. Cushman, "Pentomic Infantry Division in Combat," <u>Military Review</u> 37 (January 1958): 19-30; Letter, U.S. Continental Army Command, 8 January 1959, Subject: Changes in ROCID TOE (U), with supporting CGSC documentation; CARL, N-17935.62-U.
23. Letter, U.S. Continental Army Command, 13 January 1959, Subject: The Armored Cavalry Regiment (U), and Letter of Instruction, U.S. Army Command and General Staff College, 14 January 1959, Subject: DA approved Divisional Changes, with accompanying charts CARL N-17935.62-U.
24. Doughty, <u>Evolution</u>, 19-25; Ney, <u>Evolution</u>, 75.
25. Mataxis and Goldberg, <u>Nuclear Tactics</u>, 122; Galvin, <u>Air Assault</u>, 264.
26. Bergerson, <u>The Army Gets an Air Force</u>, 80-106; Hamilton H. Howze, "The Howze Board," <u>Army</u> Part I (February 1974), 12-14.
27. Howze, "The Howze Board," Part II (March 1974), 18-24, and Part III (April 1974), 18-24; Howze, "Tactical Employment of the Air Assault Division," <u>Army</u> (September 1963), 44-45, 52.
28. Galvin, <u>Air Assault</u>, 280-87, 293; John J. Tolson, <u>Airmobility, 1961-1971</u> (Washington, D.C., 1973), 51-59.
29. Tolson, <u>Airmobility</u>, 25-28.
30. Ibid., 32, 43-44; Bergerson, <u>The Army Gets an Air Force</u>, 119.

31. Dave R. Palmer, Summons of the Trumpet: U.S.-Vietnam in Perspective (San Rafael, CA, 1978), 98-102; Galvin, Air Assault, 294-95.

32. Tolson, Airmobility, 88, 102-4, 195, 201-2.

33. Ibid., 120.

34. This account of Lam Son 719 is based on U.S. Army, Headquarters, 101st Airborne Division (Airmobile), "Final Report-Airmobile Operations in Support of Operations Lam Son 719" (24 April 1971), Vol. I; CARL N-18430.56-A; Tolson, Air Assault, 236-52; Palmer, Summons, 238-43.

35. 101st Airborne Division, I-12, I-15.

36. Ibid., I-52.

37. Ibid., I-42 to I-43; Tolson, Airmobility, 251-52.

38. Simpkin, Mechanized Infantry, 25; Jean Marzloff, "The French Mechanized Brigade and its Foreign Counterparts," International Defense Review 6 (April 1973): 178; Terry Gander, Encyclopedia of the Modern British Army, 2d ed. (Cambridge, UK, 1982), 17-23, 89.

39. France, Ministère de la Guerre, École Superieure de Guerre, Études Opérations 1er Cycle, 1953-1954 (Paris 1953), Book I, Annex 3; Marzloff, "French Mechanized Brigade," 176-8; International Institute of Strategic Studies, "The Military Balance 1977-78," Air Force Magazine 60 (December 1977): 80-81; Philippe C. Peress, "The Combined Arms Battalion Concept in the French Army," unpublished student study project, U.S. Army Command and General Staff College, 1977, 1-41, CARL N-13423.472; Ecole Superieure de Guerre, "Memorandum on Nuclear Weapons," undated, 1976 translation No. K-6556 by U.S. Department of the Army, Assistant Chief of Staff for Intelligence, 17-8.

40. Peress, "Combined Arms Battalion," 1-41.

41. Marzloff, "French Mechanized Brigade," 177-78; Edgar D. Arendt, "Comparative Analysis of Contemporary Non-U.S. Army Small Infantry Unit Organizations" (Washington, DC, 1967), 17-22.

42. Moshe Dayan, Moshe Dayan: Story of My Life (New York, 1976), 45-49, 97-98, 100-20.

43. Moshe Dayan, Diary of the Sinai Campaign (New York, 1966), 34-5.

44. This account of Abu Agheila in 1956 is derived from S.L.A. Marshall, Sinai Victory (New York, 1967), 94-140; and Edward Luttwak and Dan Horowitz, The Israeli Army (New York, 1975), 148-49, 151.

45. Avraham Adan, On the Banks of the Suez (San Rafael, CA, 1980), 207-13.

46. Trevor N. Dupuy, Elusive Victory: The Arab-Israeli Wars, 1947-1974 (New York, 1978), 231, 612-13; Edgard O'Ballance, No Victor, No Vanquished: the Yom Kippur War (San Rafael, CA, 1978), 55.

47. Adan, Banks of the Suez, 57; Jac Weller, "Armor and Infantry in Israel," Military Review 57 (April, 1977): 3-11.
48. Adan, Banks of the Suez, 491-92.
49. Mohamed Heikal, The Road to Ramadan (New York, 1975), 14-43, 208, 240-41; Charles Wakebridge, "The Egyptian Staff Solution," Military Review, 55 (March 1975): 3-11; Chaim Herzog, The War of Atonement: October 1973 (Boston, 1975), 273; O'Ballance, No Victor, 115.
50. Adan, Banks of the Suez, 141; Herzog, War of Atonement, 194.
51. Herzog, War of Atonement, 84-113; 205.

CONCLUSION ENDNOTES

1. Howze, "The Howze Board," Part II, 23.

205

BIBLIOGRAPHY
UNPUBLISHED WORKS

Conner, Fox. Letter to Major Malin Craig concerning division organization, 24 April 1920. Copy in Military History Institute, UA 25 C65.

Fisher, Ernest F. Jr. "Weapons and Equipment Evolution and Its Influence Upon Organization and Tactics in the American Army from 1775-1963." Washington, DC: Office of the Chief of Military History, n.d.

France, Ministère de la Guerre. École Supérieure de Guerre. "Memorandum on Nuclear Weapons." Translated by direction of U. S. Department of the Army, Office of the Assistant Chief of Staff for Intelligence, No. K-6556, from undated original.

_____. "Urbanization: Its Consequences on Equipment and Composition of Army Units." Translated by direction of U. S. Department of the Army, Office of the Assistant Chief of Staff for Intelligence, No. K-5892, from 1974 original.

Glantz, David M. "Soviet Airborne Forces in Perspective." Typescript. Fort Leavenworth, KS: Combat Studies Institute, U. S. Army Command and General Staff College, 1983.

Great Britain. War Office. Letter 20/GEN/6059 (S.D. 1) concerning reorganization of divisions, dated 1 October 1942. CARL N-6136.

Great Britain. War Office. Middle East Command. "Notes on Main Lessons of Recent Operations In the Western Desert." Typescript dated 10 August 1942. Mimeographed reproduction by U. S. War Department General Staff, Military Intelligence Service. Washington, DC: War Department, 1942. CARL N-3915.

Lange, H. W. W. "The French Division-Concept of Organization and Operation." U. S. Department of the Army, Office of the Assistant Chief of Staff for Intelligence, Report No. 2137175, R-217-60, 16 March 1960. Typescript. CARL N-15835.18.

Marshall, Samuel L. A. "CCF In the Attack (Part II)." Typescript. Operations Research Office Report ORO-S-34 (EUSAK). Tokyo: Operations Research Office, 1951. CARL N-16454.59.

McKenney, Janice E. "Field Artillery Army Lineage Series." Typescript. Washington, DC: Center of Military History, 1980.

Peress, Philippe C. "The Combined Arms Battalion Concept in the French Army." Handwritten student study project, U. S. Army Command and General Staff College, 1977. CARL N-13423.472.

Pershing, John J. Wrapper Indorsement Forwarding Report of the A. E. F. Superior Board on Organization and Tactics, General Headquarters, American Expeditionary Force, Washington, DC, dated 16 June 1920. Copy in Military History Institute, UA 25 C65.

Reinhardt, Hellmuth (ed.) "Small Unit Tactics: Infantry, Part 1." Typescript. U. S. European Command German manuscript series No. P-060d, 10 November 1950. CARL N-17500.16-A.

United States. Department of the Army. European Command, Historical Division. "Small Unit Tactics, Artillery." Foreign Military Studies, Vol. 1, No. 7, 1952. German Manuscript series #P-060h. CARL R-17500.6-A.

United States. Department of the Army. General Staff. Assistant Chief of Staff for Intelligence (G2). "The Soviet Army: A Department of the Army Assessment, May 15, 1958." typescript.

United States. Department of the Army. 101st Airborne Division (Airmobile). "Final Report-Airmobile Operations In Support of Operation Lam Son 719, 8 February-6 April 1971." 2 vols. Mimeographed, Republic of Vietnam, 1971.

United States. Department of the Army. United States Continental Army Command. Letters of instruction on Pentomic division. "Changes in ROCID TOE (U)," dated 8 January 1959; "The Armored Division (U)," dated 13 January 1959, and "The Armored Cavalry Regiment (U)," dated 13 January 1959, with supporting documentation by U. S. Army Command and General Staff College. CARL N-17935.62-U.

United States. War Department. Army Ground Forces. "The New Inf, Armd, and A/B Divisions." Typescript explanation and tables, 24 January 1947. CARL N-15338-B.

United States. War Department. 1st Armored Division. "After Action Report, 1st Armd Div. 25 Jan-31 Dec 43." Typescript with maps. U. S. Army Armor School Library.

United States. War Department. General Staff. War College. "Provisional Manual of Tactics for Large Units." Typescript. Washington Barracks: Army War College, 1923-24.

United States. War Department. General Staff. Military Intelligence Division. Special Bulletin No. 2: "Soviet-Finnish War: Operations From November 30, 1939, to January 7, 1940." G2 document No. 2657-D-1054.

United States. War Department. 2d Division. "Special Report Based on Field Service Test of the Provisional 2d Division, conducted by the 2d Division, U. S. Army, 1939." Typescript. Copy in Military History Institute.

PUBLISHED DOCUMENTS

Adan, Avraham. On the Banks of the Suez: An Israeli General's Personal Account of the Yom Kippur War. San Rafael, CA: Presidio Press, 1980.

Addington, Larry H. The Blitzkrieg Era and the German Staff. 1865-1941. New Brunswick, NJ: Rutgers University Press, 1971.

Agar-Hamilton, J. A. I. and L. C. F. Turner. The Sidi Rezegh
    Battles, 1941. Union War Histories series. Cape Town, South
    Africa: Oxford University Press, 1957.
Alferov, S. "Wartime Experience: Breakthrough of Enemy Defenses
    by a Rifle Corps." USSR Report: Military Affairs, no. 1771
    (2 June 1983): 36-43. JPRS 83593. Translated by the
    Foreign Broadcast Information Service from the Russian
    article in Voyenno-istoricheskiy zhurnal [Military History
    Journal], March 1983.
Alfoldi, Lazlo M. "The Hutier Legend." Parameters, Journal of
    the U. S. Army War College 5 (June 1976): 69-74.
Allen, Robert S. Lucky Forward: The History of Patton's Third
    U.S. Army. New York: Vanguard Press, 1947.
Altham, E. A. The Principles of War Historically Illustrated.
    Vol I. London: MacMillan and Company, Ltd., 1914.
Altmayer, René. Études de Tactique Générale. 2d ed. Paris:
    Charles-Lavauzelle, 1937.
Anthérieu, Étienne. Grandeur et Sacrifice de la Ligne Maginot.
    Paris: Durassie et Cie., 1962.
Ardant du Picq, Charles Jean. Battle Studies: Ancient and
    Modern Battle. Translated by John N. Greely and Robert C.
    Cotton. Harrisburg, PA: Military Service Publishing Co.,
    1958.
Arendt, Edgar D. "Comparative Analysis of Contemporary Non-U. S.
    Army Small Infantry Unit Organizations (U)." Washington,
    DC: Booz-Allen Applied Research, Inc., 1 September 1967.
    Report No. DA-04-495-AMC-845 (X) for U. S. Army Combat
    Developments Command, Infantry Agency, Fort Benning, GA.
    CARL N-18760.57.
Army League, Great Britain. The Army in the Nuclear Age: Report
    of the Army League Sub-Committee. London: Saint Clements
    Press, Ltd., 1955.
_____. The British Army in the Nuclear Age. London: Army
    League, 1959.
Atkinson, C. T. The Seventh Division, 1914-1918. London: John
    Murray, 1927.
Baily, Charles Michael. "Faint Praise: The Development of
    American Tanks and Tank Destroyers During World War II."
    Ph.D. dissertation, Duke University, 1977.
Balck, Wilhelm von. Development of Tactics-World War.
    Translated by Harry Bell. Fort Leavenworth, KS: The General
    Service Schools Press, 1922.
Barnett, Correlli. The Desert Generals. 1st edition. New
    York: Viking Press, 1961.
Beaver, Daniel R. "Politics and Policy: The War Department
    Motorization and Standardization Program for Wheeled
    Transport Vehicles, 1920-1940." Military Affairs 47 (October
    1983): 101-8.

Becker, G. L'Infánterie d' Après-Guerre en France et en
    Allemagne. Édition de 1924, mise à jour et completée.
    Paris: Berger-Levrault, 1930.
Beesly, Patrick. Very Special Intelligence: The Story of the
    Admiralty's Operational Intelligence Centre, 1939-1945.
    London: Hamish Hamilton, 1977.
Belfield, Eversley. The Boer War. London: Leo Cooper, 1975.
Bell, Raymond E. "Division Cuirassée, 1940." Armor 83
    (January-February 1974): 25-29.
Bennett, Ralph. Ultra in the West: The Normandy Campaign,
    1944-45. New York: Charles Scribner's Sons, 1979.
Bergerson, Frederic A. The Army Gets an Air Force: Tactics of
    Insurgent Bureaucratic Politics. Baltimore, MD: Johns
    Hopkins University Press, 1980.
Bernhardi, Friedrich von. The War of the Future in the Light of
    the Lessons of the World War. Translated by F. A. Holt. New
    York: D. Appleton and Co., 1921.
Bidwell, Shelford and Dominick Graham. Fire-Power: British Army
    Weapons and Theories of War, 1904-1945. Boston: George
    Allen and Unwin, 1982.
Binkley, John C. "A History of U. S. Army Force Structuring."
    Military Review 57 (February 1977): 67-82.
Binoch, Jacques. "L'Allemagne et le lieutenant-colonel
    Charles de Gaulle." Révue Historique, 248 (July-September
    1972): 107-16.
Biriukov, Grigoriy F. and G. V. Melnikov. Tank Warfare.
    Mimeographed translation by U. S. Department of the Army,
    Office of the Assistant Chief of Staff for Intelligence, no.
    J-4398, from the Russian book, Bor'ba s Tankami. Moscow: no
    publisher, 1967.
Blumenson, Martin. Breakout and Pursuit. United States Army in
    World War II. Washington, DC: Office of the Chief of
    Military History, 1961.
_____. Kasserine Pass. Boston: Houghton Mifflin, 1967.
_____. (ed.) The Patton Papers. Vol. II: 1940-1945.
    Boston: Houghton Mifflin, 1974.
Bolton, E. "Talks on the Soviet Art of War." Soviet Military
    Review 1967, No. 2: 46-48; No. 6: 42-45; No. 10: 26-29;
    No. 11: 45-48.

Bond, Brian. British Military Policy Between the Two World
    Wars, Oxford, UK: Clarendon Press, 1980.
_____. Liddell Hart: A Study of His Military Thought. New Brunswick, NJ:
    Rutgers University Press, 1977.
Bonnal, G. A. B. E. Henri. La premiere bataille; le service de deux ans;
    Du caractere chez les chefs; Discipline-Armee nationale; Cavalerie.
    Paris: R. Chapelot et Cie., 1908.
Braun, _____. "German and French Principles of Tank Employment."
    Typescript translation by F. W. Merten, U. S. War Department, General
    Staff, War College Division, January 1938. From the German article in
    Militar-Wochenblatt, 22 October 1937.

210

Brindel, _____. "La Nouvelle Organisation Militaire," Révue des Deux Mondes, 7th Series, Vol. 51 (1929): 481-501.

Brodie, Bernard and Fawn M. Brodie. From Crossbow to H-Bomb. Revd. and Enl.ed. Bloomington, IN: Indiana University Press, 1973.

Browne, D. G. The Tank in Action. Edinburgh: William Blackwood and Sons, 1920.

Bruckmüller, Georg. The German Artillery in the Break-through Battles of the World War. 2d ed. Translated by J. H. Wallace and H. D. Kehm, U. S. Army, n.d., from the German book published Berlin: E. S. Mittler and Son, 1922.

Burgess, H. Duties of Engineer Troops in a General Engagement of a Mixed Force. Occasional Papers No. 32, U. S. Army Engineer School. Washington, DC: Press of the Engineer School, 1908.

Caemmerer, Rudolf von. The Development of Strategical Science During the 19th Century. Translated by Karl von Donat. London: Hugh Rees, Ltd., 1905.

Caidin, Martin. The Tigers are Burning. New York: Hawthorn Books, 1974.

Camut, _____. L'Emploi des Troupes du Génie en Liaison Avec les Autres Armes. Paris: Librairie Militaire R. Chapelot, 1910.

Callahan, Raymond. Burma, 1942-1945. The Politics and Strategy of the Second World War. Newark, DE: University of Delaware Press, 1978.

Carver, Richard M. The Apostles of Mobility. New York: Holmes and Meier Publishers, 1979.

Cave Brown, Anthony. Bodyguard of Lies. New York: Harper and Row, 1975.

Chandler, David G. The Campaigns of Napoleon. New York: The Macmillan Co., 1966.

Cherniavskiy, M. "Experience in the Action of Tanks in the East Prussian Operation." Mimeographed translation by U. S. Department of the Army, Office of the Assistant Chief of Staff for Intelligence, no. F-6606A, from the Russian article in Zhurnal bronetankovkh i mekhanizirovannykh voisk [Journal of Armored and Mechanized Forces], 1945.

Chuikov, Vasili I. The Fall of Berlin. Translated by Ruth Kisch. New York: Holt, Rinehart and Winston, 1968.

Clark, Alan. The Donkeys. New York: William Morrow and Co., 1962.

Clarke, Jeffrey J. "Military Technology in Republican France: the Evolution of the French Armored Force, 1917-1940." Ph.D. dissertation, Duke University, 1969.

Clayton, Aileen. The Enemy Is Listening. London: Hutchinson & Co., Ltd., 1980.

Cole, Hugh M. The Ardennes: Battle of the Bulge. United States Army in World War II. Washington, DC: Office of the Chief of Military History, 1965.

_____. The Lorraine Campaign. United States Army in World War II. Washington, DC: Historical Division, U. S. Army, 1950.

Coll, Blanche D., Jean E. Keith, and Herbert H. Rosenthal. The Technical Services: The Corps of Engineers: Troops and Equipment. United States Army in World War II. Washington, DC: Office of the Chief of Military History, 1958.

Comparato, Frank E. Age of Great Guns: Cannon Kings and Cannoneers Who Forged the Firepower of Artillery. Harrisburg, PA: Stackpole, 1965.

Conan Doyle, Arthur. The British Campaign in France and Flanders, 1915. London: Hodder and Stoughton, 1917.

Contamine, Henry. La Revanche 1871-1914. Paris: Berger-Levrault, 1957.

Cooper, Bryan. The Battle of Cambrai. New York: Stein and Day, 1968.

Cooper, Matthew and James Lucas. Panzer: The Armoured Force of the Third Reich. New York: St. Martin's Press, 1976.

Court, Geoffrey D. W. Hard Pounding, the Tactics and Technique of Antitank Warfare with Observations on its past, present, and future. Washington, DC: U. S. Field Artillery Association, 1946.

Craig, Gordon A. The Battle of Königgrätz: Prussia's Victory over Austria, 1866. Philadelphia: J. B. Lippincott, 1964.

Crozier, Brian. De Gaulle. New York: Charles Scribner's Sons, 1973.

Culmann, F. Tactique Générale d'après l'Experience de la Grande Guerre. 4th Revd. ed. Paris: Charles-Lavauzelle et Cie., 1924.

Cushman, John H. "Pentomic Infantry Division in Combat." Military Review 37 (January 1958): 19-30.

Deichmann, Paul. German Air Force Operations In Support of the Army. U. S. A.F. Historical Studies No. 163. Maxwell Air Force Base, AL: U. S. A. F. Historical Division, Research Studies Institute, 1962.

Dayan, Moshe. Diary of the Sinai Campaign. New York: Harper and Row, 1966.

_____. Moshe Dayan: Story of My Life. New York: William Morrow and Co., Inc., 1976.

Deygas, F. J. Les Chars d'Assaut: Leur Passé, Leur avenir. Paris: Charles Lavauzelle et Cie., 1937.

Doughty, Robert A. "The Enigma of French Armored Doctrine, 1940." Armor 83 (September-October 1974): 39-44.

_____. The Evolution of U. S. Army Tactical Doctrine, 1946-76. Leavenworth Papers No. 1. Fort Leavenworth, KS: Combat Studies Institute, U. S. Army Command and General Staff College, 1979.

Drea, Edward J. Nomonhan: Japanese-Soviet Tactical Combat, 1939. Leavenworth Papers No. 2. Fort Leavenworth, KS: Combat Studies Institute, U. S. Army Command and General Staff College, 1981.

Dremov, I. "The Forcing of a River Line By a Mechanized Brigade
(from Combat Experience)." Mimeographed translation by U. S.
Department of the Army, Office of the Assistant Chief of
Staff for Intelligence, no. E-6585A, from the Russian
article in Zhurnal bronetankovykh i mekhanizirovannykh voisk
[Journal of Armored and Mechanized Forces], 1946, no. 7: 4-8.
Dupuy, Trevor N. Elusive Victory: The Arab-Israeli Wars,
1947-1974. New York: Harper and Row, 1978.
Dutil, L. Les Chars d'Assaut: Leur Création et Leur rôle
Pendant la Guerre,1915-1918. Paris: Berger-Levrault, 1919.
Edmunds, James E. and Archibald F. Becke. History of the Great
War: Military Operations France and Belgium, 1914. Vol. 1,
3d ed. London: Macmillan and Co., 1933.
Edmunds, James E. and Graeme C. Wynne. History of the Great
War: Military Operations France and Belgium, 1915. London:
Macmillan and Co., 1927.
Ellis, L. F., G. R. G. Allen, A. E. Warhurst, and James Robb.
Victory in the West, Vol. I: The Battle of Normandy.
History of the Second World War. London: Her Majesty's
Stationery Office, 1962.
Ellis, L. F. and A. E. Warhurst. Victory in the West, Vol. II:
The Defeat of Germany. History of the Second World War.
London: Her Majesty's Stationery Office, 1968.
Ellis, William D. and Thomas J. Cunningham, Jr. Clarke of St.
Vith: The Sergeants' General. Cleveland, OH:
Dillon/Liderbach, 1974.
English, John A. A Perspective On Infantry. New York: Praeger,
1981.
Eremenko, Andrei. The Arduous Beginning. Translated by Vic
Schneierson. Moscow: Progress Publishers, [1966].
Erickson, John. "The Ground Forces in Soviet Military Policy."
Strategic Review 4 (April 1976): 64-79.
_____. The Road to Berlin: Continuing the History of Stalin's
War with Germany. Boulder, CO: Westview Press, 1983.
_____. The Road to Stalingrad: Stalin's War with Germany,
Volume 1. New York: Harper and Row, 1975.
_____. "Soviet Combined-Arms: Theory and Practice."
Typescript. Edinburgh, UK: University of Edinburgh, 1979.
_____. The Soviet High Command: A Military-Political History,
1918-1941. New York: St. Martin's Press, 1962.
_____. Soviet Military Power. London: Royal United Service
Institute for Defense Studies, 1971.
Ernest, N. "Self-Propelled Artillery in Offensive Combat by the
Combined Arms." Mimeographed translation by U. S. Department
of the Army, Office of the Assistant Chief of Staff for
Intelligence, no. F-6592, from the Russian article in Voennyy
vestnik [Military Herald], 1945, no. 22.
Essame, Hubert. The Battle for Europe, 1918. New York: Charles
Scribner's Sons, 1972.

Estienne, Jean-Baptiste Eugène. Conférence Faite le 15 Février 1920 sur Les Chars d'Assaut: Historique Technique-Historique Tactique-Vues d'avenir. Paris: Librairie de L'Enseignement Technique, 1920.

Everett, H. W. "The Secret War in the Desert." British Army Review 60 (December 1978): 66-68.

Falls, Cyril. Armageddon: 1918. Philadelphia: J. B. Lippincott Co., 1964.

_____. The Battle of Caporetto. Philadelphia: J. B. Lippincott Co., 1966.

Farrar-Hockley, Anthony. Goughie: The Life of General Sir Hubert Gough, CGB, GCMG, KCVC. London: Hart-Davis, MacGibbon, 1975.

Fehrenbach, T. R. This Kind of War: Korea, A Study in Unpreparedness. New York: Pocket Books, 1964.

Ferré, Georges. Le Défaut de l'Armure. Paris: Charles-Lavauzelle, 1948.

Foch, Ferdinand. The Memoirs of Marshal Foch. Translated by T. Bentley Mott. London: William Heinemann, Ltd., 1931.

_____. Des Principes de la guerre: Conférences faites en 1900 à l'École superieure de guerre. 4th ed. Paris: Berger-Levrault, 1917.

France. Ministère de la Défense. Etat-Major de l'Armée de l'Air. Le Haut Commandement français face au progrès technique entre les deux guerres. Vincennes: Service Historique de l'Armée de l'Air, 1980.

France. Ministère de la guerre. Décret du 2 decembre 1904 Portant Réglement sur les manoeuvres de l'infanterie. Paris: Charles Lavauzelle, 1909.

_____. Décret du 28 octobre 1913 portant réglement sur la conduit des grandes unités. Paris: Berger-Levrault, 1913.

_____. Décret du 28 octobre 1913 portant réglement sur la service des armées en campagne. Paris: Librairie Chapelot, 1914.

_____. Instruction du 28 décembre 1917 sur Liaison pour les Troupes de Toutes Armes. with changes 1-3 and Annex dated 5 July 1919. Paris: Charles-Lavauzelle et cie., 1921.

_____. Instructions for the Tactical Employment of Large Units, 1937 [sic. 1936]. Typescript translation by Richard U. Nicholas, U. S. Army, n.d.

_____. Instruction sur l'Emploi tactique des Grandes Unités, 1936. Paris: Charles-Lavauzelle, 1940.

_____. Instruction Provisoire sur l'Emploi tactique des Grandes Unités, 1921. Paris: Charles-Lavauzelle, 1922.

_____. Provisional Field Service Regulations, French Army, Annex No. 1 to Provisional Instructions for the Employment of Large Units. 1924. Translated by U. S. Army, General Service Schools. Fort Leavenworth, KS: General Service Schools Press, 1924.

_____. Réglement des Unités de Chars légers. 2 vols. Paris: Charles-Lavauzelle, 1930, and Imprimerie-Librairie Militaire Universelle L. Fournier, n.d.

France. Ministère de la Guerre. Ecole Superieure de Guerre. Études Operations ler Cycle, 1953-1954. Mimeographed. Paris: Ecole Superieure de Guerre, 1953.

_____. Tactique Générale. Rambouillet, FR: Pierre Leroy, 1922.

France. Ministère de la Guerre. Direction de la Cavalerie. Instruction Provisoire sur l'Emploi et la Manoeuvre des Unités d'Autos-Mitrailleuses de Cavalerie. Vol. 1. Paris: Charles-Lavauzelle, 1921.

France. Ministère de la Guerre. Etat-Major de l'Armée. Instruction Provisoire sur l'Emploi des Chars de Combat comme Engins d'Infanterie, 23 March 1920. Paris: Charles-Lavauzelle, 1920.

_____. Instruction sur l'Emploi des Chars de Combat. Paris: Charles-Lavauzelle, 1930.

France. Ministère de la Guerre. Etat-Major de l'Armée. Service Historique. Les Armées Françaises dans la Grande Guerre, Vol. 1, 2d ed. Paris: Imprimerie Nationale, 1936.

Fuller, John F. C. Armament and History: A Study of the Influence of Armament on History from the Dawn of Classical Warfare to the Second World War. New York: Charles Scribner's Sons, 1945.

_____. Armored Warfare: An Annotated Edition of Lectures on F. S. R. III (Operations Between Mechanized Forces). Harrisburg, PA: Military Service Publishing Co., 1943.

_____. The Foundations of the Science of War. London: Hutchinson and Co., 1925.

_____. Memoirs of an Unconventional Soldier. London: Ivor Nicholson & Watson, 1936.

_____. On Future Warfare. London: Sifton Praed & Co., Ltd., 1928.

Galvin, John R. Air Assault: The Development of Airmobile Warfare. New York: Hawthorn Books, Inc., 1969.

Gamelin, Maurice G. Servir. 3 Vols. Paris: Librairie Plon, 1946-47.

Gander, Terry, Encyclopaedia of the Modern British Army. 2d ed. Cambridge, UK: Patrick Stephens, 1982.

Gastilovich, A. "Experience in Offensive Actions in Mountainous Terrain." Mimeographed translation by U. S. Department of the Army, Office of the Assistant Chief of Staff for Intelligence, No. F-6088B, from the Russian article in Voyennaya mysl', 1946, No. 6.

Gaulle, Charles de. Vers l'Armée du Métier. Paris: presses Pocket, 1963.

Gavin, James M. Airborne Warfare. Washington, DC: Infantry Journal Press, 1947.

le Général J. B. Estienne, Père des Chars. Paris: Imprimerie Union, n.d.

Germany. Federal Republic. TF 59: Truppenfuhrung 1959.
Translated as Operations Manual of the Federal German Army by
Headquarters, U. S. Military Assistance Advisory Group, 1961.

Germany. Federal Republic, Federal Ministry for Defense. Army
Regulation 100/100: Command and Control in Battle. Weimar,
BRD: Federal Office of Languages, 1973.

Germany. [Weimar] Ministry of National Defense. Truppenamt.
Command and Combat of the Combined Arms, 1921. Translated by
U. S. Army General Service Schools. Fort Leavenworth, KS:
General Service Schools Press, 1925.

Gilbert, Gerald. The Evolution of Tactics. London: Hugh Rees,
Ltd., 1907.

Gillie, Mildred H. Forging the Thunderbolt: A History of the
Development of the Armored Force. Harrisburg, PA: Military
Service Publishing, 1947.

Glantz, David M. "Soviet Offensive Military Doctrine Since
1945." Air University Review 34 (March-April 1983): 24-35.

_____. "Soviet Operational Formation for Battle: A
Perspective." Military Review 63 (February 1983): 2-12.

Grandmaison, Louis L. de. Deux Conférences faites aux officiers
de l'Etat-major de l'armée, février 1911. La notion de
sûreté et l'engagement des grandes unités. Paris:
Berger-Levrault, 1912.

_____. Dressage de l'Infanterie en vue du combat offensif. 2d
ed. Paris: Berger-Levrault, 1906.

Graham, Dominick. "Sans Doctrine: British Army Tactics in the
First World War." in Timothy Travers and Christian Archer
(eds.) Men at War: Politics, Technology and Innovation in
the Twentieth Century. Chicago: Precedent Publishers, 1982.

Great Britain. War Office. Field Service Regulations 1923-24
(Provisional). 2 Vols. London: His Majesty's Stationery
Office, 1923-24.

_____. Field Service Regulations, Vol. II: Operations (1929).
London: His Majesty's Stationery Office, 1929.

_____. Field Service Regulations, Vol. II: Operations-General
(1935). London: His Majesty's Stationery Office, 1935.

_____. Field Service Regulations, Vol. III: Operations-Higher
Formations (1935). London: His Majesty's Stationery Office,
1936.

_____. Infantry Training: Vol. II: War (1926). London: His
Majesty's
Stationery Office, 1926.

_____. Infantry Training: Vol. II: War (1931). London: His
Majesty's Stationery Office, 1931.

_____. Instruction for the Training of Divisions for Offensive
Action. Reprinted and edited by U. S. Army War College.
Washington, DC: Government Printing Office, 1917.

_____. Tank and Armoured Car Training: Vol. II-War (1927)
Provisional. London: His Majesty's Stationery Office, 1927.

_____. Report of the Committee on the Lessons of the Great War.
London: War Office, 1932.

Great Britain. War Office. 1st Army. "German Methods of Trench
Warfare." 1 March 1916. London: War Office, 1916.

Great Britain. War Office. General Staff. "German Armoured
Tactics in Libya," in "Periodic Notes on the German Army."
London: His Majesty's Stationery Office, 1942.

_____. SS. 210. "The Division in Defence." London: His
Majesty's Stationery Office, 1918.

_____. German Army Handbook April, 1918. reprinted. London:
Arms & Armour Press, 1977.

_____. SS. 135. "The Training and Employment of Divisions,
1918." Revd. ed. London: His Majesty's Stationery Office,
1918.

Green, Constance M., Harry C. Thomson, and Peter C. Roots. The
Technical Services: The Ordnance Department: Planning
Munitions for War. United States Army in World War II.
Washington, DC: Office of the Chief of Military History,
1955.

Greenfield, Kent Roberts. Army Ground Forces and the Air-Ground
Battle Team, Including Organic Light Aviation. Army Ground
Forces Study No. 35. Washington, DC: Historical Section,
Army Ground Forces, 1948.

Greenfield, Kent R., Robert R. Palmer, and Bell I. Wiley. The
Organization of Ground Combat Troops. United States Army in
World War II. Washington, DC: Historical Division,
Department of the Army, 1947.

Greenhous, Brereton. "Aircraft versus Armor: Cambrai to Yom
Kippur," in Timothy Travers and Christon Archer (eds.) Men
at War: Politics, Technology, and Innovation in the
Twentieth Century. Chicago, IL: Precedent Publishers, 1982.

_____. "Evolution of a Close Ground-Support Role for Aircraft in
World War I." Military Affairs 39 (February 1975): 22-28.

Greer, Thomas H. The Development of Air Doctrine in the Army Air
Arm, 1917-1941. U. S. A. F. Historical Studies No. 189.
Reprinted Manhattan, KS: Aerospace Historian, n.d.

Guderian, Heinz. "Armored Forces." The Infantry Journal 44
(September-October, November-December 1937): 418-21, 522-8.

_____. Panzer Leader. Translated by Constantine Fitzgibbon.
New York: E. P. Dutton and Co., Inc., 1952.

Hamilton, Nigel. Monty: The Making of a General, 1887-1942.
New York: McGraw-Hill Book Co., 1981.

Hay, Ian. Arms and the Men. The Second World War, 1939-1945: A
Short Military History Series. London: Her Majesty's
Stationery Office, 1977.

Hazen, David W. "Role of the Field Artillery in the Battle of
Kasserine Pass." M.M.A.S. thesis, U. S. Army Command and
General Staff College, 1973.

Heikal, Mohamed. The Road to Ramadan. London: William Collins
& Co., Ltd., 1975.

Hermes, Walter G. _Truce Tent and Fighting Front_. United States Army in the Korean War. Washington, DC: Office of the Chief of Military History, 1966.

Herzog, Chaim. _The Arab-Israeli Wars: War and Peace in the Middle East_. New York: Random House, 1982.

_____. _The War of Atonement: October, 1973_. Boston: Little, Brown & Co., 1975.

Hinsley, F. H., E. E. Thomas, C. F. G. Ransom, and R. C. Knight. _British Intelligence in the Second World War: Its Influence on Strategy and Operations_. 2 Vols. London: Her Majesty's Stationery Office, 1979, and New York: Cambridge University Press, 1981.

Hogg, Ian V. _Barrage: The Guns in Action_. Ballentine's Illustrated History of World War II, Weapons Book No. 18. New York: Ballentine Books, 1970.

_____. _The Guns, 1914-18_. Ballentine's Illustrated History of the Violent Century, Weapons Book No. 27. New York: Ballentine Books, 1971.

Horne, Alistair. _To Lose a Battle: France, 1940_. Boston: Little, Brown, & Co., 1969.

House, Jonathan M. "The Decisive Attack: A New Look at French Infantry Tactics on the Eve of World War I." _Military Affairs_ 40 (December 1976): 164-69.

Howard, Michael E. _The Franco-Prussian War_. New York: Collier Books, 1969.

_____. (ed.) _The Theory and Practice of War: Essays Presented to Captain B. H. Liddell Hart on his Seventieth Birthday_. London: Cassell, 1965.

Howze, Hamilton H. "The Howze Board." _Army_ Magazine 24 (February, March, April 1974): 8-14, 18-24, 18-24.

_____. "Tactical Employment of the Air Assault Division." _Army_ Magazine 13 (September 1963): 36-53.

Hughes, Judith M. _To the Maginot Line: The Politics of French Military Preparations in the 1920s_. Cambridge, MA: Harvard University Press, 1971.

Hurley, Alfred F. _Billy Mitchell: Crusader for Air Power_. 2d ed. Bloomington, IN: Indiana University Press, 1975).

Ingles, Harry C. "The New Division." _Infantry Journal_ 46 (November-December 1939): 521-29.

International Institute for Strategic Studies. "The Military Balance 1977/78." _Air Force_ 60 (December 1977): 59-126.

Isely, Jeter A. and Philip A. Crowl. _The U. S. Marines and Amphibious War: Its Theory, and its Practice in the Pacific_. Princeton, NJ: Princeton University Press, 1951.

Jackson, Robert. _Air War Over France, May-June 1940_. London: Ian Allan Ltd., 1974.

Jacobs, W. A. "Air Support for the British Army, 1939-1943." _Military Affairs_ 46 (December 1982): 174-82.

Jacomet, Robert. _L'Armement de la France, 1936-1939_. Paris: Editions LaJeunesse, 1945.

Kauffmann, Kurt. The German Tank Platoon: Its Training and
    Employment In Battle. 2d ed. Panzer Kampfwagenbuch.
    Berlin: Verlag Offene Worte, n.d. Mimeographed translation
    by U. S. Army, Headquarters Armored Force, from the German.
Kennedy, Robert M. The German Campaign in Poland (1939).
    Department of the Army Pamphlet 20-255. Washington, DC:
    Office of the Chief of Military History, 1956.
Kireyev, N. and N. Dovbenko. "From the Experience of the
    Employment of Forward Detachments of Tank (Mechanized)
    Corps." USSR Report: Military Affairs, No. 1736 (17 January
    1983), 25-35. Translated by the Foreign Broadcast
    Information Service from the Russian article in
    Voyenno-istoricheskiy zhurnal [Military History Journal]
    September 1982.
Klotz, Helmut. Les Leçons Militaires de la Guerre Civile en
    Espagne. 2d ed. Paris: by the author, 1937.
Klyuchkov, A. "The Tank Battalion in the forward Element."
    Mimeographed Translation by U. S. Department of the Army,
    Office of the Assistant Chief of Staff for Intelligence, No.
    F-6585B, from Zhurnal bronetankovykh i mekhanizirovannykh
    voisk [Journal of Armored and Mechanized Forces] 1946, No.
    7: 9-14.
Kobrin, N. "Encirclement Operations." Soviet Military Review,
    1981, No. 8: 36-39.
Lackland, Frank D. "Attack Aviation." U. S. Army Command and
    General Staff School Student Paper, 1931 reproduced in U. S.
    Army Command and General Staff College Reference Book 20-18,
    Selected Readings in Military History: Evolution of Combined
    Arms Warfare. Fort Leavenworth, KS: Combat Studies
    Institute, U. S. Army Command and General Staff College, 1983.
Lafitte, Raymond. 1'Artillerie d'Assaut de 1916 à 1918. Paris:
    Charles-Lavauzelle, 1921.
Leeb, Wilhelm von. Defense. Translated by Stefan T. Possony and
    Daniel Vilfroy. Harrisburg, PA: Military Service Publishing
    Co., 1943.
Lester, J. R. Tank Warfare. London: George Allen and Unwin,
    Ltd., 1943.
Lestringuez, Pierre. Sous 1'Armure: Les Chars d'Assaut Français
    Pendant La Guerre. Paris: La Renaissance du Livre, 1919.
Liddell Hart, Basil H. "French Military Ideas Before the First
    World War." in Martin Gilbert (ed.) A Century of Conflict.
    New York: Athenium, 1967.
_____. Foch: The Man of Orleans. London: Eyre and
    Spottiswoode, 1931.
_____. The German Generals Talk. New York: William Morrow &
    Co., 1948.
_____. The Ghost of Napoleon. New Haven, CT: Yale University
    Press, 1935.

_____. _History of the Second World War_. New York: G. P. Putnam's Sons, 1971.

List, Single (pseud.) _The Battle of Booby's Bluffs_. Washington, DC: U. S. Infantry Association, 1922.

Losik, C. A. _Stroitel'stvo i boevoe primenenie sovetskikh tankovykh voisk v gody velikoi otechestvennoi voiny_. [Construction and Combat Use of Soviet Tank Forces in the years of the Great Patriotic War] Moscow: Voennoe Izdatel'stvo, 1979. Portions translated by LTC David M. Glantz.

Lucas, Pascal Marie Henri. _l'Evolution des Idées Tactiques en France et en Allemagne Pendant la Guerre de 1914-1918_. 3d ed., revd. Paris: Berger-Levrault, 1932.

Luttwak, Edward and Dan Horowitz. _The Israeli Army_. New York: Harper and Row, 1975.

Macksey, Kenneth J. _Afrika Korps_. Ballentine's Illustrated History of the Violent Century, Campaign Book No. 1. New York: Ballentine Books, 1968.

_____. _Armoured Crusader: A Biography of Major-General Sir Percy Hobart_. London: Hutchinson & Co., 1967.

_____. _Guderian: Creator of the Blitzkrieg_. New York: Stein and Day, 1976.

_____. _Rommel: Battles and Campaigns_. London: Arms & Armour Press, 1979.

_____. _The Tank Pioneers_. London: Jane's Publishing, 1981.

_____. _Tank Warfare: A History of Tanks in Battle_. New York: Stein and Day, 1972.

Malinovskiy, R. Y. and O. Losik. "Wartime Operations: Maneuver of Armored and Mechanized Troops." _USSR Report: Military Affairs_, no. 1553 (29 December 1980), 18-26. JPRS 77064. Translated by the Foreign Broadcast Information Service from the Russian article in _Voyenno-istoricheskiy zhurnal_ [Military History Journal], September 1980.

Marshall, George C. _Memoirs of My Services In the World War, 1917-1918_. Boston: Houghton Mifflin Co., 1976.

Marshall, Samuel L. A. _Commentary on Infantry Operations and Weapons Usage in Korea, Winter of 1950-51_. Operational Research Office Report ORO-R-13. Chevy Chase, MD: Operations Research Office, 1951. CARL R-16454.151-2.

_____. _Operational Punch and the Capture of Hill 440, Suwon, Korea, February, 1951_. Operations Research Memorandum ORO-T-190. Chevy Chase, MD: Operations Research Office, 1952.

_____. _Pork Chop Hill: The American Fighting Man in Action: Korea, Spring, 1953_. New York: Morrow, 1956.

_____. _Sinai Victory_. New York: Morrow, 1967.

_____. _The River and the Gauntlet: Defeat of the Eighth Army by the Chinese Communist Forces November, 1950, in the Battle of the Chongchon River, Korea_. New York: Time Reading Program, 1962.

_____. World War I. New York: American Heritage Press, 1971.

Marshev, M. "Action of a tank platoon during combat in the depths of the enemy defenses." Mimeographed translation by U. S. Department of the Army, Office of the Assistant Chief of Staff for Intelligence, No. F-4488B, from the Russian article in Voyennyy vestnik [Military Herald] 1948, No. 23: 28-33.

Martel, Giffard LeQ. In the Wake of the Tank: The First Eighteen Years of Mechanization in the British Army. 2d ed. London: Sifton Praed & Co., Ltd., 1935.

_____. Our Armoured Forces. London: Faber and Faber, 1945.

_____. An Outspoken Soldier: His Views and Memoirs. London: Sifton Praed & Co., Ltd., 1949.

Martin, Michel L. Warriors to Managers: The French Military Establishment Since 1945. Chapel Hill, NC: University of North Carolina Press, 1981.

Marty-Lavauzelle, I. Les Manoeuvres du Bourbonnais en 1909. Paris: Charles-Lavauzelle, n.d.

_____. Les Manoeuvres de l'Ouest en 1912. Paris: Charles-Lavauzelle, 1913.

_____. Les Manoeuvres de Sud-Ouest en 1913. Paris: Charles-Lavauzelle, 1913.

Marzloff, Jean. "The French Mechanized Brigade and its foreign counter-parts." International Defense Review 6 (April 1973): 176-80.

Mataxis, Theodore C. and Seymour L. Goldberg. Nuclear Tactics, Weapons, and Firepower in the Pentomic Division, Battle Group, and Company. Harrisburg, PA: Military Service Publishing Company, 1958.

McCormick, Robert R. The Army of 1918. New York: Harcourt, Brace and Howe, 1920.

McKenna, Charles Douglas. "The Forgotten Reform: Field Maneuvers in the Development of the United States Army, 1902-1920." Ph.D. dissertation, Duke University, 1981.

Meller, R. "Federal Germany's Defense Potential, Part 1: The Armed Forces." International Defense Review 7 (April 1974): 167-74.

Messenger, Charles. The Blitzkrieg Story. New York: Charles Scribner's Sons, 1976.

_____. Trench Fighting 1914-18. Ballentine's Illustrated History of the Violent Century, Weapons Book No. 28. New York: Ballentine Books, 1972.

Milner, Samuel. Victory in Papua. United States Army in World War II. Washington, DC: Office of the Chief of Military History, 1957.

Monash, John. The Australian Victories in France in 1918. New York: E. P. Dutton and Co., n.d.

Moulton, J. L. A Study of Warfare In Three Dimensions: The Norwegian Campaign of 1940. Athens, OH: Ohio University Press, 1967.

Mrazek, James E. The Fall of Eben Emael. Washington, DC: Luce, 1971.

Négrier, François-Oscar de. "Quelques Enseignemen[t]s de la Guerre Sud-Africaine." Révue des Deux Mondes, 5th Series, Vol. 9 (1902): 721-67.

Nenninger, Timothy K. "The Development of American Armor, 1917-1940." M. A. thesis, The University of Wisconsin, 1968.

Ney, Virgil. Evolution of the U. S. Army Division 1939-1968. Combat Operations Research Group Memorandum M-365. Fort Belvoir, VA: U. S. Army Combat Developments Command, 1969.

Novitskiy, K. "Coordination Between Medium and Heavy Tanks in Offensive Combat." Mimeographed translation by U. S. Department of the Army. Office of the Assistant Chief of Staff for Intelligence, No. F-6602A, from the Russian article in Tankist 1947, No. 9: 40-43.

O'Ballance, Edgar. No Victor, No Vanquished: The Yom Kippur War. San Rafael, CA: Presidio Press, 1978.

_____. The Third Arab-Israeli War. Hamden, CT: Archon Books, 1972.

Ogorkiewicz, Richard M. Armoured Forces: A History of Armoured Forces and Their Vehicles. New York: Arco Publishing Co., 1970.

_____. Design and Development of Fighting Vehicles. Garden City, NY: Doubleday, 1968.

Osadchiy, N. "Cooperation of Tanks with Motorized Infantry." Mimeographed translation by U. S. Department of the Army, Office of the Assistant Chief of Staff for Intelligence, No. F-6585C, from the Russian article in Zhurnal brontetankovykh i mekhanizirovannvkh voisk [Journal of Armored and Mechanized Forces] 1946, No. 7: 15-17.

Palat, Barthélemy Edmond. "Les Manoeuvres du Languedoc en 1913." Révue des Deux Mondes, 6th Series, Vol. 17 (1913): 799-817.

Palmer, Dave Richard. Summons of the Trumpet: U. S.-Vietnam in Perspective. San Rafael, CA: Presidio Press, 1978.

Perré, Jean Paul. Batailles et Combats des Chars Francais: La Bataille Défensive Avril-Juillet 1918. Paris: Charles-Lavauzelle, 1940.

Perrett, Bryan. A History of Blitzkrieg. New York: Stein and Day, 1983.

Pershing, John J. My Experiences In the World War. 2 Vols. New York: Frederick A. Stokes Co., 1931.

Piekalkiewicz, Janusz. The Cavalry of World War II. New York: Stein and Day, 1980.

Playfair, I. S. O., G. M. S. Stitt, C. J. C. Molony, and S. E. Toomer. The Mediterranean and Middle East, Vol. I: The Early Successes Against Italy (to May 1941). History of the Second World War. London: Her Majesty's Stationery Office, 1954.

Playfair, I. S. O., F. C. Flynn, C. J. C. Molony, and S. E.
    Toomer. The Mediterranean and Middle East, Vol. II: The
    Germans Come to the Help of their Ally (1941). History of
    the Second World War. London: Her Majesty's Stationery
    Office, 1956.
Playfair, I. S. O., F. C. Flynn, C. J. C. Molony, and T. P.
    Gleave. The Mediterranean and Middle East, Vol. III:
    British Fortunes Reach Their Lowest Ebb. History of the
    Second World War. London: Her Majesty's Stationery Office,
    1960.
_____. The Mediterranean and Middle East, Vol. IV: The
    Destruction of the Axis Forces in Africa. History of the
    Second World War. London: Her Majesty's Stationery Office,
    1966.
Pratt, Edwin A. The Rise of Rail-Power in War and Conquest,
    1833-1914. Philadelphia: J. B. Lippincott, 1916.
Prussia, Kriegsministerium. Generalstabe des Feldheeres.
    Vorshriften für den Stellungskrieg für alle Waffen. Teil
    14: Der Angriff im Stellungskrieg. 1 January 1918.
    Berlin: Kriegsministerium, 1918.
Radzievsky, A. I. Tankovyi udar [Tank Blow]. Moscow: Voennoe
    Izdatel'stvo, 1977. Portions translated by LTC David M.
    Glantz.
Raney, George H. "Tank and Anti-Tank Activities of the German
    Army." Infantry Journal 31 (February 1927): 151-8.
Reznichenko, Vasiliy G. (ed.) Tactics. Mimeographed
    translation by U. S. Department of the Army, Office of the
    Assistant Chief of Staff for Intelligence, No. J-1731, from
    the Russian book, originally published Moscow: Military
    Publishing House, 1966.
Ritter, Gerhard. The Sword and the Scepter: the Problem of
    Militarism in Germany, Vol. 1: The Prussian Tradition,
    1740-1890. Translated by Heinz Norden. Coral Gables, FL:
    University of Miami Press, 1969.
Rommel, Erwin. Infantry Attacks. Translated by G. E. Kidde.
    Washington, DC: The Infantry Journal, 1944.
_____. The Rommel Papers. B. H. Liddell Hart, ed. Translated
    by Paul Findlay. New York: Harcourt, Brace & Co., 1953.
Ross, G. MacLeod. The Business of Tanks, 1933-1945. Infracombe,
    UK: Arthur H. Stockwell, Ltd., 1976.
Rotmistrov, Pavel. "Cooperation of Self-Propelled Artillery with
    Tanks and Infantry." Mimeographed translation by U. S.
    Department of the Army, Office of the Assistant Chief of
    Staff for Intelligence, No. F-6583B, from the Russian article
    in Zhurnal bronetankovykh i mekhanizirovannykh voisk [Journal
    of Armored and Mechanized Forces], 1945, No. 7: 8-13.
_____. "Tanks-The Decisive Power of the Attack." Mimeographed
    translation by U. S. Department of the Army, Office of the
    Assistant Chief of Staff for Intelligence, No. F-6089A, from
    the Russian article in Voyennaya mysl', 1946, No. 8.

Rochenbach, Samuel D. "Tanks." Mimeographed. Fort Meade, MD: U. S. Army Tank School, 1922.

Rowan-Robinson, H. Further Aspects of Mechanization. London: William Clowes and Sons, 1929.

Russia. War Department. Field Service Regulations, 27 April 1912. Translated by U. S. War Department, General Staff, War College Division. Typescript, n.d.

Ryan, Stephen. Pétain the Soldier. New York: A. S. Barnes & Co., 1969.

Ryazanskiy, A. "The Creation and Development of Tank Troop Tactics in the Pre-War Period." Mimeographed translation by U. S. Department of the Army, Office of the Assistant Chief of Staff for Intelligence, No. J-1376, 35-46, from the Russian article in Voyennyy vestnik [Military Herald], 1966, No. 11: 25-32.

_____. "Land Forces Podrazdeleniye Tactics in the Postwar Period." Mimeographed translation by U. S. Department of the Army, Office of the Assistant Chief of Staff for Intelligence, No. J-2745, from the Russian article in Voyennyy vestnik, 1967, No. 8: 15-20.

Scales, Robert H. Jr. "Artillery in Small Wars: The Evolution of British Artillery Doctrine, 1860-1914." Ph.D. dissertation, Duke University, 1976.

Schmidt, Paul Karl [Carell, Paul]. The Foxes of the Desert. Translated by Mervyn Savill. New York: E. P. Dutton & Co., 1961.

Schnabel, James F. Policy and Direction: The First Year. United States Army in the Korean War. Washington, DC: Office of the Chief of Military History, 1972.

Seaton, Albert. Stalin As Military Commander. New York: Praeger, 1976.

Serré, C. (Rapporteur). Rapport Fait au nom de la Commission Chargée d'Enquêter sur les événements Survenues en France de 1933 à 1945. 8 Vols. Paris: Imprimerie de l'Assemblée Nationale, 1947-51.

Sheppard, E. W. Tanks in the Next War. London: Geoffrey Bles, 1938.

Showalter, Dennis E. Railroads and Rifles: Soldiers, Technology, and the Unification of Germany. Hamden, CT: Archon Books, 1975.

Shtrik, S. "The Encirclement and Destruction of the Enemy During Combat Operations Not Involving the Use of Nuclear Weapons." Translated under contract for the Defense Intelligence Agency, No. FPD 0093/68, from the Russian article in Voyennaya mysl', 1968, No. 1: 279-92.

Simpkin, Richard E. Mechanized Infantry. Oxford, UK: Brassey's Publishers, Ltd., 1980.

_____. Tank Warfare: An Analysis of Soviet and NATO Tank Philosophy.
London: Brassey's Publishers, Ltd., 1979.

Slim, William. *Defeat Into Victory*. Shorter edition. New
    York: David McKay, 1961.

Smirnov, S. A. *Tactics: A Manual for the Military Schools of
    the Red Army*. 3d Revd. ed. Moscow: Soviet Military
    Publications Division, 1935. Transcript translation by
    Charles Berman, 1936, from the Russian original.

Smith, Bradley F. *The Shadow Warriors: O. S. S. and the Origins
    of the C. I. A.* New York: Basic Books, Inc., 1983.

Snyder, James M. (ed.) *History of the Armored Force, Command and
    Center*. U. S. Army Ground Forces Study No. 27. Washington,
    DC: Army Ground Forces Historical Section, 1946.

Sokolovsky, V. D. (ed.) *Soviet Military Strategy*. 3d ed.
    Translated and edited by Harriet Fast Scott. New York:
    Crane, Russak, & Co., 1975.

Steadham, Kenneth A. "A Comparative Look at Air-Ground Support
    Doctrine and Practice in World War II, with an appendix on
    Current Soviet Close Air Support Doctrine." Combat Studies
    Institute Report No. 2. Fort Leavenworth, KS: Combat
    Studies Institute, U. S. Army Command and General Staff
    College, 1982.

_____. "The Evolution of the Tank in the U. S. Army."
    Typescript. Combat Studies Institute Report No. 1. Fort
    Leavenworth, KS: Combat Studies Institute, U. S. Army
    Command and General Staff College, 1982.

Stolfi, R. H. S. "Equipment for Victory in France in 1940."
    History 55 (February 1970): 1-20.

Stone, Norman. *The Eastern Front, 1914-1917*. New York:
    Charles Scribner's Sons, 1975.

Strokov, Alesandr A. *Vooruzhennye Sily i Voennoe Iskusstvo v
    Pervoi Mirovoi Voine* [The Armed Forces and Military Art in
    the First World War.] Moscow: Voenizdat, 1974. Portions
    translated by LTC David M. Glantz.

Subbotin, A. "Concerning the Characteristics of the Direction of
    Present-Day Offensive Operations." Mimeographed Translation
    by U. S. Department of the Army, Office of the Assistant
    Chief of Staff for Intelligence, No. F-6123A, from the
    Russian article in *Voyennaya mysl'*, 1946, No. 6.

Sunderland, Riley. "Massed Fire and the FDC." *Army* 8 (May
    1958): 56-59.

Sweet, John J. T. *Iron Arm: The Mechanization of Mussolini's
    Army, 1920-1940*. Westport, CT: Greenwood Press, 1980.

Terraine, John. *To Win a War-1918, the Year of Victory*. Garden
    City, NY: Doubleday, 1981.

Terrett, Dulany. *The Technical Services: The Signal Corps: The
    Emergency*. United States Army in World War II. Washington,
    DC: Office of the Chief of Military History, 1956.

Teveth, Shabtai. *The Tanks of Tammus*. New York: Viking,
    1968-69.

Thompson, Paul W. *Engineers in Battle*. Harrisburg, PA:
    Military Service Publishing Co., 1942.

Times, London. The Yom Kippur War. Garden City, NJ: Doubleday, 1974.

Tolson, John J. Airmobility, 1961-1971. Vietnam Studies. Washington, DC: Department of the Army, 1973.

Trupener, Ulrich. "The Road to Ypres: The Beginnings of Gas Warfare in World War I: Journal of Modern History 47 (September 1975): 460-80.

Ushakov, D. "The Role of Engineer Troops in Modern War." Mimeographed translation by U. S. Department of the Army, Assistant Chief of Staff for Intelligence, No. F-1622a-a, from the Russian article in Voyenno-inzhenerny zhurnal [Military Engineer Journal], 1946, No. 5-6: 9-13.

Union of Soviet Socialist Republics. Commissariat of Defense. Frunze Military Academy. "Planning and Execution of Problem No. 5lot: Position Defense of the Infantry Division with Employment of Trenches and Organized Outpost Area." Mimeographed translation by U. S. Department of the Army, Office of the Assistant Chief of Staff for Intelligence, No. G-2563, from the 1944 Russian original.

Union of Soviet Socialist Republics. Commissariat of Defense. General Staff. "Changes in the Articles of the Field Manual Project Pertaining to the Military Employment of Cavalry." Mimeographed translation by U. S. Department of the Army, Office of the Assistant Chief of Staff for Intelligence, No. E-9437, from the 1943 Russian original.

_____. "Collection of Materials for the Study of the War Experience, No. 2 (September-October 1942)." Mimeographed Translation by U. S. Department of the Army, Office of the Assistant Chief of Staff for Intelligence, No. F-7565, from the 1942 original.

_____. Field Service Regulations of the Red Army (1942). Mimeographed Translation by U. S. War Department, Office of the Assistant Chief of Staff for Intelligence, no no. Copy in Military History Institute.

_____. Field Service Regulations of the Red Army (1944). Mimeographed Translation by U. S. War Department, Office of the Assistant Chief of Staff for Intelligence, no no. Copy in Military History Institute.

_____. Field Service Regulations, Soviet [sic Red] Army, 1936 (Tentative). Moscow: Commissariat of Defense, 1937. Typescript translation by Charles Berman, from the Russian original.

_____. Field Service: Staff Manual (Tentative). Moscow: Commissariat of Defense, 1935. Typescript translation by Charles Berman, from the Russian original.

_____. "Instructions for Air Force and Ground Troops on Combined Operations." Translated by U. S. Department of the Army, Office of the Assistant Chief of Staff for Intelligence, No. F-3733, from the 1944 Russian original.

_____. *Manual for Combat Support Aviation*. Mimeographed translation of Chapters 6-8 by U. S. Department of the Army, Office of the Assistant Chief of Staff for Intelligence, No. F-3732a, from the Russian original (n.d.).

_____. (Draft) *Manual on the Breakthrough of Fortified Areas, 1944*. Mimeographed translation by U. S. Department of the Army, Office of the Assistant Chief of Staff for Intelligence, No. F-798, from the 1944 Russian original.

_____. *1942 Infantry Tactical Manual of the Red Army*. Decree No. 347, 9 November 1942. Mimeographed translation by U. S. Department of the Army, Office of the Assistant Chief of Staff for Intelligence, No. F-2830, from the 1942 Russian original.

_____. *Service Regulations for the Armored and Mechanized Forces of The Red Army*. Part I: *The Tank, Tank Platoon, and Tank Company*. Moscow: Commissariat of Defense, 1944. Mimeographed translation by U. S. Department of the Army, Office of the Assistant Chief of Staff for Intelligence, No. F-7176.

Union of Soviet Socialist Republics. Institut Marksizma-Leninizma. *History of the Great Patriotic War*, Vol. III: *Radical Turning Point in the Course of the Great Patriotic War*. Moscow: Military Publishing House of the Ministry of Defense, 1961. Typescript translation by U. S. Department of the Army, Office of the Chief of Military History, n.d.

United States. Department of the Army. *Field Manual 100-5: Operations*. Washington, DC: Government Printing Office, 1982.

United States. Department of the Army. The Armored School. "Armored Division Organizational and Manning Charts, TO&E 17N." Instructional Pamphlet No. CS-2, 1949. Fort Knox, KY: U. S. Army Armored School, 1949.

_____. "Armor in the Exploitation: The Fourth Armored Division Across France to the Moselle River." Student Research report, mimeographed, 1949. CARL N-21467.74.

United States. Department of the Army. U. S. Army Forces, Far East. *Japanese Night Combat*. 3 vols. Japanese Research Division report, mimeographed, 1955. CARL N-17807.28A.

United States. Department of the Army. U. S. Army Command and General Staff College. *Reference Book 100-2*, Vol. 1: *Selected Readings in Tactics: The 1973 Middle East War*. Fort Leavenworth, KS: U. S. Army Command and General Staff College, 1976.

United States. Department of the Army. General Staff. Assistant Chief of Staff for Intelligence (G2). *Soviet Army Organization: Mechanized Division (Wartime)*. Washington, DC: Office of the Assistant Chief of Staff for Intelligence, 1954.

_____. Soviet Army Organization: Tank Division (Wartime). Washington, DC: Office of the Assistant Chief of Staff for Intelligence, 1954.

_____. "Soviet Tank and Motorized Rifle Division." Intelligence Research Project No. A-1729. Washington, DC: Office of the Assistant Chief of Staff for Intelligence, 1958.

United States. Department of the Army. Office of the Chief of Military History. Department of the Army Pamphlet 20-230: Historical Study-Russian Combat Methods in World War II. Washington, DC: 1972.

United States, Department of Defense. Weapons System Evaluation Group. "A Historical Study of Some World War II Airborne Operations." WSEG Staff Study No. 3. Mimeographed, 1951. CARL R-17309.1.

_____. "A Study on Tactical Use of the Atomic Bomb." WSEG Staff Study No. 1. Mimeographed, 1949. CARL N-16687.2.

United States, War Department. Field Manual 100-5: Tentative Field Service Regulations-Operations. Washington, DC: Government Printing Office, 1939.

_____. Technical Manual TM-E20-451: Handbook On German Military Forces 15 March 1945. Washington, DC: Government Printing Office, 1945.

_____. Technical Manual TM-E30-480: Handbook on Japanese Military Forces. 15 September 1944. Washington, DC: Government Printing Office, 1944.

United States, War Department. Chief of Infantry. Infantry Field Manual, Vol. II: Tank Units. Washington, DC: Government Printing Office, 1931.

United States, War Department. U. S. Army Command and General Staff School, FM 101-10 (Tentative), Staff Officers' Field Manual. Undated, with changes to 1943.

United States, War Department. European Theater of Operations. The General Board. "Army Tactical Information Service." Study No. 18. Mimeographed, n.d.

_____. "Chemical Mortar Battalions." Study No. 70. mimeographed, n.d.

_____. "The Control of Tactical Aircraft in the European Theater of Operations." Study No. 55. Mimeographed, n.d.

_____. "Organization, Equipment, and Tactical Employment of the Airborne Division." Study No. 16. Mimeographed, n.d.

_____. "Organization, Equipment, and Tactical Employment of the Armored Division." Study No. 48. Mimeographed, n.d.

_____. "Organization, Equipment, and Tactical Employment of Tank Destroyer Units." Study No. 60. Mimeographed, n.d.

_____. Organization, Operations, and Equipment of Air-Ground Liaison in all Echelons from Division Upwards." Study No. 49. Mimeographed, n.d.

_____. "Tactics, Employment, Technique, Organization, and Equipment of Mechanized Cavalry Units." Study No. 49. Mimeographed, n.d.

_____. "Types of Divisions-Post-War Army." Study No. 17. Mimeographed, n.d.

United States, War Department. General Service Schools. General Tactical Functions of Larger Units. Fort Leavenworth, KS: General Service Schools Press, 1922.

_____. Tactics and Technique of the Separate Branches. 2 Vols. Fort Leavenworth, KS: General Service Schools Press, 1925.

United States, War Department. General Staff. Field Service Regulations 1914. With change 7, dated 18 August 1917. Menasha, WI: George Banta Publishing Co., 1918.

_____. Field Service Regulations: United States Army, 1923. Washington, DC: Government Printing Office, 1924.

_____. "Lessons From the Tunisian Campaign, 15 October 1943." Washington, DC: Government Printing Office, 1943.

_____. A Manual for Commanders of Large Units (Provisional). 2 vols. Washington, DC: Government Printing Office, 1930-31.

_____. Order of Battle of the United States Land Forces In the World War; American Expeditionary Forces; Divisions. Washington, DC: Government Printing Office, 1931.

United States, War Department. General Staff. Assistant Chief of Staff for Intelligence, G2. Determination of Fighting Strength, USSR. 2 vols. Washington, DC: Office of the Assistant Chief of Staff for Intelligence, 1942.

_____. "The Organization and Tactical Employment of Soviet Ground Formations." Mimeographed, July 1944. Study No. C5859.

United States, War Department. General Staff. Military Intelligence Division. Special Bulletin No. 36: The Battle of Salum, June 15-17, 1941. Washington, DC: War Department, 1941.

United States, War Department. General Staff. Military Intelligence Service. Special Series No. 6: Artillery in the Desert. Washington, DC: War Department, 1942.

_____. Special Studies No. 8: German Tactical Doctrine. Washington, DC: Government Printing Office, 1942.

_____. Special Studies No. 26: Japanese Tanks and Tank Tactics. Washington, DC: Government Printing Office, 1942.

_____. Information Bulletin No. 12, MIS 461: "Japanese Warfare: A Summary." Washington, DC: War Department, 1942.

_____. Information Bulletin No.1 6, MIS 461: "Japanese Warfare: A Summary." Washington, DC: War Department, 1942.

United States. War Department. General Staff. War Plans Division. A Survey of German Tactics, 1918. Monograph No. 1. Washington, DC: War Department, 1918.

United States. War Department. The Infantry School. Special Text No. 265: Infantry in Defensive Combat. Fort Benning, GA: Army Field Printing Plant, 1936.

United States. War Department. Third U. S. Army. Letters of Instruction No. 1, 2, and 3, 1944. Reprinted in Third Army After Action Report, Third U. S. Army, 1945.

Van Creveld, Martin. Supplying War: Logistics from Wallenstein to Patton. Cambridge, UK: Cambridge University Press, 1977.

Viner, Joseph W. Tactics and Techniques of Tanks. Fort Leavenworth, KS: The General Service Schools Press, 1920.

Vladimirskiy, A. "Wartime Operations: Counterattacks by the Southwestern Front." USSR Report: Military Affairs, No. 1627 (16 October 1981): 24-32. Translated by the Foreign Broadcast Information Service from the Russian article in Voyenno-istoricheskiy zhurnal [Military History Journal], July 1981, 21-28.

Volodin. N. "Assignment of Combat Engineers in the Breakthrough and Development of the Offensive." Mimeographed translation by U. S. Department of the Army, Office of the Assistant Chief of Staff for Intelligence, No. F-1522a-b, from the Russian article in Voyènna-inzhenerny zhurnal [Military Engineer Journal], 1946, No. 5-6: 21-25.

Voroushenko, V. and A. Pozdnyshev. "Heavy Tanks in Combat with Counterattacking Tanks of the Enemy." Mimeographed translation by U. S. Department of the Army, Office of the Assistant Chief of Staff for Intelligence, No. F-6606C, from the Russian article in Zhurnal brontetankovykh i mekhanizirovannkyh voisk [Journal of Armored and Mechanized Forces], 1945.

Voroushenko, V. and B. Tretyakov. "Organization of Defense of a Mechanized Corps for the purpose of holding a line until the approach of the Infantry." Mimeographed translation by U. S. Department of the Army, Office of the Assistant Chief of Staff for Intelligence, No. F-6581, from the Russian article in Zhurnal Brontetankovykh i Mekhanizirovannkyh Voisk, 1945.

Wavell, Archibald. Allenby: A Study in Greatness. New York: Oxford University Press, 1941.

_____. The Palestine Campaigns. 2d ed. London: Constable and Co., Ltd., 1929.

Weeks, John. Men Against Tanks: A History of Anti-Tank Warfare. New York: Mason/Charter, 1975.

Weigley, Russell F. The American Way of War: A History of United States Military Strategy and Policy. New York: Macmillan, 1973.

_____. "Shaping the American Army of World War II: Mobility Versus Power." Parameters, Journal of the U. S. Army War College 11 (September 1981): 13-21.

Weller, Jac. "Armor and Infantry in Israel." Military Review 55 (March 1975): 3-11.

Wheldon, John. Machine Age Armies. London: Abelard-Schuman, 1968.

Winton, Harold R. "General Sir John Burnett-Stuart and British Military Reform, 1927-1938." Ph.D. dissertation, Stanford University, 1977.

Woodward, David. Armies Of the World, 1854-1914. New York: G. P. Putnam's Sons, 1978.

Wray, Timothy A. "Standing Fast: German Defensive Doctrine On
    the Russian Front During the Second World War." M.M.A.S.
    thesis, U. S. Army Command and General Staff College, 1983.
Wynne, Graeme C. "The Development of the German Defensive Battle
    in 1917, and its Influence on British Defence Tactics." The
    Army Quarterly 24 (April, July 1937): 15-32, 248-66.
_____. If Germany Attacks: The Battle in Depth in the West.
    London: Faber and Faber, 1940.
Yamaguchi, Jiso (ed.) Burma Operations Record: 15th Army
    Operations in Imphal Area and Withdrawal to Northern Burma.
    Revd. ed. Japanese Monograph No. 134. Washington, DC:
    Office of the Chief of Military History, 1957.
Yarchevsky, P. "Breakthrough of the Tactical Defense."
    Mimeographed translation by U. S. Department of the Army,
    Office of the Assistant Chief of Staff for Intelligence, No.
    F-6090B, from the Russian article in Voyennaya mysl', 1946,
    No. 9.
Yekimovskiy, A. "Tactics of the Soviet Army During the Great
    Patriotic War." Mimeographed translation by direction of U.
    S. Department of the Army, Office of the Assistant Chief of
    Staff for Intelligence, No. J-2507, from the Russian article
    in Voyennyy vestnik [Military Herald], 1967, No. 4: 12-20.
Yekimovskiy, A. and N. Makarov. "The Tactics of The Red Army in
    the 1920's and 1930's." Mimeographed translation by
    direction of U. S. Department of the Army, Office of the
    Assistant Chief of Staff for Intelligence, No. J-2141, from
    the Russian article in Voyennyy vestnik, 1967, No. 3: 8-13.
Yunker, Stephen F. "'I Have the Formula': The Evolution of the
    Tactical Doctrine of General Robert Nivelle." Military
    Review 54 (June 1974): 11-25.
Zakharov, M. V. (ed.) 50 Let Vooruzhennykh sil SSSR [50 Years of
    the Soviet Armed Forces] Moscow: Voennoe Izdatel'stvo,
    1968. Portions translated by LTC David M. Gantz.
Ziemke, Earl F. Stalingrad to Berlin: The German Defeat In the
    East. U. S. Army Historical Series. Washington, DC: Office
    of the Chief of Military History, 1968.

Milton Keynes UK
Ingram Content Group UK Ltd.
UKHW052003310823
427823UK00005B/215